D0409891

Woman and
Temperance

Woman and Temperance

THE QUEST FOR POWER AND

LIBERTY, 1873–1900

RUTH BORDIN

Temple University Press

Philadelphia

Temple University Press, Philadelphia 19122
© 1981 by Temple University. All rights reserved
Published 1981
Printed in the United States of America

Library of Congress Cataloging in Publication Data

Bordin, Ruth Birgitta Anderson, 1917–
Woman and temperance.

(American civilization)
Includes bibliographical references and index.
1.   Woman's Christian Temperance Union—History.
2.   Temperance—History.   3.   Women in public life
—United States—History.   I.   Title.   II.   Series.
HV5229.B67   363.4′1′0973   80-21140
ISBN 0-87722-157-X   ↵

for

Anna, David, Jason,

and Martin

Contents

Contents

Illustrations

Acknowledgments

The debts any author accumulates are beyond acknowledgment. Diane Hatfield somehow translated my illegible handwriting into legible typescript. Louise Wade and Michael Homel provided encouragement and practical help. Librarians and manuscript curators at places as far apart as the Manuscripts Division of The Historical Society of Wisconsin (Josephine Harper), the Department of Archives and Manuscripts of Catholic University in Washington, D.C. (Anthony Zito), and the Serra Museum Research Library in San Diego (Sylvia Arden) helped dig out materials pertinent to this study. Kathleen Marquis stimulated me to attempt to master the literature in women's history. Marilyn Motz provided an exchange of ideas that only a current graduate student in women's studies could have supplied. Barbara Winkler read the manuscript and caught errors of fact. Rand Jimmerson assisted in the early stages by helping me understand women's role in temperance.

My greatest debt, however, is to the current staff of the Bentley Historical Library of the University of Michigan. My friends and colleagues there always provided willing and intelligent access to research materials. More important, they consistently provided collegiality, affection, moral support, and companionship at lunch. Mary Jo Pugh and Francis X. Blouin of the Bentley staff read, commented on, and helped shape this manuscript in significant ways. It could never have been completed without them.

Janet Zollinger Giele shared part of an afternoon during a busy conference schedule to exchange ideas about women and temperance. She also read the manuscript and made several useful suggestions. Allen Davis and Kenneth Arnold as well contributed helpful advice. And for forty years Edward Bordin has taken my professional aspirations seriously, whether or not they made sense in the "outer sphere." Our joined lives have not always been lived in liberated times, but he has always been a liberated man.

Introduction

This book was born as I investigated the genesis of a girls' reformatory for young offenders established by the state of Michigan in 1880. The Michigan Woman's Christian Temperance Union, an organization only four years old at the time, was clearly the sole instigator and major implementer of this project. At its convention held in Grand Rapids in 1878, the state WCTU had been moved to action by a speech of Mary Lathrap, one of the WCTU's founders and a licensed preacher in the Methodist church. Lathrap energized the convention with a speech on the "fallen woman." Asking the Union members to be concerned with their sisters, not only inebriate men, Lathrap concluded her address with a call for the WCTU to work for legislation to establish a state-supported house of shelter for delinquent girls, primarily prostitutes, "especially the youngest—who have some of life's sweetness left."[1] The Michigan Union appointed a committee, launched a statewide petition drive, and collected over twenty thousand signatures. Tens of thousands of copies of Lathrap's address were distributed around the state. As Michigan's superintendent of public instruction described the enthusiasm these petitions mobilized, "There was never, probably, a memorial placed before the general public for signatures, received with such warm approval as this."[2]

Several bills proposing a girls' reformatory were presented to the next legislature, including one drawn by the WCTU. The Union's bill was eventually passed in 1879. Perhaps its most important provision stipulated that women be appointed to a majority of the places on the institution's Board of Control. These were the first women to hold public office in the state of Michigan. Two were members of the WCTU. The Union also successfully sponsored a provision in the law that stipulated that no men, only women, could staff the new correctional institution. When the reformatory opened, the superintendent, the physician, the teachers, and the housekeepers were all women. There was only one exception: a man ran the heating plant. This exercise in local history suggested that in 1878 the Michigan WCTU was already a major force in Michigan politics, a dynamic, strong, woman's organization with program concerns ranging far beyond narrow temperance goals. But further investigation revealed that little has been written about the WCTU's activities and structure, especially by women. Why not?

At about the same time the microfilm edition of the Temperance and Prohibition Papers was being prepared. The Michigan Historical Collections of the Bentley Historical Library at the University of Michigan was a major participant in this federally funded project.[3] The raw materials from which a study of the WCTU as a major women's organization could be made were close at hand. The WCTU's records, its publications, and the scrapbooks of Frances Willard's family and her secretaries, as well as her own correspondence, were being made easily available to scholars.

The history of temperance was also taking on new life. In the single year 1979, the temperance movement was given able and provocative treatment by Jack Blocker, Larry Engelmans, and William Rorabaugh.[4] Why did our ancestors view temperance as a major social reform? Was temperance a popular reform movement of the nineteenth century for the simple reason that Americans drank too much? Or was devotion to temperance a symbolic medium for larger issues of social control or threatened status? The historians of the 1970s tended to find the answer in alcohol abuse. They observed that in the United States just after independence, a surplus of cheap grain plus technological developments in distilling vastly increased the supply of spirits. Overindulgence peaked in the early nineteenth century. The United States became a drunken society, and alcoholism a major problem. Temperance reformers slowed the pace of alcohol abuse in the 1840s and 1850s, but after the Civil War, saloons multiplied and the problem was again on the rise.

That historians asked these questions represented an abrupt turnaround in how they viewed the temperance movement. For twenty years after the repeal of Prohibition in 1933, historians ignored the depth and scope of the problem Prohibition attempted to solve. A whole generation of writers viewed temperance agitation as a frivolous interference with basic individual liberty and a preoccupation with an issue that was at best marginal to the real problems of a rapidly industrializing and urbanizing society.[5] Historians saw the saloon as a benign institution that served a vital social function as a poor man's club.

But in the 1970s alcohol again came to be seen as a drug problem of national proportions. This new approach for historians found its best summary in Norman Clark's *Deliver Us from Evil*.[6] Clark rescued Prohibition and the temperance movement from its previous association with bigoted cranks and placed it squarely in the American reformist tradition as part of a larger solution to the social problems accompanying urbanization and industrialization. He recognized the temperance movement as a rational response to a genuine social evil. A decade earlier, in his major study, *Symbolic Crusade*, sociologist Joseph Gusfield analyzed the temperance movement somewhat differently.[7] Gusfield believed temperance reform was essentially divorced from economic interests. He dubbed it "a symbolic crusade," not an instrumental reform oriented toward producing the specific goal of a temperate America. To Gusfield, neither the temperance movement nor the state and national prohibition legislation that resulted was a specific attack on alcohol abuse, but rather they represented a form of social control. Prohibition was an attempt by middle-class Protestants, who were unable to preserve the status quo, with their previous social and economic dominance threatened by the Catholic immigrant, urbanization, and industrialization, to impose at least one tenet of their personal morality—sobriety—on the larger society. Gusfield erred in not recognizing how real the problem of alcohol abuse was. Also, he did not fully understand that the temperance movement transcended class and status. While its leadership was middle and upper middle-class in the nineteenth century, the temperance cause attracted adherents from all levels of society. It also transcended Protestantism. Catholics too subscribed to temperance goals. Nonetheless Gusfield made one major contribution that may not have been equaled. He put temperance in the reformist tradition, treated it as a serious impulse of reformers, and intelligently scrutinized its leadership.

Joseph Timberlake and John C. Burnam, also writing in the 1960s, were fully aware of the prohibition movement's role as an integral part of the Progressive program.[8] Timberlake like Gusfield viewed temperance as a genuine reform, an attempt to deal effectively with many of the same problems addressed by other aspects of the Progressive program. He perceived considerable validity in the Progressive's belief that alcohol was the enemy of industrial efficiency, a threat to the working of democratic government, the abettor of poverty and disease: the besotted could not govern wisely, vote intelligently, or safely operate complicated machinery. Temperance reform to the Progressive was designed to meet genuine social problems.

I share many of the views of recent historians of temperance, and have benefited from their studies. My own concern, however, has been with women and temperance. What role did women play in the temperance movement in the last quarter of the nineteenth century? Why did women choose temperance as a congenial cause? How does their choice of temperance relate to the woman's movement? The revived interest in the history of temperance has done little to explain women's place in the movement. In many of these studies, their role has received a paragraph or two, at most a few pages.

Women were involved with temperance from its beginnings in the late eighteenth century. In their accepted nineteenth-century role as guardians of the home, they contributed to the pre–Civil War movement. Although leadership and public participation were denied them, they were encouraged to use their roles as mothers, sisters, and daughters to exercise moral suasion and set a good example within the family. However, when legislative solutions to intemperance were first adopted in the 1850s, women found their place in the movement in jeopardy because they could neither vote nor participate in political campaigns. In the post–Civil War temperance movement, women became the leaders. Women found temperance the most congenial cause through which to increase their involvement in public life. During the last quarter of the nineteenth century, women used the WCTU as a base for their participation in reformist causes, as a sophisticated avenue for political action, as a support for demanding the ballot, and as a vehicle for supporting a wide range of charitable activities. By the 1880s the Woman's Christian Temperance Union was the largest organization of women the United States had yet known. It reached into every state and territory, all major cities, and thousands of local communities.

The Union was led during its initial flowering by Frances Willard, unquestionably America's leading heroine to her contemporaries and the most famous woman of her day. Willard, president of the WCTU from 1879 until her death in 1898, was the charismatic, almost messianic, mobilizer of American womanhood for over two decades. While she did not create the Union, much less the temperance movement, and no doubt the strong surge of women into the temperance cause would have occurred without her, her superb organizing skills, effective manipulation of public opinion, and ability to inspire the personal devotion of tens of thousands of women were a major factor in the WCTU's success. Willard was a classic case of the right person, at the right place, at the right time. She also was quick to recognize the WCTU as the right place and time to fulfill her personal goals. She made maximum use of the circumstances the temperance movement provided. In another age Willard might have chosen another cause, but the marriage of the WCTU and Willard was certainly made in heaven and happy for them both.

Despite the current revived interest in temperance as a social movement and the leading part that Frances Willard and women in general played in the movement during the late nineteenth century, the Woman's Christian Temperance Union has not yet been the subject of a full-length published scholarly study. Three "official" histories have been published by the WCTU itself.[9] The history of the Union has also been the subject of two doctoral dissertations.[10] No biography of Frances Willard has been published since 1944.[11] Only brief accounts of the activities of the WCTU are included in several recent scholarly treatments of the temperance movement.[12] Perhaps because the WCTU in the mid–twentieth century became a cheap joke, the epitome of bluestocking bigotry, and was equated with cartoons of Carry Nation wielding her ax or with elderly spinsters finding an outlet for subconscious hostility against males by denying the gracious niceties of comfortable living to their fellow citizens, the WCTU and Frances Willard have not received the attention they deserve. Women historians in the present day have almost completely ignored the temperance movement. Two exceptions are Janet Zollinger Giele and Ellen DuBois, who discuss the success and tactics of the WCTU in contrast to the suffrage movement.[13]

Why have the WCTU and Frances Willard herself suffered such neglect, while much attention has been focused on the suffrage and social purity movements? Mary Earhart, Willard's biographer, holds Anna Gordon, Willard's private secretary, responsible for unwittingly diminishing her heroine by consciously limiting Willard's significance to her role in the struggle over temperance. Gordon was so intent on Willard's sanctification that she felt compelled to hide Willard's radical social philosophy and the breadth of her concern with social issues. By carefully destroying controversial correspondence and fostering adulatory mythmaking, Gordon was able to make Willard into a sanitized, idealized woman whose work was devoted solely to defending that sacred nineteenth-century institution, the home.[14] Certainly her purging of Willard's papers may have made Willard less interesting to latter-day students of the woman's movement than she would otherwise have been. However, Gordon cannot be held responsible for the recent lack of attention paid by women to the role of women in the temperance movement as a whole. The feminists of the 1960s and 1970s have been personally concerned with egalitarianism and sexual freedom. Living in a libertarian age, they quite naturally discovered an interest in the suffrage and social purity movements, which represented antecedents for their own concern with social and political equality and control of their own bodies, rather than temperance, which seemed part of the anti-libertarian tradition. But it was in the temperance movement that large numbers of women were politicized, and it was through temperance that they experienced wider spheres of public activity in the nineteenth century.

This volume attempts to remedy in part this lack of scholarly attention. It focuses on the period from 1873 to 1900, when the WCTU was both the leading temperance organization and the leading women's organization in the United States. After 1900 the Anti-Saloon League took over as prime mover of the temperance cause, the National American Woman Suffrage Association became the main force in the women's movement, and the General Federation of Women's Clubs eclipsed the WCTU in size of membership, although it was never to rival it in political force. During the last quarter of the nineteenth century the Woman's Christian Temperance Union was the major vehicle through which women developed a changing role for themselves in American society. Through both private charity and support of legislation the WCTU attempted to meet the myriad social problems arising from urbanization, industrialization, and immigration in the United States. The Union played two important roles: it was the national voice through which women expressed their views on social and political issues, and it was also a vast grass-roots organization that worked for charitable and political solutions to social problems.

Woman and
Temperance

A Maternal Struggle

AN OVERVIEW OF THE WCTU,

WOMAN AND TEMPERANCE

The phrase "A maternal struggle" is an apt one to describe the outpouring of attention and concern that women focused on the temperance movement in the 1870s.[1] Although temperance was not a new cause for women in the last quarter of the nineteenth century, the character of women's participation changed drastically in the 1870s, as did their relationship to the temperance movement as a whole. Temperance became a cause that large numbers of women actively embraced, and women in turn became the most important force in the temperance movement. Also, by the 1880s temperance had become the issue that drew tens of thousands of women to rally behind general women's and reformist causes and demand a more equal share in the political process. Through temperance, which women saw as protection of the home, women from many social and economic strata were caught up in feminist goals.[2] Women joined the Woman's Christian Temperance Union, the major temperance organization for women, in numbers that far surpassed their participation in any other women's organization in the nineteenth century and that made the WCTU the first women's mass movement.

By 1892 the WCTU had nearly 150,000 dues-paying members. Including auxiliaries, such as the Young Woman's Christian Temperance Union (known as the Y's), its membership was well over 200,000. In 1892 only

The chapter title is from Senator Henry William Blair's description of women's rise to command in the temperance movement, in his *The Temperance Movement*, 504.

3

20,000 women were affiliated with the General Federation of Women's Clubs, and in 1893 there were roughly 13,000 dues-paying members of the National American Woman Suffrage Association. Temperance was clearly the cause women found most attractive in the late nineteenth century. The WCTU was the largest organization of women that had existed until that time, and the size and influence of other women's groups were not comparable.

Because women found the temperance cause so congenial, women dominated the temperance movement from 1873 until the rapid growth of the Anti-Saloon League in the early twentieth century. Women also provided the movement's creative thrust. Temperance workers at the time recognized this. In his history of the temperance cause published in 1888, Henry William Blair, who was a senator from New Hampshire and had an active voice in temperance affairs himself, credits the WCTU with being the leading force in late nineteenth-century temperance reform.[3] Women were the precinct workers in local-option elections. The WCTU almost single-handedly pushed legislation for compulsory temperance education in the schools through Congress and the state legislatures. Temperance women led the campaigns for prohibition amendments in several states in the 1880s and 1890s.

The temperance cause itself was hardly new.[4] The General Conference of the Methodist church had imposed strict limitations on the use of distilled liquor as early as 1790, although it did not urge total abstinence until 1832. Benjamin Rush had published his famous treatise "An Inquiry into the Effects of Ardent Spirits on the Mind and Body" in 1785. The earliest temperance society of more than local consequence, the Union Temperate Society, had been organized by William Clark at Saratoga in 1808, and the Massachusetts Society for the Supression of Intemperance followed in 1813. By 1833 there were so many American temperance organizations that temperance adherents saw the need for national affiliation, and the United States Temperance Union was formed in 1833. Its affiliated societies totaled a million members. Pre–Civil War temperance agitation reached its peak in the early 1850s and resulted in the adoption of various types of legislative prohibition in several states. The consumption of distilled liquor dropped sharply.

Women made up a substantial proportion of antebellum temperance adherents, but they were not among the leaders. Since drink was seen to present a threat to the home, both men and women perceived temperance as a woman's issue. Women entered the temperance movement in substantial numbers in the 1840s and were encouraged to advocate temperance at their own hearths, to exercise the powers of moral suasion that were part of the domestic sphere that women were assigned in the nineteenth century. The Daughters of Temperance, the female auxiliary of the popular Sons of Temperance, peaked at 30,000 members in 1840. However, women began to show dissatisfaction with their nonpublic role when the temperance movement entered the political arena in the 1850s.[5] Legislative solutions to temperance presented problems for women. Women could not vote in elections where prohibitory legislation was an issue. They were not accepted as speakers from temperance platforms. In fact, the first state women's temperance society was founded by Susan B. Anthony in 1852, after she was informed on rising to speak to a motion at a New York temperance convention that the sisters were there not to speak but to listen and learn.[6] Although most women responded less aggressively than Anthony to male domination of the public phases of the movement, women nonetheless felt displaced.

Women began to play a more prominent role after the Civil War. They were accepted as equal members in the Independent Order of Good Templars, a fraternal temperance lodge, and held office. Martha Brown, one of the founders of the WCTU, was Grand Chief Templar of Ohio in 1872. But the post–Civil War temperance movement did not gain momentum until the woman's Crusade of 1873–74, which radically changed women's overall importance in the temperance cause. Why did women flock in such impressive numbers to the temperance cause in the mid-1870s? Why this sudden acceleration in commitment? The answer requires first of all some explanation of the general attractiveness of temperance as a women's issue in the nineteenth century.

There seems little doubt that the temperance movement developed in response to a social evil that was both real and widespread. Nineteenth-century Americans were heavy users of strong drink, and alcohol was believed to be necessary as food, as a beverage, and as a generally available medicinal drug and anesthetic. Water in urban areas was frequently scarce or unsafe, and milk was dangerous, carrying tuberculosis, undulant fever, and other diseases even when it was fresh. Milk was also expensive. Distilled spirits were cheap. Alcohol was also thought to be necessary for supplying the energy for hard physical labor and providing the internal warmth that made outdoor work bearable in cold northern winters. Spirits were the most commonly available anesthetic and analgesic, and alcohol's place in the pharmacopeoia was generally accepted by the medical profession.[7] In other words, strong drink was an accepted part of nineteenth-century life.

Although the use of alcohol seems to have fallen precipitously as a result of the antebellum temperance movement, production and use rose again rapidly during the Civil War, and the number of saloons grew quickly in the generally prosperous postwar period. By 1873 Ohio supported one such establishment for every 200 people.[8] By 1900, one out of every 116 Americans was employed in some aspect of the liquor industry, including over half a million people who engaged directly in the liquor trade. Americans spent well over $1 billion on alcoholic beverages in 1900, when they spent only $900 million on meat, $150 million to support their churches, and less than $200 million on public education.[9] This heavy use continued into the next century. In 1909 they spent $1.8 billion on alcoholic beverages in contrast to $2 billion on all food products and nonalcoholic beverages combined.[10] In Chicago by the end of the nineteenth century the number of saloons equaled the total of the city's grocery stores, meat markets, and dry goods stores, and a survey in 1895 showed that on an average day the number of saloon customers was equal to one-half the city's population.[11] It was generally conceded that in the 1880s and 1890s working-class sections of American cities had about one saloon to every fifty males over fifteen years of age. In 1886 the Board of Excise Commissioners reported 9,168 licenses in force in New York City for the retail sale of liquor, but they also estimated that there were at least a thousand dealers selling without a license.[12] Along with heavy use came the inevitable abuse, and the saloon was rightly seen as a major social curse in the late nineteenth century. In fact, in his major interpretive essay on the temperance movement, Norman Clark has described the United States as a drunken society.[13]

The liquor interests were also deeply involved in politics. They were identified with corruption, crime, and vote buying. Of the 1,002 political meetings held in New York City on the local level in 1886, nearly 800 were held in saloons.[14] The liquor business controlled a disproportionate number of public offices, especially on the local level. For example, one-third of the aldermen of Detroit and Milwaukee in the 1890s were saloon-keepers, as were half of the Democratic precinct workers in Chicago at the turn of the century.[15] The National Brewers Association paid the costs of testing the Kansas prohibition law before the Supreme Court in 1883.[16] Distillers and brewers had money to buy political influence, and they used it.

Alcohol abuse was a real and pressing personal and social problem. It was also perceived as a problem from which women suffered disproportionately although they were not the offenders. In the late nineteenth century serious drinking was considered a male prerogative, and the American saloon, except for hangers-on like prostitutes, was almost exclusively a male institution. At the same time, women saw the saloon as a pervasive and pernicious influence on their lives. This perception was based on reality. The nineteenth-century drunkard's reputation as a wife beater, child abuser, and sodden, irresponsible nonprovider was not undeserved. Susan B. Anthony, addressing the National American Woman Suffrage Association at its meeting in Chicago in 1875, emphasized that women were the greatest sufferers from drunkenness, and graphically pictured the virtuous woman in legal subjection to a drunken husband.[17] Anthony was repeating a widely held belief, echoing what was considered a truism at the time.[18] Any reading of letters, diaries, newspaper articles, and books written by women in the 1870s shows that it was as victims of alcohol abuse that women were attracted to the temperance movement even before they had their own temperance organizations.

A woman also suffered severe legal disadvantages in the 1870s that left her especially vulnerable to the abuses of an alcoholic husband. Women did not usually control their own wages and had no claim on their husbands' earnings. A husband could not only drink up his pay, but anything a wife might earn as well. Although between 1839 and 1850 most states had passed some kind of legislation that recognized the right of married women to own property, this legislation did not remove all legal restrictions, and previous gains were sometimes lost in the courts.[19] An 1879 Ohio decision stated outright that a husband had a property interest in his wife. She was not entitled to her own wages and must rely solely on her husband's pledge and promise to support her.[20] As late as 1900, in thirty-seven states, a woman possessed no rights to her children, and all her possessions were her husband's property.[21] Nowhere in the 1870s did women possess full suffrage, although some women could vote in school elections in Kentucky and Kansas.[22] Given a woman's limited legal rights, the drunkard as head of the household was seen as a true oppressor of his wife and family. The drunken husband epitomized the evils of a society in which women were second-class citizens, in ways that no sober (however tyrannical) husband and father could.

Although women were attracted to the temperance cause from its beginnings because they were frequent victims of alcohol abuse, other factors contributed to the enthusiasm with which they flocked to its banners. Not unimportant was the congeniality of temperance as a cause with the nineteenth century's dominant sexual ideology, the doctrine of spheres. Men functioned in the world of politics and commerce; women presided over the spiritual and physical maintenance of home and family.[23] Woman, as the protector of the home and the nurturer of children, had a compelling duty to save these sacred trusts from external threat. In the early temperance movement she was expected to exercise this duty through practicing moral suasion and setting a good example.[24] The emphasis of the early temperance movement was on individual redemption and personal abstinence, and women were expected to use their influence at home to convert their husbands, sons, and brothers from drinking. However, in a sense the drink issue was itself to prove subversive to the maintenance of a strict division between the sexual spheres. As soon as the temperance movement began to look to coercive legal solutions such as local option or prohibition, moral suasion was admitted to be an ineffective weapon, and it became apparent that if women were to continue their commitment to temperance, their role must inevitably move into the public realm. At the same time the old concept provided the rationale for this leap into the outer world. If the saloon was a threat to home and hearth, was it not a woman's duty to invade the public sphere to defend what was universally acceded to be her special area of responsibility? To many temperance women, therefore, participation in the post–Civil War movement took place on a basis that did not fundamentally alter the ideology that held women responsible for the welfare of the home.

Jill Conway has pointed out that while women activists were achieving a real change in female behavior after the Civil War, this new activism did not for most of them result in a similarly new view of the female temperament or women's sphere.[25] They still accepted women's role as one of nurturant domesticity. They wielded power, but their conceptions of what women could do did not immediately change to fit this new-found power. In the temperance movement women could view themselves as protecting the home. In this sense it was a maternal struggle. If they committed public acts, took public stands, it was only in their role as nurturant mothers who must insure a good environment for those dependent on them. The WCTU was a "safe" women's movement. But its members nonetheless were never completely sure about the nature of their public role. They frequently avowed their complete disinterest in activism for anything but altruistic purposes, and at the same time they pointed with pride to the widening spheres of women. These women were much like the settlement-house women who followed them, moralists and idealists who believed literally in their responsibility to help their fellow human beings—in this case by removing them from contact with the evils of drink.

June Sochen has labeled women who joined organizations like the WCTU "pragmatic feminists," in contrast to the ideologists. They identified specific grievances from which women suffered and tried to do something about them. They did not want to change traditional sex roles. They did not argue, at least at first, for women's rights as such. They were firm believers in "true womanhood," but they did push for widening spheres. They marked out an area that they felt concerned them deeply, the evils of drink, and directly attempted to do something about it.[26] Frances Willard could describe the WCTU as an organization whose "broad sympathies . . . ministered to all good and true women who are willing to clasp hands in one common effort to protect their homes and loved ones from the ravages of drink . . . . without a peer among the sisterhoods that have grouped themselves around the cross of Christ."[27]

Another factor that no doubt contributed to the ease with which women flocked to temperance in the 1870s was the presence of an already existing network through which women could function in the temperance cause. The missionary societies of the several Protestant denominations, as well as the churches themselves, provided already functioning female networks that could be converted into WCTU chapters. The temperance movement, the WCTU in particular, was ecumenical from the beginning, and in this it differed from church groups such as missionary societies; but the WCTU was certainly church-oriented, and almost all of its members were church-going Protestants. In one Michigan town, for example, membership on the executive committee of the temperance union that launched that town's Crusade in the spring of 1874 was allocated equally among the six participating Protestant churches.[28] In essence, then, a woman was the Methodist or Presbyterian or Quaker representative on that board. If she resigned she was replaced by another from the same denomination. The same practice was followed by the Ann Arbor Union as late as 1894.[29] As Mary Ryan has pointed out, this phenomenon, the use of existing church networks, the movement from denominational groups into ecumenical reform societies, occurred in Utica within the Female Moral Reform Societies of the 1830s.[30] In both situations the ideal of reform that was embraced was one that suited the teachings of the churches in a way that a reform aimed at the political system, such as woman suffrage, would not.

None of this, however, explains why the last quarter of the nineteenth century was the time when women's participation in the temperance cause markedly accelerated. Several factors combined to make a mass movement exclusively of women both possible and successful at this time. First, American society by the 1870s and 1880s had a large enough body of middle and upper middle-class women to support such a movement, and these women had, in turn, sufficient leisure to permit them to devote themselves to supplying its organizing force. Only in the late nineteenth century did child-care and homemaking become a full-time job for urban middle-class women. Before that time even many upper-class women were frequently engaged in making a direct economic contribution to the family's welfare. Rural women always produced part of the family's cash income whether they lived on small family farms or large plantations. The tradesman's wife and daughters were expected to help in the shop. In the craftsman's family, women assisted with cabinetry or candlemaking. The innkeeper and his wife were business partners. Widows continued to manage and run businesses their husbands left behind. But a change occurred in urban areas in the latter half of the century. Urban working-class, immigrant, and black women were still fully sharing responsibility for the family's economic burdens through employment either at the factory or mill or by doing piecework at home. Immigrant women who were not employed in industry found jobs as servants. In many areas in 1880 women made up 30 to 40 percent of the industrial labor force. In other cities most women workers were domestics or laundresses.[31]

However, by the last decades of the century a clear line had been drawn between the proper sphere of economic activities for poor women and their middle and upper-class sisters. As industrialization removed the urban worker from the home-related store or workshop, the working-class woman remained part of the work force, but the owner-entrepreneur-manager, even the clerk, left the women of his family at home solely occupied with domestic duties. The middle-class woman was no longer expected to make a direct contribution to family income. She was to be supported by her male relatives. Being able to support women in relative leisure and not to depend on their wages became a significant criterion of a man's movement into the middle class. The immigrant who had prospered to the point where his wife and daughters no longer went out to work for wages had moved up the social ladder. For the first time, rearing children and managing the household became a full-time job for large numbers of women.[32] Housekeeping and parenting have considerable economic value, as anyone who has purchased these services outside the family well knows; still, by the last quarter of the nineteenth century, middle and upper-class urban women had lost their role as direct financial contributors to family income.

It is easy to exaggerate the degree of leisure that resulted. However, this relinquishing of economic responsibility was accompanied by ready availability of servants who provided relief from much of the sheer drudgery of household tasks. Aileen Kraditor believes the feminist movement was at least in part a result of the mass Irish migration that began in the mid-nineteenth century, providing American middle-class women with a large measure of domestic service for the first time and giving them the leisure to participate in reform activities.[33] This service was performed for urban middle-class Southern women by freed blacks who had left the plantations after the Civil War. The availability of servants also left the young mother less closely confined by the care of small children. Women had some hours in the afternoon when they were free of immediate household responsibility.

Moreover, the birth rate was falling. The average number of children born to a white woman fell from 7.04 in 1800 to 4.24 in 1880 to 3.56 in 1900.[34] Since women were having fewer children, less time was absorbed by pregnancy and the care of infants and young children, which increased their leisure and left them with more energy for outside concerns.

The number of women enjoying this leisure had to be large enough to support a mass movement. Thousands of presidents, secretaries, and superintendents were necessary to staff the WCTU's many chapters at the local level. Anyone who has participated in an activist, reformist, volunteer club knows how much time leadership, even on the local level, can require. By the 1870s enough women had the necessary leisure.

Also, they were gathered in urban areas where they could associate easily. Over six million people lived in urban places by 1860, nearly ten million by 1870, over fourteen million by 1880, and thirty million by

1900.[35] Most of these towns and cities could easily be canvassed on foot. This made possible easy interaction and collaboration by women with a common cause. While many of the women now congregated in urban areas worked for a living, some of their middle-class sisters were probably in need of meaningful occupation.[36] Women whose services were less visibly essential to the family's economic well-being would have a void to fill. They would search for and be easily enlisted in activities that were complementary and appropriate to the sphere in which they were expected to function, the home. And the problems the WCTU attacked were closely related especially at first to the domestic sphere, although this base rapidly broadened. The Industrial Revolution had created a class of women with leisure who were likely to be receptive to new ideas and activities. Simultaneously it created a society with glaring social evils to which women responded by urging reform—women who had time to see, investigate, and respond to these problems.[37]

Another factor that promoted the mass growth of the WCTU was the marked increase in the number of women exposed to at least a common school education. There was by the 1870s an educated clientele for a mass movement. As early as 1850 more than 50 percent of school-age white females were attending school. What probably is equally important, most United States elementary schools were coeducational. As the number of children exposed to a common school education came to represent a major segment of the United States population, more and more women reached adulthood having already shared a common experience with men outside the home. Although both sexes received the same schooling, as adults women were not accepted on equal terms as potential leaders in organizations where they shared membership privileges with men. The WCTU offered them opportunities for creative service and self-fulfillment that they were unlikely to find elsewhere. The National American Woman Suffrage Association had male officers as well as male members. Men clearly played a major part in managing its affairs. The right of women to take leadership roles in Protestant churches was severely limited. But not in the WCTU. Here the women themselves were exclusively in charge.

These factors—urbanization, industrialization, universal education, growing leisure—all contributed to creating social and economic patterns that made a mass movement of women possible by the 1870s. At the same time the reality of woman's disproportionate suffering from the problems of alcohol abuse, the compatibility of temperance with the doctrine of spheres, and the convenient existence of church networks that could be converted to temperance reform activity insured that temperance would become the major thrust of the women's movement.

Breadth of program (albeit with temperance as its core) was also to contribute to the WCTU's appeal. The multifaceted program that the WCTU was to adopt by the end of its first decade attracted a broad spectrum of women with varying goals and interests. Although the WCTU began as a temperance group, dedicated to closing down the retail liquor trade and reforming individual drunkards by moral suasion as had the Washingtonians and Templars before it, the Union soon expanded both the means it used and the ends to which it was committed. Because it was an organization of women in a society where drunkenness was seen as primarily a male vice, it could not concentrate on bringing ex-drunkards into its own organization, but instead was forced to concentrate on expediting and abetting the reform of those outside its membership. The Union was compelled to look for legislative solutions to the problem of alcohol abuse almost from the beginning. Most historians have seen the WCTU during the period of Annie Wittenmyer's presidency, 1874–1879, as primarily an evangelical movement devoted to moral suasion, but in fact political means were accepted and used by the WCTU as early as 1874, and legislative solutions were never eschewed. However, with Frances Willard's election to the presidency in 1879, an office she was to hold until her death in 1898, support for legislative goals became increasingly important. The WCTU, frustrated in its attempts to find legislative solutions to the problems of alcohol, inevitably took the next step: general (if not total) support of the ballot for women as the only way such legislation could be achieved. The fourth phase, in which a multitude of social problems were attacked and the spectrum of the organization's concerns significantly widened, reflected the leadership's growing conviction that drunkenness was result as well as cause. By the 1880s the Union's leaders were becoming convinced that an unjust society made alcohol an inevitable escape from poverty, that the poor had no other surcease, that the deprived child and overburdened mother would eventually turn to alcohol to ameliorate their sufferings; that only fundamental changes in the environment would heal in the last analysis. To implement this fourth phase, the WCTU promoted general prison reform, special facilities for women offenders, the eight-hour working day, model facilities for dependent and neglected children, the kindergarten movement, and shelters for the care of the children of working mothers, social rooms other than saloons for the urban poor, federal aid to education, mothers' education, vocational training for women, and a dozen other causes that they believed would improve the lot of the underprivileged, especially the urban poor. In this they foreshadowed the settlement-house movement by a decade. Jane Addams began her work in 1889 in Chicago, the same city where the Woman's Christian Temperance Union had its headquarters and where the WCTU was already sponsoring the kindergarten, had campaigned for and achieved the appointment of police matrons, had provided working-class recreational clubhouses to replace the saloons, had worked to provide clubs for newsboys and other young street workers, and even founded a hospital. Possibly the settlement-house movement was motivated by a different philosophy of purpose, a more broadly conceived view of the causes of social ills. The WCTU in its early years certainly viewed drink as a main cause of poverty and was drawn into wider concerns because of its initial commitment to fighting alcohol abuse, but by the late 1880s the Union was beginning to see poverty as cause rather than result. Whatever its motivation, in the 1880s the WCTU was the major organizer and supporter of organized charity in most metropolitan areas.

A Western Prairie Fire

THE WOMAN'S CRUSADE

OF 1873–1874

The Woman's Christian Temperance Union grew out of a spontaneous woman's crusade against saloons and retail liquor sellers which began in Ohio, swept the Midwest like a prairie fire and spread through the West and parts of the East during the winter of 1873–74. Thousands of women in hundreds of communities took to the streets and invaded saloons and shops that sold alcoholic beverages, in an attempt to disrupt and close down the liquor trade. Although many results of this Crusade were temporary, the women's efforts met with spectacular immediate success, their victories demonstrating that direct attack on a social evil by women could be effective. The Crusade, by involving large numbers of women in a program of militant action, produced significant results for the women's movement in the United States, drawing many women toward feminist goals that they themselves did not always at first recognize. Because the Crusade story is the moving tale of women suddenly finding new strengths, strengths that propelled them from their homes into public life and political positions, it illustrates the spontaneous appeal and unconscious feminism of the movement, and merits closer attention. [1]

On December 22, 1873 a professional lecturer in Massachusetts, Dr. Diocletian Lewis, deep into his fall tour, gave a public address called "Our

The chapter title is Frances Willard's metaphor of the rise and spread of the Crusade, reported in Anna Gordon's *Frances E. Willard*, 85.

15

Girls" at the music hall in Hillsboro, Ohio. Educated at Harvard and trained in homeopathic medicine, Lewis was a leading advocate of physical exercise and an active life for women. He was also an ardent temperance man. His appearance was part of the regular winter course of lectures sponsored by the local lecture association. Admission was charged, he received his usual fee. Lewis had a free day before he had to appear in a neighboring town, and Judge Albert Matthews, a temperance adherent, suggested that Lewis give a temperance lecture in Hillsboro the next evening, Sunday, December 23. The lecture was to be free, and Lewis would collect no additional fee, but the cause was one in which Lewis thoroughly believed, and he agreed willingly enough. Lewis's usual practice was to give free temperance lectures on Sundays, and he called his address "The Duty of Christian Women in the Cause of Temperance."

That night Lewis told his audience his customary story about his own family. Forty years before, his father had been a drinking man, and his mother, sorely distressed by his father's regular patronage of a local saloon in Saratoga, New York, appealed in desperation to the owner to cease selling spirits, prayed in the saloon with several of her friends, and actually succeeded in getting the saloonkeeper to close his business. Lewis suggested that if his mother had been able to do this many years ago, the women of Hillsboro could do the same thing in 1873. His appeal fell on fertile ground. The women in the audience took up the challenge with enthusiasm.

Actually there was nothing new about Lewis's appeal to the Hillsboro women. Lewis was repeating the same lecture he had prepared when he first went on the lecture circuit in 1854. By December 1874 his appeal on the power of women's prayers in the grog shops had been given about three hundred times, and the plan he outlined had already been tried some twenty times without notable success, the first time in Dixon, Illinois, in 1858, when fifty women marched praying into the saloons and continued their nonviolent assault for six days until all the community's saloons had closed.[2] But earlier results had always been temporary and local. Lewis had made the same speech ten days before in Fredonia, New York. Over two hundred women had followed his suggestion and marched to the saloons next day for prayer and song. The next morning they organized a temperance society, but they did not continue their marches.[3]

Eliza Jane Thompson, a respected Hillsboro matron of fifty-seven, was busy with domestic duties that evening and did not go to the lecture, although Lewis was her husband's houseguest, but her daughter and seventeen-year-old son attended. They came home in a state of high excitement, telling their mother what Lewis had suggested. Fifty women had agreed to try the approach in Hillsboro next day, and sixty or seventy men in the audience said they would back them. In her memoirs, Thompson wrote that her son told her, "You are on some committees to do work in the Presbyterian Church in the morning, and the ladies expect you to go with them to the saloons."[4]

Her children's enthusiasm did not dispel Thompson's reservations about joining this new activist temperance committee. She knew she would first need her husband's consent. This would not be easy. James Henry Thompson was a prominent attorney and now a judge. Eliza Thompson herself came from an influential Ohio family. She attended Catharine Beecher's school in Cincinnati as a child and there met Harriet Beecher Stowe.[5] Her father had been governor of Ohio and her uncle a United States senator. She saw herself as a lady and was accustomed to behaving like one. Taking public positions was not part of her self-image. And while she was an ardent supporter of the temperance cause, she was not in the habit of expressing her convictions in a public way. Also, her husband was reluctant to see her join in what he called "tomfoolery," although her children urged her on. And Thompson had compelling personal reasons for her devotion to temperance. Her older son, Allen, a promising young minister, purportedly acquired a taste for alcohol through a physician's prescription and died prematurely in an inebriate asylum in Binghamton, New York.[6]

Thompson slept little the night of December 22. She prayed for guidance but reached no decision. She feared the subject would come up at breakfast when the family gathered in the dining room with its mahogany furniture and shining silver service. It did not. After the morning meal the family adjourned to the library for prayer. As they walked into the room her son asked her what she would do. Judge Thompson paced the floor and suggested they leave his wife alone to pray. "I turned the key, and was in the act of kneeling before God and His Holy Word, to see what would be sent me, when I heard a gentle tap at my door; upon opening it I saw my dear daughter with her little Bible open, and the tears coursing down her young cheeks, as she said, 'I opened to this, mother. It must be for you.' "[7] The young woman's Bible had opened to Psalm 146, which promises the opening of the eyes of the blind. To Thompson this meant the call to the meeting was the work of God.

The type of good- character they had in the WCTU

Because of the respect in which Thompson was held in the community, she was the logical choice for president of the little band that organized in the Presbyterian church next morning, and she was promptly elected to the chair on her arrival. The Presbyterian minister temporarily presided. When he called her forward to replace him, Thompson could not move. "My limbs refused to bear me. The dear ladies offered me assistance, but it was not God's time." Her brother, Colonel Isaac Trimble, who was present, said he thought that "the ladies will do nothing until the gentlemen of the audience leave the house." And the men adjourned to "leave this work with God and the women."[8] As the last man left, Thompson's strength returned and she walked to the front, read from the Bible, and called on Mrs. Joseph McDowell to lead in prayer. McDowell had never prayed in public before. She was so shy that even when she prayed with her own children, she whispered, but "she prayed that morning as if a live coal from the altar had touched her lips, and there was no dry eye in the house."[9] Thompson then asked the women to sing the old hymn "Give to the Winds Thy Fears." They formed a line, and two by two marched singing out of the church and down the cold and sunless street, a few snowflakes falling on their cloaks and shawls. "Every heart was throbbing and every woman's countenance betrayed her solemn realization of the fact that she was going about her Father's business."[10]

Lewis had instructed the women precisely how to proceed. They must first attempt to ask the various dispensers of alcoholic beverages—druggists, grocers, physicians, innkeepers and saloon owners—to sign pledges that they would cease to sell. If they refused, the women would begin prayer and song services in the establishments selling liquor. Only women should participate. Male support, both financial and moral, was important, but the men were to remain passive and in the background. Otherwise the emotional force of the movement would be lost.[11] Druggists, who sold liquor in the nineteenth century, were first on the Crusaders' list, undoubtedly because with them the chance of success would be greater than at the saloons. One druggist signed the pledge after much persuasion, two signed willingly, and a fourth postponed his decision.

Now the real work began. The Crusaders made their way next day with solemn steps to the hotels and saloons where the liquor trade was a major part of the business. As they walked singing down the street there were no taunts from passersby, no crowds of shouting boys dogging their footsteps. The farmers in town doing errands stopped their teams of horses and watched with awe. Throughout the day songs and prayers were heard at establishments selling liquor. The women returned to the church in the early evening, and they at last broke ranks to walk home in the moonlight of Christmas Eve. They gathered again at nine the next morning and prayed together for awhile, adjourning later to attend their own churches and be with their families to give them "the attention due the established usage of Christmas Day."[12] But on December 27 they were on the snowy streets again, visiting hotels and saloons. One proprietor gave them "smooth words and fair promises but no signatures."[13] Another was not at home. One polite hotel keeper wished them success but protested that he could not of course close his bar unless everyone else did. Finally they marched on the saloons, which none of these women had ever entered before. They began with the better-class houses, and the astonished proprietors soon had women kneeling in prayer on their sawdust floors and singing evangelical hymns.[14]

The Methodist Episcopal church was the site of an ecumenical mass meeting on Sunday evening, December 28, and the women, Protestants all, were tolerant enough to ask the Catholic priest to join them.[15] He refused. They continued throughout the winter to have prayer meetings and marches every morning and mass meetings in the churches once a week. When saloon doors were locked against them, they knelt in the street, and by the end of the first week of the Crusade, one saloonkeeper was expressing a great desire to get out of business.[16] In a few weeks businesses dispensing intoxicating liquors were reduced from thirteen to four, and those four sold their wares with considerable trepidation.[17] One saloonkeeper became a fishmonger, and fish enjoyed at least temporary favor among Crusade housewives.[18]

Hillsboro was not the only place caught up in the white heat of temperance fervor that winter. Lewis gave the same lecture in the music hall of nearby Washington Court House, Ohio, on December 24. Again his message caught fire. At his suggestion the women gathered at ten the next morning, Christmas Day. The holiday was forgotten, Christmas dinners were cooked by servants or not at all. Committees to frame appeals were appointed, the entire group of women present constituted itself a visitation committee to visit the liquor dispensers next morning, and as their morning session adjourned (with the afternoon well gone) they agreed to gather again in the evening to hear from committees still working, whose reports would be considered for adoption by the larger group. Next morning after a prayer service the women of Washington Court House were on the streets, visiting the drugstores first, but moving on to hotels and saloons, not stopping for dinner or lunch. The men gathered in the church to pray, and the church bells tolled at the end of every hour.[19] On the third day the Washington Court House women tasted success for the first time: a liquor dealer began pouring his stock in the gutters. Unlike most, this praying band was led by a male minister, but when the barrels were rolled out,

> axes were placed in the hands of the women who had suffered most
> [presumably the wives of drunkards], and swinging through the air,
> they came down with ringing blows, bursting the heads of the
> casks, and flooding the gutters of the street. One good woman, put-
> ting her soul into every blow, struck but once for a barrel, splash-
> ing Holland gin and old Bourbon high into the air amid the shouts
> of the people. Four barrels and one cask were forced open, the
> proprietors giving a hearty consent.[20]

For the next three days new victories were reported constantly. The bells continued to toll. The whole town was in a temperance frenzy. At a mass meeting on January 2, the victorious women announced that every dealer had surrendered. Their eight-day campaign had closed eleven saloons and produced pledges from the proprietors of three drugstores to cease selling liquor except on prescription. The women had also confronted physicians and property holders and framed pledges for them to sign.[21] Success had come more quickly than in Hillsboro.

Dio Lewis continued to play a role in the movement. He remained in Ohio lecturing and telling his inspirational story for another two weeks. As the Crusade swept along, he became so involved that he canceled his regular winter lecture series as much as his commitments permitted and returned once more to Ohio, where the Crusade had really caught hold, to provide leadership. His participation helped keep the movement going. The religious press began to report on the work of the Ohio women and the *New York Tribune* sent a reporter, Moses P. Handy, to accompany Lewis.[22] Newspaper coverage contributed significantly to the spread of the work. The press had usually been closed to temperance agitators, but the Crusade, with its spontaneity, its color, and its female participation and leadership, was excellent copy, and it opened newspapers to the temperance cause.

The idea of the temperance Crusade spread, and within three months of

A Saloonkeeper Surrenders, and Signs the Pledge,
Scene from the early crusade.

Reprinted from Jane E. Stebbins, *Fifty Years History of the Temperance Cause* (1876).

the Hillsboro march, women had driven the liquor business out of 250 villages and cities.[23] In Ohio 130 towns had experienced Crusades; Michigan had 36, Indiana 34, Pennsylvania 26, and New Jersey 17.[24] By the time the marches ended, at least 912 communities in 31 states and territories had experienced crusades.[25]

In one small Michigan town, Adrian, the movement began on March 3, 1874. The women involved met daily to plan a mass meeting for March 9, a meeting that was so successful it overflowed the opera house and also an improvised second assemblage at the Presbyterian church. The first march took place two days later. For several weeks the women who participated were totally committed. They must have had time for little else. Committees met early in the morning. Prayer meetings followed. Praying bands were sent out twice a day, and more meetings were held after the marches. Women on the executive committee were most heavily involved, since they had no alternative to daily participation, and two or three were forced to resign because of illness in their families. But bands of 150 were being sent out daily, and over one thousand Adrian women (the population of the city was approximately eight thousand) had pledged to assist in the movement. Certainly the cause had been embraced by many women who did not belong to a leisured upper class, although it was probably the upper middle class that found large blocks of time to give. On March 14, the Adrian women celebrated their first success. One saloonkeeper promised to give up his business by May. The next day three out of twenty-two grocers agreed not to sell intoxicating beverages. Another consented three days later.[26]

Capitulation did not come easily. One saloonkeeper locked in two women for several hours while refusing admission to the larger group gathered outside. The local newspaper reported that

> visions of disaster dire filled the hearts of the rank and file who were left outside. One lady, in a state of breathless excitement, hurried to the Methodist church, where the Executive committee were in session, and informed them that their leaders had been locked into the saloon, and what terrible fate was in store for them, could not be imagined. Instantly the ladies comprising the Executive committee arose, and sallied forth to rescue their comrades. Arrived in front of the saloon, the band was found outside, the ladies inside, and the door locked. What could be done except to wait for them? And they waited. The door was tried and found to

be locked, and then the siege began. Chairs were brought for the ladies and placed on the sidewalk, but so as to have a free passage; later in the evening coffee and other refreshments were furnished by friends of the ladies, the back-door of the saloon was picketed, and the siege was only raised at 11 P.M., when the ladies left for their homes. A great crowd filled the street, and many and various were the comments on the movement. During the progress of the siege it is safe to say that not much business was done at the bar of that saloon.[27]

The Adrian Crusade was well covered by the local press. Each weekly issue of the paper regaled its readers with blow-by-blow accounts of the women's confrontations with Adrian's barkeeps, and the stories were not unsympathetic.[28] Speeches delivered at mass meetings were reported in detail. Many of the addresses were by men, but women were also among the speakers. One woman facing the opera house audience admitted she was so reluctant to speak that she hid behind the curtain. She preferred visiting saloons to forensics.[29]

By summer the open selling of liquor had virtually ceased in Adrian. The marches had been replaced in April by vigilance committees that recorded how many and who entered bars that were still open, and also reported (the Crusaders even hired Pinkerton detectives at one point) on the backdoor business of dealers who were purportedly shut. The daily prayer sessions and weekly mass meetings continued in Adrian until summer. Meanwhile, surrounding communities had joined the movement. The Adrian Crusade was less spontaneous and less dramatic than those in Hillsboro and Washington Court House, but it was effective. And it was marked by an impressive grass-roots fervor and level of commitment.[30]

The first Crusaders met little overt resistance. Their highly charged nonviolent protest demoralized and immobilized the liquor dealers. Saloon patrons were abashed. Who could enjoy drinking as usual when a Bible lay on the bar and the beer-scented air was alive with prayers and hymns? Most patrons stayed home. Many saloonkeepers and liquor dealers were simply bewildered. One Mount Vernon, Ohio, grocer was reported as saying, "Ladies, you look at this whole matter from one standpoint only. You will not consider it from my view nor will you allow me to argue the case with you. When I begin to discuss this question, you begin to sing and pray, and any one of your tongues can make twice as much noise as mine." When a woman began to sing "Nearer My God to Thee," and the others took up the song, the grocer exclaimed, "There you go. I told you you were afraid to hear me."[31] As one contemporary put it, "When a band of women, whom he [the saloon keeper or merchant] knew as the wives and mothers of the best citizens, came, with tender words and earnest prayers, it was an enemy he hardly knew how to fight."[32] Most of the owners began to lock their doors when the women were abroad. But eventually business began to strike back.

The Crusade began in Ohio and so did the resistance of the liquor industry. Cincinnati wholesale liquor dealers early became alarmed at developments in Washington Court House. After most of the existing saloons closed, they staked a young Irishman to the tune of five thousand dollars to open a new saloon in Washington Court House. When the new saloonkeeper's liquor was unloaded from the drays, forty women were on hand. They followed the casks inside and began a prayer meeting that continued uninterrupted until eleven that night. They returned next morning, and the new proprietor locked them in for two hours. On this occasion the women eventually won, and the new proprietor surrendered after four days. His unsold stocks were returned to Cincinnati.[33]

Owners now turned to the courts. Eventually they obtained an injunction restraining the women from singing and praying at an out-of-town beer garden that had remained open when those within the city limits of Washington Court House were closed. The injunction did not stop the women from continuing to pray, and they were taken into court. The defendants were proud of being among the Crusade martyrs and eager to be on the list of those hailed into court, but they did eventually obey that court order, and only the area within the city limits remained dry.[34] The women of Hillsboro were also subjected to injunctions and cease and desist orders.[35] In some communities women were showered with sour beer and threatened with violence, but there was remarkably little physical aggression against them. The women in turn learned to use the law to assist them in their cause. They kept watch and made careful records to prove that liquor was being illegally sold after hours or to minors, and brought the barkeepers to court.[36] They fought hard. They did not give up, as they had in the abortive crusades that Lewis's early lectures had inspired, and their success was conspicuous.

The Crusade never did as well in cities as in small towns, but even cities felt the movement. In Dayton, Ohio, the praying bands were organized in late February 1874, with some assistance from Lewis and the cooperation of most of the city's churches. The women planned their campaign well and did not sally onto the streets until March 6, splitting into two bands and visiting each of the city's saloons in turn. They were not met by the awestruck wonder of passersby as they had been in small-town Hillsboro where everyone knew them. At first they marched in the rain, but the sun came out and crowds began to gather to watch their progress. Sausage and beer were thrown at them. Women joined their male relatives in screaming at the praying temperance bands. But the hostility backfired. Sober, respectable citizens gathered in the churches for evening mass meetings, and the number of marchers increased. The struggle came to a head in a municipal election in April, when the "wets" carried both mayoralty and council races, and the women were barred from the streets by the police. Street crusading ceased, but the temperance cause had won adherents.[37]

Cleveland, Ohio, also experienced a militant Crusade. On one occasion nearly five hundred women marched in a procession a quarter of a mile long. In one part of the city a mob, headed by the brewers, rushed upon the kneeling women, kicking some and bruising others with brickbats. Dogs were set on them at one saloon, but their leader put her hands on the dogs' heads and they knelt quietly at her feet instead of attacking. However, some passersby took off their hats as the marchers went by, and small children frequently joined in the hymns.[38]

In large cities Crusaders met stronger and more violent opposition than they encountered in small towns, but they also attracted sympathy, and the fury of their opposers made converts of those who earlier found marching women unseemly. Midwestern urban centers experienced real Crusades, although in most Eastern Seaboard cities the movement hardly got off the ground. Temperance mass meetings were held, but street activity did not materialize. Dio Lewis addressed a large and enthusiastic audience in Brooklyn on March 12, 1874, and his women listeners promised to proceed "western style," but nothing came of it immediately.[39] However, next October, Brooklyn women did take to the streets, visiting drugstores and claiming to close over a hundred, at least temporarily.[40] Philadelphia was also an exception. More was accomplished in Philadelphia than in any other eastern city. By mid-April Philadelphia Crusaders claimed to have nearly 25,000 women on the streets at one time or another, to have visited 406 saloons, to have persuaded 38 church members to cease renting property for use as saloons, and to have convinced 80 barkeepers to resign.

They also claimed to have obtained pledges from 281 saloonkeepers; pledges to do what, they failed to say, although to cease selling was implied.[41] However, nationwide 750 breweries closed, the production of malt liquor dropped over 5.5 million gallons, and federal excise tax receipts dropped off sharply.[42]

Women were attracted to the Crusade for the same reasons they were attracted to the overall temperance cause—their special vulnerability at the hands of abusers of alcohol, the congeniality of temperance to the doctrine of spheres, and the acceptability of temperance work to many Protestant churches. The general demographic factors that made the 1870s ripe for substantial expansion of women's organizational efforts also contributed to the Crusade's success. But why did the Crusade take off in December of 1873? Its special techniques had been tried before with at most temporary local victory. Why that specific winter rather than some year that preceded or followed it? Several attempts have been made to answer this question. Among others, one of the official historians of the WCTU has suggested that women who were previously involved in the antislavery movement and in the Sanitary Commission (a civilian organization that provided humanitarian services for the armed forces) during the Civil War had already tasted activism. With Reconstruction drawing to a close they were now ready to espouse a new cause, and they found it in the Crusade and the temperance movement.[43] This may be some part of the answer, but from what we know of the appeal of the Crusade on the local level, too many women were involved; the Crusade was too broadly based to be explained by the need of a few already activist women for a new cause. In Adrian, Michigan, nearly half the adult women of the community were participating in some way. Over 32,000 women by actual count participated in the Crusades in Ohio, and nearly 60,000 nationwide, and this is most probably an underestimate.[44]

Also, there is evidence that the Crusade leadership included many women who had no previous experience outside the home or their local parish church. Of the thirty temperance leaders who were singled out for formal portraits in Willard's *Woman and Temperance*, most of whom had participated in the Crusade, eighteen had no previous experience other than as housewives before they joined the temperance movement. True, of the remaining twelve, three had been active with the Sanitary Commission during the Civil War, nine had been professional educators or lecturers, three were lay preachers, three had been leaders in the women's missionary society movement, and one was an attorney (some had of course participated in more than one of these activities).[45] But eighteen of the thirty were venturing forth for the first time. Certainly in a score of states, women who previously led quiet lives, who had always appeared shy and subservient to their husbands, suddenly organized, took to the streets, were locked into airless, smelly saloons, risked arrest, and generally behaved as if nothing counted any longer in their lives except their dedication to the temperance Crusade. Mary Woodbridge, mother of three by the time she was twenty, who had previously devoted herself exclusively to her family, became overnight, when the Crusade came to her home town in Ohio, a talented, moving speaker in the evangelistic style. Before many months Woodbridge was in constant demand as a platform lecturer and eventually became editor of a temperance paper and a national WCTU officer. She had changed from homebody to career woman almost instantly, and obviously she relished her new roles.[46] Eliza Thompson of Hillsboro was certainly not accustomed to organizing and militant leadership, and she always retained some of her original reticence, but she also could and did address hundreds formally from public platforms for the rest of her life.

Some of these leaders were ministers' wives, accustomed to speaking and public visibility. Abbie Fisher Leavitt, whose husband was a Baptist minister, quickly joined the Crusade when it was organized in Cincinnati. She was arrested and jailed briefly in May 1874 while praying on the sidewalk in front of a saloon.[47] She may previously have had experience in leading prayer meetings, but she was not in the habit of running afoul of the law. However, she took incarceration in stride and continued her prayers and hymns for the benefit of the inmates of the jail. Others among the new temperance leaders had worked with the Sanitary Commission during the Civil War and had acquired leadership skills they now put to new use. Eliza Stewart was one of these; she brought praying bands into courtrooms, organized mass meetings, and eventually became a prominent temperance lecturer whose skill on the podium was hailed in Great Britain as well as the United States.[48] But in her commemorative volume on the early leadership of the woman's temperance movement, Frances Willard describes just as many women who changed suddenly, becoming public figures overnight without any previous experience in public causes.

The panic that hit the United States in September 1873 may especially have left rural areas in a more unsettled condition than usual that winter.

The Crusade began in towns and small cities whose economic base rested on agriculture. Norman Clark believes economic instability and the attendant gloom, uncertainty, and confusion, contributed to an atmosphere in which demonstrations could occur.[49] But there was no overt expression of any such connection by the women involved, and the leadership at least was not suffering directly from the panic.[50] In fact the marching women of central Ohio were acting directly against their economic interests. In Hillsboro agricultural commodities were a major source of income. Wheat and corn supplied the raw material for its major industries, five flour mills and two distilleries, and the distilleries far outstripped the flour mills as a source of manufacturing income.[51] However, economic conditions are mentioned in no contemporary accounts of the Crusade.

The United States Centennial was approaching. Were women thinking it was time to put another room of the Republic in order? The Crusaders later participated in the Centennial and saw it as a forum for the temperance cause in just that way. But did they make any connection earlier? Again there is no evidence that they did.

A recent study contends that alcohol was more available through retail outlets in 1873 than it had been since before the Civil War and that the number of saloons per thousand population was increasing rapidly, although it fell equally rapidly the next year. Also, the Crusade was most successful in communities where the saloon was the greatest threat.[52] This explanation must be taken seriously, although the data on which it is based may well present problems; but again why December 1873?

Ohio, where the Crusade began, was in the midst of a constitutional convention that winter of 1873–74, a convention that was considering the issue of liquor licenses and the regulation of the liquor traffic in general. At this time Ohio did not license liquor dealers and forbade the sale of spirits in saloons, where only beer and wine could be vended. Also, under existing Ohio law individuals had to be refused permission to purchase liquor or beer if a relative asked that it not be served. Liquor interests wanted the convention to license saloons to sell spirits, but Ohio's temperance forces vigorously opposed such regulation on the grounds that state licensing of drink implied state approval of intemperance. Divided over the issue, the constitutional convention shifted resolution of the licensing amendment to the voters. In the August 1874 election Ohioans defeated licensing but at the same time turned down the new constitution that would have enforced the decision.[53] The end result was a stalemate, but the debate was hot during the winter of 1873–74 and created the environment in which the Crusade could take off in Ohio: a convention in which women could not participate and in which they were unrepresented, but that addressed an issue that concerned them deeply.

At the same time, the church networks through which women could express and organize a public protest were already in place and functioning: Every meeting of which we have any record at which Crusades were organized and launched took place in Protestant churches. By the 1870s women were well organized for church-related activities. The Crusade permitted them to gather together in an ecumenical cause that built on their individual denominations. This was not the first time this had been done. The moral reform societies of the antebellum period used a similar process. However, the moral reform society of Utica in the 1840s was led by women from one denomination, the Presbyterians, although they were joined by Baptists and others.[54] In the 1870s ecumenical equality was the watchword on the local level. Leadership was carefully and equally apportioned among the several denominations. If exclusion from participation in the Ohio convention's decisions on regulation of the liquor traffic set the stage for the Ohio protest marches, interdenominational solidarity and the ability to organize within the church gave women the means for direct action.

But once the Crusade gained momentum in Ohio, it tapped the growing, if frequently unconscious, need of women everywhere to assert themselves.[55] One cannot read the minutes of the Adrian temperance society for that memorable spring of 1874 without feeling the excitement experienced by these women, and their conviction that anything was possible. Somehow staying home and supervising or performing household tasks would be dull stuff after this heady brew.

In an article in the *Union Signal*, the official organ of the Woman's Christian Temperance Union, in 1883, Margaret Parker, a British temperance worker, suggested to her American counterparts that the Crusade had been the major factor in changing the role of women in the American temperance movement and even in American society. She wrote, "We have had no wonderful crusade in England—no such baptism of power and liberty." Her use of those words, power and liberty, was significant. Parker was seeing the Crusade as an experience that taught large numbers of women to speak and act in public and undertake leadership roles, roles that English women ten years later still dared not assume. She reported that English women in 1883, unlike their American sisters, still believed that "woman's voice should only be heard within the four walls of her own home. English women are utterly dumb at all the meetings which they themselves have with infinite labor got up."[56] Parker's point was well taken, because the Crusade of 1873–74 did effect a change in a considerable segment of conservative middle-class American women, giving them a new sense of identity, a whiff of public power, a taste for the public platform. The Crusade significantly altered their relationship to the larger society.

Mark Twain predicted at the time that the temperance results of the Crusade would prove ephemeral, but he believed that the Crusade would lead inevitably to suffrage for women.[57] Mary Livermore, a prominent temperance leader and suffrage lecturer, agreed with Twain when she assessed the results of the Crusade on its tenth anniversary, saying that she believed its contribution to the temperance movement per se was probably its least important result. Livermore saw the Crusade as unifying women, giving them moral courage and teaching them the power of association: it "taught them to work intelligently, wisely adapting means to ends . . . , [to be] patient, tolerant, able to agree to disagree on minor matters, and yet standing as one where principle is concerned."[58] Henry Blair, the senator and temperance leader from New Hampshire, also saw the Crusade as much more than "an assault on the liquor traffic." He interpreted the Crusade as an unleashing of "strange, rapt and enthusiastic labors, in which man took no part save only as an attendant, a maternal struggle by which the whole sex brought forth a new institution, a woman force, which should be perpetual, and should work out the higher, the supreme life of the womanhood of the future."[59]

Frances Willard, who participated only briefly in the Crusade that spawned the movement she was to lead for twenty years, contended that the Crusade had four major effects. First, women stepped "outside the denominational fence" and "broke down sectarian barriers." They were willing to join hands with anyone on this issue, and the ecumenicism of the movement was a new force in American Protestantism. Second, women were brought face to face with a side of life they had not personally encountered before, and were exposed to life patterns alien to their sheltered homes. They saw poverty and wretchedness firsthand, an exposure that sparked the women's temperance movement towards its later deep concern with broad social issues. Third, the Crusade "taught women their power to transact business, to mould public opinion by public utterance, and opened the eyes of scores and hundreds to the need of the Republic for the suffrages of women, and made them willing to take up for their homes and country's sake the burdens of that citizenship they would never have sought for their own." And fourth, it showed middle-class women how to use their growing leisure in a positive and profitable way.[60]

Willard's biographer credits the Crusade with ushering in the new women's movement.[61] In the sense that relatively conservative women were attracted to the women's movement for the first time, this is certainly true. Characteristic of the Crusade is that conservative women used radical and militant means to obtain their ends. Why were these women able to behave in ways that at first glance seem so out of character? In dozens of communities women organized, marched, prayed, and sang hymns in saloons or on the streets, formed picket lines to prevent the delivery of liquor to the establishments that dispensed it, took down the names of patrons who dared brave these same picket lines, and organized and addressed temperance mass meetings. Why were they able to act in such aggressive ways? In part because they were confronting an evil they saw as a personal threat to themselves and their families, but also because their cause, temperance, had an aura of respectability about it. Almost none of these women in 1874 would have campaigned for so radical a cause as woman suffrage or even admitted to wanting the vote. But in actively, aggressively agitating for temperance, a woman was less likely to meet the unqualified opposition of her male relatives. Her church often found her zeal admirable rather than misplaced. Because the cause was respectable, respectable women could join it.

Frequently, but not always, these Crusaders came from the upper ranks of the society of their towns. Mark Twain characterized them as young girls and women who were "not the inferior sorts, but the very best in their village communities."[62] In a study of ninety-five of the original Hillsboro Crusaders who could be identified, Charles Isetts has shown that these women were "socially and economically the dominant force in Hillsboro at that time." Over 90 percent of Crusader households were native white Americans of two generations' standing or more, and Crusader families controlled two-thirds of Hillsboro County's wealth.[63] Nonetheless the broad appeal of the Crusade should not be underestimated. There were artisans' wives among the Crusaders of both Hillsboro and Adrian. Although the middle-class and upper middle-class networks were present and leading, the cause both attracted and welcomed women from other backgrounds. However, in Adrian, Hillsboro, and Washington Court House women of high social standing clearly predominated in the leadership of the Crusade.[64] Undoubtedly this high social standing, coupled with a sense of righteous womanhood, permitted the Crusaders to feel a keen sense of the justice of their cause and their own moral superiority. They believed their work was in the best interests of society. Certainly this helps to explain their self-confidence and tactical militance.

But beneath the surface, what gave the Crusade its thrust and its real importance was that these women were experiencing power. They were discovering that they could force both governmental bodies and individuals to accede to their demands. Even though they saw this work as defense of a traditionally defined woman's sphere, the radical and public methods they endorsed represented a real if only partially conscious commitment to the idea that women could legitimately function in the public realm. Their work was that of an effective pressure group, and in many instances they succeeded in forcing a male-dominated society to do what they wanted, at least temporarily.

Mary Livermore was right in her insistence that the Crusade should not be measured by its temperance achievements. As she wrote, "That phenomenal and exceptional rising of women in Southern Ohio ten years ago, floated them to a higher level of womanhood. It lifted them out of a subject condition . . . to a plateau where they saw that endurance had ceased to be a virtue."[65] The women themselves, the participants in the Crusade, saw it as a watershed, an experience that had changed their concept of themselves. They articulated these feelings at WCTU conventions and whenever, wherever, they gathered for the rest of their lives. The Crusade had an emotional impact equivalent to a conversion experience and moved these women to feminist principles, whether they recognized them or not.[66] On the tenth anniversary of the Crusade in 1883, both the national convention of the WCTU and the *Union Signal* commemorated the anniversary at length. The anniversary issue of the *Signal* carried two columns of brief anonymous quotes from women who had been Crusade participants; their letters responded to the question "What has the Crusade done for you?" Again and again they expressed the Crusade's meaning to them in terms that today we can only interpret as recognition of its effect on their personal growth and development. Their statements run like this: It "startled me into an active thinking life." It gave me "broader views of woman's sphere and responsibility." Because of it I "developed a new and grander purpose in life." One said it "opened doors of opportunity and tender-hearted fellowship." Another said it "brought me from the retirement of my home into public work." Still another, "The Crusade taught women to do noble deeds not dream them."[67] These conservative, middle-class, churchgoing women obviously realized the larger effects of the Crusade and even after ten years felt very warmly about its influence on their personal and public lives.

At subsequent anniversaries Crusaders continued to describe their experience as a watershed. For one, it "led me out from private literary pursuits, first into work with the masses in opera house, jail, factory, and shop, then into churches, schools, colleges, and the platform."[68] As Eliza Stewart wrote in 1889, "Beautifully, step by step, were those praying women led as the work opened up before them, and soon women who had not dreamed they held such rich gifts in their keeping, were found on pulpits and rostrums with burning words swaying great audiences."[69] A *Signal* editorial in 1889 argued that the Crusade "revolutionalized woman's place and work in the church. Men are slowly coming to recognize God's hand in the unsealing of women's lips and are following the lead of his providence."[70]

The Crusade was a liberating force for a group of church-oriented women who could not have associated themselves directly with the equal rights or suffrage movements. Talented and ambitious women began to break through the social constraints imposed by widely held notions of women's role in the first decades of the nineteenth century and began to build organizations that they themselves controlled.[71] More women joined these early innovators as the antislavery movement gained momentum. Still others were engaged by the activities of the Sanitary Commission during the Civil War and the Freedman's Bureau afterwards. But it took the Crusade of 1873–74 to touch off a mass movement of women that resulted in a nationwide organization with units in thousands of cities and towns, attracting tens of thousands of women members. As Frances Willard wrote, the Crusade "was like the fires we used to kindle on the western prairies, a match and a wisp of grass were all that was needed, and behold the spectacle of a prairie on fire sweeping across the landscape, swift as a thousand untrained steeds and no more to be captured than a hurricane."[72]

The Sober Second Thought

CREATING A NATIONAL

ORGANIZATION

The enthusiastic, evangelical outpouring of antisaloon sentiment that
characterized the Crusade established temperance as an area where women
could effectively organize. But the wild fervor of the fire lit in Ohio during
the winter of 1873–74 was tamed into a purposeful and productive movement at Lake Chautauqua in New York in August 1874. Nearly every town
and city that produced a Crusade also spawned some kind of female
temperance society. The new association in Fredonia, New York, called
itself the Woman's Christian Temperance Union, the first use of that name.
Only Ohio, however, had done much about state organization, holding
several state conventions during the Crusade winter and spring from late
February to June 1874. The Ohio meetings were real organizational
attempts but they were not national, and men as well as women were
involved.[1] Local committees and associations were frequently in touch
with each other, but plans for a national organization did not mature until
summer.

Once again church networks, this time on a national level, came into
play and assisted in the creation of a national organization for temperance
women. In August 1874 a group called by John Heyl Vincent, a Methodist

The chapter title is Frances Willard's euphemistic phrase for the founding convention and
formal organization of the WCTU, recorded in her autobiography, *Glimpses of Fifty Years*,
349.

bishop who developed teaching methods for the rapidly growing sabbath-school movement, gathered at Fair Point on Lake Chautauqua in New York. In association with Lewis Miller, a Methodist Sunday-school super-intendent, Vincent organized and conducted that summer the first national Sunday-school teachers' institute.[2] Women were prominent in the Sunday-school movement, especially as writers of instructional materials, and many women attended the Fair Point Institute, several of whom had participated in the previous winter's Crusade. Inevitably they reminisced about their experiences around the evening campfires. Martha McClellan Brown, a Crusader from Ohio with a long record as a temperance worker, suggested during one of these nostalgic conversations that temperance women needed an organization on a national scale, one that could unite the ardent but frequently isolated women's temperance efforts. Another Ohio Crusader, Mrs. G. W. Manly, suggested they take immediate steps toward organization. Vincent's aid was enlisted, and he read from the Assembly Hall's pine-board platform the women's call for a temperance organization meeting.

Vincent's reputation helped to launch the new organization. When he associated himself with the first call for a meeting, his considerable prestige became attached to the movement and lent it national stature. However, it was Jennie Willing of Illinois, a guest at the assembly who had been corresponding secretary of the Woman's Foreign Missionary Society of the Methodist church and also a professor of English language and litera-ture at Illinois Wesleyan University, who took the lead in planning and presided over the first meeting, which was attended by some fifty women. Willing and Emily Huntington Miller, who acted as secretary, used their church network contacts to circulate a letter to be sent to all women's temperance organizations urging them to hold conventions and elect from each congressional district a delegate to a national organizing convention to be held in Cleveland in November.[3] The decision to base delegate representation on congressional districts proved an important one, although why political divisions were chosen seems to have been forgotten in the course of time. The Crusade had been organized by city or town. However, the emphasis on moral reform and local control that marked the Crusade was soon joined with larger political goals, and the initial pattern of organization by congressional district, used until 1888, may have enabled the WCTU to embrace this dual emphasis more easily. Without doubt it expedited political action in the early years.

The committee on organization that was appointed at Chautauqua was widely based. No two members came from the same state, and the membership spanned the continent from the Eastern Seaboard to California.[4] Jennie Willing, Emily Miller, and Martha Brown were best known of the group, having already achieved solid national reputations, but only Brown had been prominent earlier in national temperance organizations. Both Miller and Willing had made their previous contributions through the missionary societies of the Methodist church. Brown had participated not only in the Crusade, but in the conventions in Ohio the previous spring, and had also worked earlier with the Templars. The letter circulated by Willing and Miller brought a good response, and conventions were held in a number of states. In Illinois, for example, delegates gathered on October 27 in Bloomington. They not only selected delegates for a national convention, but elected officers and set up a state organization as well.

On Wednesday, November 18, 1874, the first national convention of the Woman's Christian Temperance Union gathered in Cleveland, Ohio, in the lecture room of the Second Presbyterian Church. Sixteen states were represented and 135 women registered; unofficial visitors who accompanied the delegates brought the total to 300.[5] Its members were acutely aware of the larger significance of the assembly. The presiding officer found it appropriate to remark that such a conference of women would have been impossible a generation or two earlier, when "woman was often no more than a slave to man." Another participant saw it as one of the "most hopeful of conventions since that one in Philadelphia when they wrote of 'life, liberty and the pursuit of happiness.' "[6] The delegates proceeded to organize, elect permanent officers, and adopt a constitution, a brief document outlining general structure, which was drawn up by a committee headed by Judith Ellen Foster, an Iowa attorney and suffragist. There was discussion about including "Christian" in the name of the organization. That this was discussed shows the ecumenicism of the movement, but since the large majority of the delegates were Protestant, the proponents of explicit Christian commitment soon won the contest. So that the WCTU would not become a national movement in name only, in effect controlled from the Atlantic Seaboard or the heartland of the Midwest, broad geographical representation was insured by a provision that there should be a vice-president from each state.[7]

Men participated as guests, not members, of the Cleveland convention. Men were never voting members of the WCTU as they were in the National

American Woman Suffrage Association. The planning committee of the first convention did ask a man to preside over one session, but the minutes carefully note that it was not a business meeting. In succeeding years men were asked occasionally to address public evening programs or make welcoming remarks in their capacity as public officials. They were also urged to contribute financially as honorary members, but they could not vote, hold office, or participate in debate.

To exclude men from membership and substantive participation in the Union was a decision that markedly increased the WCTU's potential for capturing top place as an outlet for the woman's movement in the nineteenth century. Because the WCTU from the beginning banned males from voting membership, men never became competitors in the WCTU for leadership roles. On state, local, and national levels, women did the work, set the policies, and monopolized the offices. No other existing organization provided women with a similar forum over which they exercised complete control. For example, in 1892 over 3,500 of the nearly 4,000 members of organizations associated with the National Conference of Charities were women. However, women held only 20 percent of the national and 40 percent of the state offices.[8] The National American Woman Suffrage Association was led exclusively by women for some years after 1869, but it represented the more radical suffragists who followed Susan B. Anthony and Elizabeth Cady Stanton, and could scarcely be called a mass organization. Women began through the Woman's Board of Missions to assume partial control over the work of some female foreign missionaries in 1868, but did not exercise complete control nationally or in the mission field.[9] The decision to exclude men from membership in the WCTU broke new ground and was crucial to the role the WCTU would play in the woman's movement.

The first convention also adopted a plan of work that foreshadowed some aspects of the program the Woman's Christian Temperance Union would be pursuing for the rest of the century. The convention agreed to the principle of total abstinence, and its delegates circulated and signed temperance pledges that were unequivocal. They committed themselves to strongly promoting the introduction of temperance education in both Sunday schools and public schools. They supported continuing the evangelical methods, mass meetings, prayer services, and the like that had been used with success during the Crusade. They agreed to welcome and actively seek publicity and publish and distribute literature, to urge newspapers to let them contribute temperance columns, and to urge the public press to take notice of their meetings and other activities.[10]

These first program commitments were never repudiated, although later much expanded, and the convention's first set of resolutions was more modest than in later years. The 1874 resolutions opposed intemperate men in office, called for banishing liquor and wine from public banquets and the tables of public officials, demanded a congressional committee to investigate the liquor traffic, and admonished physicians to use care in prescribing alcohol as medicine.[11] Several more extreme resolutions were introduced and rejected. One, which called for the disfranchisement of rum-sellers under certain conditions, was tabled. Another, which censured the churches for equivocating on the temperance question, was replaced by a mild, sisterly call for cooperation in temperance work from organized Christianity. A third, which suggested it was better for physicians to allow patients to die than prescribe alcohol as medicine, resulted in spirited debate. One group of delegates felt it was legitimate for physicians to prescribe alcohol as medicine just as they would any poison, such as arsenic, that had specific medicinal uses. Others adamantly believed that any use of alcohol was wrong. A moderate substitute motion urging physicians to use caution in the prescription of alcohol was suggested by Frances Willard of Illinois and unanimously adopted.[12] The more controversial but rejected resolutions, however, were picked up by the press; the convention was credited with adopting them, and newspapers cited them to show the irresponsibility of the movement. The new officers wrote letters to the editor to set the record straight.

A spirited contest developed over the choice of a national president. Nine names were placed in nomination. Technically no names were withdrawn, but several nominees asked not to be considered, among them Jennie Willing, the presiding officer of the organizing convention. Willing could probably have been elected had she not asked to be excused.[13] Three obvious candidates were eager for election. Martha Brown, who had provided the spark at Chautauqua that generated the convention and who had the longest and clearest record of leadership in the temperance cause, wanted very much to be the first president. Abbie Fisher Leavitt, who had been active in the Cincinnati Crusade and was secretary of the Ohio Baptist Missionary Society, was also a prime contender. But the best known of the three front-runners was Annie Wittenmyer, founder of the Methodist Home Missionary Society, editor of the *Christian Woman*, a Methodist newspaper, and a woman who had distinguished herself in her work with the Sanitary Commission during the Civil War.[14] Abraham Lincoln had endorsed her pass in his own hand when as agent of the Sanitary Commission, she introduced a system of diet kitchens into the general hospitals of the Union armies.[15] In 1874 Wittenmyer was a vigorous widow of forty-seven, with control of an established newspaper, the columns of which could be used to assist the temperance cause. Her willingness to lend her prestige to this infant movement could be and was of tremendous importance to its success. On the first ballot Wittenmyer and Leavitt were tied, each receiving thirty-one votes. Brown came in a poor third with only nine votes; she was disappointed and withdrew from the organization.[16] A motion to move a unanimous ballot for Leavitt failed. Instead Leavitt served as vice-president for Ohio, and Wittenmyer was elected president, although a number of delegates abstained.

In the elections of supporting officers, Frances Willard of Illinois, a professional educator and a recent adherent of the temperance cause, was chosen corresponding secretary. Mary Johnson of Brooklyn, New York, who had been Willard's runner-up, was elected recording secretary, and Mary Ingham of Cleveland, who had been part of the Chautauqua group, became treasurer.[17] The states were represented through the vice-presidents; the Ohio Crusaders and the Chautauqua founders each had a member on the Board of Managers; the sympathy of conservative church-women was insured by Wittenmyer's presidency; and Willard represented the militant and aggressive Illinois contingent.

The convention also stimulated fellowship and cameraderie. Crusade experiences were exchanged and relived. The delegates and visitors were housed, with some exceptions, in the homes of Cleveland's temperance sympathizers, providing ample opportunity for sisterly friendships to develop. Four mass meetings occupied the evening hours, to which the general public was invited and at which the movement's most spellbinding speakers were to be heard. It was a dramatic moment when Mary Lathrap of Michigan, a licensed preacher of the Congregational church, stretched out her hands to give the apostolic benediction, a woman officiating at a religious rite in a conservative Presbyterian church.[18]

Press reports of the convention were remarkably favorable. The *Cleveland Advocate* stated that "no one could have witnessed the proceedings

Annie Wittenmyer, President of the WCTU 1874–1879.

without having his estimate of the strength of woman's intellect perceptibly raised," and that few were prepared to see so many women able to speak so well, especially extemporaneously.[19] Jennie Willing, as presiding officer, was consistently praised. The *Cleveland Herald* described her as discharging her duties "most admirably, evincing a knowledge of parliamentary rules rarely seen in a woman, and a delicate tact in keeping the ladies in order, and occasionally preventing threatened friction by the oil of a few well chosen words, that were a pleasure to witness."[20] Willard was characterized by one newspaper as "the embodiment of sprightly intellectual ability, highly cultured," and Wittenmyer as "a woman of great zeal and earnestness, entrenched behind a volley of words, always ready for the siege."[21] Although many of the delegates were middle-aged housewives whose primary concern was temperance, the convention roster included three ministers licensed to preach, a lawyer, and several college professors, writers, and editors. Women with many talents were on hand.

The convention was businesslike and efficient and its decisions conservative, despite the fact that it was seen as "the first in the history of our mixed race where women reveled in their own sweet councils without the obtrusion of a masculine voice."[22] The large contingent of delegates whose primary allegiance was to missions and the various Protestant denominations gave it an unquestioned air of respectability. By the last quarter of the nineteenth century women were generally accepted as church workers although not usually as members of church governing bodies. Women exercised local leadership in the missionary societies of several Protestant churches. Again the Union was building on women's experience in the churches. But for many experienced churchwomen the convention was their first identification with the temperance movement in a public capacity except for the Crusade itself. It was also their first experience with a nonsectarian organization not auxiliary to a specific Protestant denomination, and their first experience with an organization led exclusively by women. These innovations were offset, however, by the conservative implications of the convention's clear connection to Protestant Christianity. The means were radical but the goals widely accepted. The convention also showed its conservatism by eschewing politics. No reference was made to woman suffrage in its deliberations. No political party was endorsed, although the Prohibition party had been in existence since 1869. And the convention's choice of a president underlined its conservative aura. Wittenmyer had addressed by invitation the congregations of several Cleveland Methodist churches before the opening of the convention, which indicates the esteem in which she was held by clergy and laity alike.[23]

When the first national convention adjourned on November 20, responsibility for sustaining the movement's initial momentum fell to the national officers, specifically the four general officers. The vice-presidents were occupied with holding the state organizations together and perfecting their structure. And though Mary Johnson and Mary Ingham made their contributions, the major burden of national leadership was borne by Annie Wittenmyer and Frances Willard. As women they represented quite different qualities. Wittenmyer was a national figure with proven organizational competence, a large following among organized churchwomen, and a secure reputation as an editor. Her devotion to the temperance cause was well established. Frances Willard was a relative newcomer to the temperance movement. She was not one of the original Crusaders, and her professional career had been in education. In her most recent position she had been dean of women and professor at Northwestern University, and until the summer of 1873, when Evanston College for Ladies was absorbed by Northwestern, she had been its president. After the merger Willard became subordinate to Northwestern's new president, Charles Fowler, a man to whom she had been briefly affianced in 1861. She was far from happy at this shift to junior status, and she and Fowler bitterly disagreed on the extent of Willard's jurisdiction over the women students whose president she had recently been. Willard was a fighter, but Fowler eventually stooped to petty harassment, and their differences led to her resignation in June 1874. One result of this personal crisis was that Willard was absorbed in her own struggles during the winter of 1873–74, and was not caught up in the Crusade fervor.

Willard made much of her early temperance proclivities in her later writing. In her autobiography she tells how her father was an honorary member of the Washingtonian Society as early as 1835, and how she herself had taken the pledge at sixteen, cutting its words from a juvenile magazine called the *Youth's Cabinet* and pasting it in the family Bible. She described the make-believe city she and her sister created as children, a city that needed no jail because it housed no saloons or billiard halls.[24] But Willard freely admitted, even after she had become "Queen of Temperance," that she had used wine and beer as beverages during her European travels from 1868 to 1870 and that she had attended only two temperance lectures in her life before joining the WCTU.[25] After she became president of the WCTU, Willard made a conscious effort to associate herself with the Crusade. In her autobiography she asserts that in 1873–74, "all through that famous battle winter of Home *versus* Saloon, I read every word that I could get about the movement," and that she assigned temperance topics for themes in her rhetoric and composition classes at Northwestern.[26] However, her Crusade experience was at best contrived and minimal. On her way back to Chicago from the East in the fall of 1874, Willard stopped at Pittsburgh to visit the Female College, where she had taught in 1863–64. The Pittsburgh Crusade was still in progress, and Willard asked her friends to arrange for her to join a praying band. They introduced her to the Pittsburgh Crusaders, and she stood on the curb singing and praying for a couple of hours at a saloon where the Crusaders were denied entrance. She later wrote of this brief experience, "Never in my life, save beside my sister Mary's dying bed, had I prayed as truly as I did then. This was my Crusade baptism."[27] And it was the only time that Willard personally took direct action against the liquor business. Willard differed from other early national leaders of the WCTU in not having previously allied herself with the temperance cause. All the others had been Crusaders. Several had belonged to the Templars or other temperance groups.

Women assumed leadership of the temperance movement at an opportune time for Willard. Her career in higher education was falling apart, and she was casting about for a new direction to her life. Perhaps because her recent professional associations with men had been unpleasant, she was involving herself more and more with the growing woman's movement. She was among the signers of the call for the Woman's Congress that had met in October 1873 to protest the leadership of Susan B. Anthony and Elizabeth Cady Stanton in the suffrage movement and that eventually resulted in the founding of the Association for the Advancement of Women. She attended the congress and was elected a vice-president, a tribute to her prominence as a leading woman educator. This post enhanced her visibility in those circles where church and temperance leaders moved. She must have known that if she joined the temperance cause, she would be in a strategic position to play a leadership role.

Both Willard and Anna Gordon, her confidant and private secretary, report that Willard went east in the summer of 1874 with the acknowledged purpose of studying the temperance movement and conferring with its leaders.[28] Willard visited Boston, where she met Dio Lewis, and New York

Yours for Home Protection,
Frances E. Willard
Jan. 30, 1889.

Frances E. Willard, President of the WCTU 1879–1898.
From her autobiography, *Glimpses of Fifty Years*.

City, where she spoke with several women active in the temperance cause. But the highlight of the trip was the Gospel Temperance Camp Meeting at Old Orchard Beach, Maine, organized by Francis Murphy, an Irish temperance reformer, which Willard attended with two of her new temperance friends, Mary Johnson and Mary Hartt of Brooklyn.[29] Willard later saw this experience as the turning point in her life.

A prestigious group had gathered at Old Orchard Beach. Maine's ex-governor, Nelson Dingley, was among the organizers, as was the presiding elder of the Methodist church. Several women who had participated in the Crusade in Chicago and other parts of the West were also on hand. Willard was asked to address one of the evening meetings, at which the audiences ran to two or three thousand people.[30] She performed well. One unidentified listener, writing to her children, commented, "Her language was remarkable for eloquence and simplicity. She told her story of her first awakening to the need of women in the great 'Temperance Crusade.' There was pathos in some of the pictures which she drew, which caused even the men to weep. Having been principal of a female school she was very refined and highly cultivated. A straight elegant figure, an oval face, a wealth of brown hair and a clear bell-like voice made her a very effective speaker. It was the first woman I had ever heard in public."[31]

Willard found visibility on her eastern trip. She was attracting a national audience, and her forensic talents were being admired in temperance circles both east and west. In the early fall of 1874 the Chicago Union, already militant and well organized, invited her to be their president. She accepted with no apparent second thoughts, although nothing was agreed about salary and she had no savings or income other than what she earned.[32] The Illinois Union elected her corresponding secretary at its convention in October. In November she assumed national office. For most of the next twenty-five years she was a professional temperance worker. But she came to this commitment late, and she was to see the role of women in the movement and the proper program for the Union to follow, quite differently from her older colleague, Annie Wittenmyer.

As Wittenmyer and Willard took up their work together, it was soon obvious that Wittenmyer's primary commitment was to gospel temperance. Wittenmyer believed the Union's program should emphasize personal reform of the drunkard and of the whole liquor industry by moral suasion. This was the route the Crusade had taken—religious conversion, Christian commitment, acknowledgment of sin, and willingness to abandon evil ways. Wittenmyer used political action on occasion, but recoiled from legislative activity that might lead women to seek the ballot. Wittenmyer sincerely believed that asking women to campaign for the vote would "strike a fatal blow at the home."[33]

On the other hand, Willard's primary commitment may not have been to temperance. From the beginning, women's rights probably commanded her deeper loyalty. Evidence suggests that Willard's first allegiance was to the women's movement and that temperance provided her with means rather than ends. As early as 1868–70, when she was touring Europe with her friend Kate Jackson, Willard decided to devote her life to the "woman question."[34] By 1871 she was giving a public lecture on "The New Chivalry," which formally committed her to mild feminist goals. She did not, however, join the Evanston equal suffrage organization, because her mother convinced her it would be a risky and controversial step for a college president.[35] But her basic commitment to the goals of the women's movement, including suffrage, was clear. In this sense Willard was an opportunist. She always had an eye for the expedient course. This aided rather than detracted from her ability to lead women along new paths.

Willard put her commitment to temperance first in her autobiography, stating she originally urged the woman's ballot in 1876 solely as a weapon to protect the home from the abuses of drink, rather than as an end in itself.[36] Willard was sincerely committed to temperance as a necessary reform, but it was the special role assumed by women in the winter of 1873–74 that made the temperance cause attractive to her. She looked with interest and sympathy at conservative women asserting themselves in an acceptable cause, organizing programs, determined to influence social patterns, and creating an exclusively women's organization. From childhood Willard had chafed against the bonds of conventional womanhood. Her closest friends called her Frank, the nickname she adopted as a very young girl. She wept when her mother told her at adolescence that she must put up her untamed hair and abandon the trousers in which she roamed the family farm, for more seemly skirts. She was angry when her brother voted for the first time, for she realized that casting a ballot would never be her privilege.[37] She demanded and got a larger portion of higher education than was normal for middle-class girls of her generation.[38] She earned her living because she had to, but also because she liked the independence it gave her. Once free of her brief conventional betrothal, she seems never again to have been tempted by the financial and social security of marriage.

Wittenmyer and Willard shared and competed for the leadership of the Woman's Christian Temperance Union until Willard won the battle in 1879. On the surface their differences were tactical, a debate over means. Should the Union's primary weapon be moral suasion or political solutions? Should the organization adhere strictly to temperance issues or work for broader social and political programs? But there were deep personal differences as well, the old leader versus the newcomer, stolid solidity versus brilliant innovation, middle age versus relative youth. However, Willard frequently treated the older woman as her mentor, leader and spiritual advisor. "Tell me what to do and I'll obey," she wrote in March 1875.[39] She accepted Wittenmyer's complaints about her abominable penmanship and tried to write more legibly.[40] In the first year of their relationship Willard frequently expressed warm affection towards Wittenmyer.[41] They began as friends and stayed friends at least into 1876. Willard was sometimes impatient, Wittenmyer occasionally annoyed, but they cooperated in holding the WCTU together and brought it through its first difficult months.

Together they faced and attempted to solve a number of problems. One of the most pressing was money. Financial backing was almost nonexistent at the national level. No provision had been made for the officers' expenses and travel, much less their salaries. Annie Wittenmyer had her newspaper and her missionary society work to sustain her and was probably not completely without private resources; her husband had been a man of some wealth. Mary Johnson was the daughter of a Brooklyn banker. Mary Ingham had a husband to help support her, and she also earned something from her writings. Willard had no private income. She depended on the salary promised her by the Chicago Union, which was not always forthcoming. Of all the officers Willard made the greatest personal sacrifice. Dues were woefully inadequate to support the work at the national level. The bylaws specified that the state unions would pay the national organization five cents for each member of a local affiliate, but frequently this assessment was not paid. Receipts for 1874–75 totaled less than $400.00, and over half of that came from a single state, Ohio. Even the state of Maine, where the temperance cause had long been successful, contributed only $1.50 to the national treasury; Illinois, where the Union was flourishing, a mere $4.50.[42]

But money was only one problem facing the leaders of the new organization. They had no literature and no publications. How were they to organize, expand, or even hold the original group together? Requests for copies of the national constitution had to go unmet because there were none to send. Not even a tract with a simple statement on how to organize new unions existed. There was no manual that would bring the constitution, advice on organizational strategy, and names and addresses of officers under one cover. Willard went to work on a manual, but the press of other work constantly interfered, and the manual did not appear until September 1875.[43] Women were writing approximately three-quarters of the temperance tracts and books published in the United States by 1875.[44] But all of these were done under other auspices, chiefly the National Temperance Society and Publication House, and the WCTU was largely dependent on this literature its first two years. By convention time in 1875 six issues of a monthly paper, the *Woman's Temperance Union* (which later became part of the consolidated *Union Signal*), had appeared under WCTU auspices.[45] Wittenmyer was publisher, and Jennie Willing editor. Willard and Mary Johnson acted as contributing editors.[46] Financial backing was inadequate, and not until 1883 did the organization support an official organ with ease.

Finding ways to appeal to membership at the local level was a problem suffrage groups were unable to solve in the nineteenth century. The Union was to be much more successful. The early WCTU attempts to facilitate communication were primitive at best, but perhaps their very naïveté helped the cause along. Mary Livermore, suffragist, Unitarian, and president of the Massachusetts Union, urged Willard in the fall of 1876 to stop trying to save that "worthless paper" that she saw as "dull, stupid and loaded with 'pious blarney.' "[47] Livermore's advice was not followed and the WCTU continued to grow, even if it was a struggle to keep information flowing to the boondocks.

Program also caused problems that first year. In its care to not antagonize possible supporters, the organizing convention did not commit itself to much. As Willard complained to Wittenmyer later in the fall, "no one of all its utterances favored prohibition."[48] Pressing tactical questions needed to be settled. Was the WCTU to remain as the Crusade itself had originally been conceived, an organization committed only to moral suasion, to reforming individuals? Was this a purely religious movement? Or did it have political aims, of which prohibition need be only a part? Willard favored prohibition and woman suffrage but was still concerned in 1874 about the expediency of openly espousing these aims.[49] She was fully supportive of the gospel temperance meeting approach at first. Willard saw gospel temperance as replacing the saloon visiting of the Crusade, and she herself actively participated in the daily meetings at Lower Farwell Hall in Chicago. She and her Chicago colleagues spent much time working with individuals, bringing them to the point of taking the pledge, helping them keep it once taken, and assisting and counseling the families of drunkards. Working directly with derelicts in the center city, Willard became acutely conscious of the problems of the unemployed, but at the time she envisioned no broader solution than continuing her temperance work among them. She suggested to Wittenmyer that they sponsor a national day of prayer. Willard felt that only "as I come close to God and through Christ's blood am made a new creature, am I ready for this work so blessed and so high."[50] Gospel temperance provided the initial thrust of the movement's program even for Willard.

While Willard was unsure of the expediency, but not the basic rightness, of political action, Wittenmyer in turn was not opposed to using government to publicize the evils attendant on the liquor traffic. For example, Wittenmyer did not hestitate to lead a petition campaign memorializing Congress to set up a committee to investigate the evils of drink, a major WCTU project during its first year. Ten thousand petitions were printed, and well over forty thousand signatures obtained. Wittenmyer and a colleague took the petition, a huge roll tied in blue ribbons, to Washington in February. The women, unskilled in political action, were not sure in which house to introduce the document. They decided to have a look at both. They went first to the gallery of the House, but the whiskey and tobacco fumes rising from the floor drove them away. As Annie Wittenmyer was acquainted with several senators, they moved their scene of operations to that chamber. Wittenmyer's senatorial acquaintances had been cordial enough before, but now were less than pleased to see her, and several found themselves too busy to pay her any mind. Eventually Senator Oliver Perry Morton of Indiana came to their assistance. The women had brought the petition in a carriage because it was too heavy to carry. Morton sent a page to lug it onto the Senate floor, where its size attracted many a curious stare. A senator was speaking on Louisiana and Reconstruction, but Morton soon found time to introduce the petition. It was referred to the Committee on Finance (presumably because of the federal excise taxes on liquor). The women followed it there and were permitted to testify in its behalf. The committee eventually reported itself favorable to an investigation, but the measure did not receive a place on the calendar before adjournment, and quietly died. Wittenmyer was not abashed. She was comfortable enough with this kind of political action and urged they continue petitioning Congress until they had achieved success.[51] At the same time, Willard was aware that the WCTU could be accused of inconsistency if it attempted "to move the arm of the law while we declare that ours is 'a purely religious movement.' "[52] She originally accepted the premise that political action should be used with caution.

Despite questions about program, the Union's primary problem in the first years was organizational spread: the WCTU must move into states where state unions did not exist, and multiply the number of local unions in states that were already organized. This was an area for which Willard assumed primary responsibility from the beginning and was one of her major contributions long before she became president. Much of the original organizing was done by mail. Again the Union made use of existing church networks. Willard wrote prominent clergymen in every state and territory asking for the names and addresses of women active in or committed to the temperance cause. She claimed to have written two thousand letters in eighty days during the summer of 1875 without any secretarial assistance. She wrote the national vice-presidents querying them on what they were doing in the states.[53] She corresponded with local unions. Her years of extensive travel would come later, but as the year moved on she traveled more and more, begging railroad passes and lodging, depending on free-will offerings for the rest of her expenses. At first her trips were to nearby communities, but her wide correspondence was building her a national constituency. Before the 1875 convention she had visited Missouri, Minnesota, Chautauqua, Rhode Island, and New York, attending state conventions and addressing sympathetic groups.[54] Her travel and her letter-writing not only facilitated the growth of the Union but enhanced her personal prestige as well.

Willard was rapidly becoming more visible to the rank and file membership and the public at large than Wittenmyer. She was also more frequently giving, rather than asking, advice in her counsels with the president. She told Wittenmyer what to put in the *Union*, urged her to pay attention to the wording of convention calls, and suggested printing the program for the national convention. She sent long itemized lists of instructions for the national convention, ranging from changes in the constitution and bylaws to how to decorate the pulpit. By late 1875 Willard was subtly pushing for commitment to broader political programs.[55] In a letter of October 27, she stated that the convention must "pronounce directly that our object is not only to pull drowning men from the stream but to make our influence felt at the fountains of power."[56] Unfortunately, Wittenmyer's letters to Willard do not exist. Either Willard did not save them or they were destroyed by Anna Gordon when she went through Willard's papers after her death. We do not know how Wittenmyer responded to this growing spate of advice and command.

The convention that met in Cincinnati in November 1875 was a success. By this time twenty-one states were organized, in contrast to sixteen states the previous year. No major changes were made in organization or program. The convention adopted a set of resolutions almost identical to those of the year before except for a fuzzy acceptance of the idea that women and men should both have a voice (the women by petition and the men by ballot) on the question of prohibiting saloons in their communities.[57] The resolution was adopted without debate and with little real understanding of its implications by the rank and file. Much of its support derived from general respect for its sponsor, Zerelda Wallace of Indiana, the stepmother of Lew Wallace, author of *Ben Hur*.[58] Most WCTU leaders opposed the resolution and permitted its presentation only in deference to Wallace's prestige. All the officers except the treasurer were reelected, Wittenmyer unanimously. The convention carefully sidestepped controversy, replying with great caution to greetings from the National American Woman Suffrage Association, then meeting in New York, that hailed the approaching day when women would be armed with the ballot and help to make the laws. The WCTU replied with an ambiguous platitude about abiding "God's will awaiting his future providence," written by Frances Willard herself.[59]

During the Union's first year, patterns had been established that would last out the century. Most significant was the emphasis on organization at the local level, a policy that insured the mass base necessary for effective action. Little evidence of the WCTU's later breadth of program was as yet apparent, but Willard's increasing visibility as leader of the movement already foreordained future goals far beyond temperance, goals that would be partially defined and articulated in the 1870s and fully implemented under Willard as president in the 1880s.

Grasping the Sword

THE WCTU IN THE 1870s:

PROGRAM, TACTICS AND

LEADERSHIP

The Woman's Christian Temperance Union easily outstripped other women's organizations in size and importance during the 1870s. Nearly 1,200 local unions with 27,000 members, plus another 25,000 members in 300 juvenile clubs composed of children and young girls, created an organizational network reaching to the community level over much of the East and Midwest. Ohio had the largest number of unions (208), followed by Massachusetts (160), Michigan (150), and Illinois (129).[1] The WCTU was still weak in the South. Beginnings had been made in Maryland, the District of Columbia, Missouri, and West Virginia, but states below the Mason-Dixon line were essentially unorganized. The 1878 convention was held in Baltimore in the hope that proximity would spur on the cause in the South, but as one brave Tennessee woman had reported earlier, "The prejudices of the Southern people are all against women doing anything in public, and especially opposed to the Woman's Temperance Crusade. Particularly is this true of our ministers. They quote St. Paul, and tell us we are wonderfully out of our places."[2] Attempts had been made to organize the Rocky Mountain area and the Far West, but the results were inconse-

The chapter title is from a hymn sung at early conventions, as reported in Frances Willard's *Glimpses of Fifty Years*, 349: "Hear the call, / O gird your armor on; / Grasp the Spirit's Mighty Sword."

quential. Although the Union was impressive in size, it suffered from substantial geographical gaps.

Despite its numerical strength, the WCTU was a shoestring operation financially. With less than $500 in the bank, the national Union's receipts for the fiscal year 1879 were slightly over $1,200. Only two state unions, New Jersey and Iowa, paid over $100 into the national treasury, and Florida and Arkansas contributed seventy-five and ten cents respectively. In the first five years of its existence, the national organization disbursed a paltry $3,051.[3] Local and state unions were much more affluent in the early years. The national treasurer reported receipts of $657 in 1876, but the Chicago Union alone spent over $2,000.[4] Total funds raised and expended nationwide were many times the national budget, and because the count was based on the payment of dues to national headquarters, national membership figures underestimate the actual membership of local unions. National dues were frequently delinquent, but perhaps the fact that money was spent more freely on the local level is what made the WCTU strong. Certainly by building on Crusade enthusiasm the Union had marshaled a strong corps of supporters by the end of the decade.

Program played one part in enlisting grass-roots support. Through the 1870s the program of the WCTU emphasized gospel temperance. Locals concentrated on convincing people to sign the pledge and on holding an occasional mass meeting with temperance speakers. A logical extension of gospel temperance was to visit jails, almshouses, and prisons. Six states reported some kind of prison work by 1878, which usually consisted of little more than holding prayer meetings, urging inmates to sign the pledge, and distributing temperance tracts.[5] Active work was under way in all the New England states, most of the Midwest, and the Middle Atlantic states, and by 1879 progress had been made. More important, the quality and focus of the Union's jail and prison efforts was changing. Jail visiting, if only to hold a prayer meeting, was calling women's attention to serious evils in the prison system. Men, women, and children frequently occupied common and squalid prison quarters in the 1870s. Prostitutes, elderly drunks, felons, and young children might all share a single cell. The prison committees of the WCTU first concentrated their attention on obtaining special facilities for women, stating firmly that "they are our sisters, and particularly our charge."[6] Most women prisoners were prostitutes, and in 1878, the national convention set up its Committee on Work for Fallen Women, which repudiated the double standard, suggested refuges for women who wished to reform, and advocated legislation to prohibit the employment of women in saloons.[7] Local and state unions also fostered prison reform. The Michigan WCTU in 1879 had pushed through to success a massive petition campaign to secure a model reformatory for girls.[8] Prison work slowly broadened the WCTU's spectrum of concerns.

A much larger share of local union effort, however, went into the campaign to banish wine from the communion table. This thorny issue had been avoided at the first convention, but at the second, a committee had been authorized to investigate the propriety of using wine in celebrating the sacraments. This committee reported in 1876, citing a plethora of Biblical scholarship to show that fermented wine was not condoned by scripture or necessary for the sacraments. The committee argued that the word *wine* was actually a mistranslation which referred to an unfermented grape juice in common use among Jews in the first century, and that the Bible taught total abstinence from alcohol except when used as medicine.[9] The report was adopted by the convention, and the battle against communion wine began. It was most successful. Over the next few years grape juice replaced wine in almost all Methodist, Baptist, and Congregational churches and some Presbyterian churches, although the change met with much more initial resistance from that denomination. Episcopalian, Lutheran, and Catholic churches were unmoved. By 1879 appeals had been sent to church boards, ministers, and conference governing bodies to adopt unfermented wines. Pressure was put on Protestant churches at every level, and WCTU members of these churches abstained from partaking in the rite of holy communion until their congregations fell into line.[10] The membership was universally enthusiastic about this phase of the action program.

Another area in which the Union behaved aggressively in the 1870s was the promotion of temperance education in Sunday schools. Initially the leaders of the Sunday-school movement were not in sympathy with temperance education, or at least wished to devote little time to it. The quarterly series prepared by the International Sunday School Committee was in most general use. The WCTU proposed that one temperance lesson per quarter be included in the series, substituted for the review lesson if necessary. Meanwhile the Union improvised. Emily Huntington Miller and Lucia Kimball, both experienced in writing for children, prepared temperance lesson plans that could be substituted for the quarterly review lesson. These were printed in WCTU publications and efforts were made to get local churches to use them. By 1879 the national WCTU had secured minimal cooperation from the publishers of all Sunday-school lessons except the *Sunday School Times*, and even the *Times* was publishing some temperance lessons as alternatives in its regular series. After five years of effort about two-thirds of the Sunday schools in Maine, New Hampshire, and Vermont were doing something about temperance education. In other states success was spotty.[11] The International Sunday School Committee did not incorporate temperance into its regular series until 1887. Again the full membership was enthusiastic in support of this phase of the Union's program. However, little was done in the 1870s to put temperance education in the public schools, an aim to which Union members had also committed themselves at their first convention.

The Union had a small publications program by 1879, although most of the literature it distributed was the product of the National Temperance Society. It published a few leaflets and tracts, some for children, and a few handbills on beer. The *Woman's Temperance Union*, which had been retitled *Our Union*, was still in trouble, suffering from the competition of several newspapers published by state unions.[12] Every local and state union of any size wanted its own organ.

By 1879 the WCTU had made significant beginnings in the area of political action. The petition was a weapon it had learned to use effectively. The great national petition campaigns produced no legislative results, but Congress paid them notice, and federal politicians were less wary of allying themselves with temperance forces. The Union was committed to a political solution, prohibition, firmly at the state level, ambivalently at the federal level, as the only real answer to the liquor problem. As late as 1878 there was debate over this commitment at the national conventions, but the minority opposing it was small.[13]

Once the WCTU accepted the need for prohibitory legislation and no longer emphasized moral reform of the individual, the Union's interest in political activity was bound to grow. California women assisted in successfully carrying a local option law in 1876. They provided free lunches, carried bouquets and prohibition tickets to the polls, sang gospel songs, kept ice-water buckets well supplied, and saw local option voted in, only to have the California Supreme Court declare the law unconstitutional.[14] Colorado, with a single local union, managed to save its local option law in 1876.[15] Several other state unions were working toward either prohibitory or local-option legislation. By 1879 four states, Maine, New Hampshire,

Vermont, and Iowa, had some kind of prohibitory legislation, and four states had some variety of local option, but most of this legislation ante-dated the WCTU, having resulted from earlier temperance efforts, and was frequently ignored in practice. But by 1879 most WCTU members saw local option as at best an unsatisfactory compromise and disapproved of licensing on principle as giving state sanction to the liquor traffic, as well as being ineffective. Saloons dispensed with licenses and operated outside the law. Many Union members who did not favor federal prohibition were committed to state prohibitory laws, which the national Union endorsed in 1876. As yet no unanimity existed on that issue, but the Union's general stance in favor of legislative solutions to the problem of alcohol abuse put it on the radical side of the temperance movement. By contrast, Dio Lewis opposed prohibition in the 1880s and continued to stick with moral reform. It is possible that women, feeling more aggrieved, were more receptive to legal compulsion than men.[16]

In the 1870s almost all temperance women pursuing political goals felt they must work through the established parties, usually the Republicans. Many of their leaders, on all levels, had acquired lobbying skills and knew their way around legislative chambers; they could testify before commit-tees and were well aware of the harassment value of the right of petition. They represented the largest and most geographically widespread body of women to acquire political action skills in the history of the republic to that date.

Although the Woman's Christian Temperance Union grew in numbers and strength under the joint leadership of Wittenmyer and Willard during the last half of the 1870s, the tactical conflict between the two women continued to deepen. The planning for the Woman's International Tem-perance Convention with which the WCTU commemorated the United States Centennial in 1876 sharpened the growing gap between them, their unresolved differences on support of the woman's ballot providing the focus. Willard wrote in her autobiography that during a trip to Ohio in the spring of 1876, while alone on her knees in prayer, "there was borne in upon my mind, as I believe from loftier regions, the declaration, 'You are to speak for the woman's ballot as a weapon of protection to her home and tempted loved ones from the tyranny of drink.' "[17] As she put it later, God himself had spoken and approved her open espousal of the suffrage cause, and Willard saw the Woman's International Temperance Congress in

Philadelphia as an appropriate place to make her declaration. But she was not ready to act without Wittenmyer's approval. Wittenmyer refused, firmly but kindly, to let her speak on suffrage at the international convention, and Willard accepted the veto without argument. She agreed that Wittenmyer was probably right about keeping the suffrage question out of the convention, adding, "but it's close at home—I don't know how long I can stand it."[18] Willard did speak out, however, before the summer was over, at the camp meeting at Old Orchard Beach, Maine. And it was Margaret Parker of Scotland, elected president of the Woman's International Temperance Union at Philadelphia a few weeks before, who gave Susan B. Anthony a firsthand account of Willard's "public committal." Anthony wrote to Willard that she was delighted that Willard had overcome "all the timid conservative *human* counsels. . . . I wish I could see you and make you feel my gladness, not only for your sake personally, but the *cause' sake*—for temperance and *virtue's* sake and for woman's sake."[19] Willard made her avowal at a conservative gathering of churchpeople and couched her reasons in highly religious terms, including, untypically, an indictment of immigrants and Catholics. She was quoted as saying she "had long hesitated but now that the ballot has been prostituted to undermine the Sabbath, and rob our children of the influence of the Bible in our schools," she thought it time "that Woman, who is truest to God and our country by instinct and education, should have a voice at the polls, where the Sabbath and the Bible are now attacked by the infidel foreign population of our country."[20] Once having spoken publicly, Willard must have felt she could no longer remain silent within the Union itself, even in the face of Wittenmyer's disapproval. She returned to Illinois in September and repeated her plea for suffrage at the Illinois WCTU convention. Here she emphasized its importance for temperance rather than for insuring sabbatarianism and a proper religious atmosphere in the schools. She introduced a resolution proposing that "the mothers and daughters of America" have a voice in the decision by which "the door of the rum shop is opened or shut beside their homes."[21] The wording was somewhat ambiguous, but the intent was clear. Willard spoke eloquently on behalf of the resolution, and it passed unanimously. She went to the national convention at Newark with Illinois solidly behind her.

In October, before the national WCTU meetings, she spoke for suffrage at the Woman's Congress meeting in St. George's Hall in Philadelphia, calling it the "home-protection ballot" for the first time.[22] Willard settled on the phrase "home protection" after she heard an address by a Canadian, Letitia Yeomans, in which Yeomans alluded to tariffs as "home protection."[23] Willard recognized immediately the potential usefulness of the phrase for describing women's political activities supporting temperance. Her home-protection slogan was a masterstroke of public relations, which made suffrage palatable to many, both men and women, who would not otherwise have been able to swallow it. It was a major factor in successfully convincing the Union to embrace suffrage as a goal, and it provided a fresh way of interpreting and justifying political demands.[24] The effect of the home-protection concept in the 1870s was certainly positive. The suffrage movement was quick to recognize its usefulness, although suffragists did not make the argument their own until later in the century. Lucy Stone editorialized in the *Woman's Journal* in 1879 that "the one standing objection to Woman Suffrage has been that the home was the province of women and if they attended to it they would have no time for politics. The women of the Christian Temperance Unions said: 'The home is the special care of women. Home protection shall be our watchword.' "[25]

In a sense the home-protection argument was implicit in women's participation in the temperance movement from the beginning. Many women had always seen the drunken husband as a threat to the home, no matter whose husband he was, or in whose home. Also, Catharine Beecher certainly had made use of woman's traditional role within the home, and the need to defend and protect that role, as justification for women moving outside the home into the public sphere as teachers to assume responsibility for the education of the young.[26] In that sense the Union in its conscious political use of the doctrine of domesticity to move women into public life and participation in the public sphere was following patterns established earlier. But it was Willard in 1876 who attached the concept of home protection to woman's demand for the ballot. Although in her autobiography Willard indicates this move was inspired by a genuine commitment to home protection as a defense of the domestic sphere, the fact that she first used other arguments to support the ballot for women indicates that considerations of strategy were more compelling than ideology.[27]

Willard presented the suffrage question in the guise of home protection before the national union at an evening mass meeting at the Newark convention in 1876 as a personal statement that called for no action by the convention. She reported that her address was received in shocked silence. Wittenmyer was on the platform, manifestly displeased and muttering,

"You might have been a leader, but now you'll only be a scout."[28] Still, there was no open break between them. Willard herself nominated Wittenmyer for president in the "first year of our new century," and both supported the mild home-protection resolution, calling for women's consent to licensing by petition, which replaced the ambiguous call of 1875 for a female voice on questions dealing with liquor.[29] The resolution was a compromise. It did not offend the conservatives by asking for the woman's ballot outright, even such a restricted ballot as Zerelda Wallace had asked for in 1875, but it did recognize the principle of home protection, that women had a special interest in the regulation and restriction of the saloon. Wittenmyer found this level of compromise acceptable, and the resolution formed the basis of the Union's petition campaign at all levels of government for the next two years.

While the national organization held back and equivocated, several state chapters attempted before 1879 to obtain legislation giving women limited suffrage. In Michigan a few women already had the right to vote in school elections, and they reported to their state convention in 1879 how their exercise of the franchise had been received by the rest of the electorate.[30] The Vermont Union was working for suffrage on school questions and home protection. The Illinois Union made an unsuccessful effort, led by Frances Willard, to obtain a home-protection ballot (by collecting 180,000 signatures on petitions) during the 1878–79 legislative session. Wisconsin had done the same.[31] Mary Livermore had pushed the Massachusetts Union to back municipal suffrage for women as early as 1877 and had convinced the entire Bay State executive committee to sign a petition for a woman suffrage amendment to the federal Constitution.[32] Most local and state unions, however, followed the national WCTU's cautious policy toward support of the franchise.

Although Willard's support of the franchise for women met with a mixed reaction in WCTU ranks, her commitment came at a time when the suffrage movement could use new allies. The postwar Equal Rights Association had split in 1869 over the issue of whether to inject the woman suffrage issue into the Reconstruction battle over the enfranchisement of blacks. Susan B. Anthony and Elizabeth Cady Stanton led a campaign to give women as well as blacks the vote by constitutional amendment, demanding specifically that the word "sex" join that of "color" and "previous condition of servitude" in the Fifteenth Amendment. The militants lost, and Anthony and Stanton organized the National Woman Suffrage

Association, which limited its membership to women and which unquali-
fiedly supported a federal constitutional amendment giving women the
vote. The American Woman Suffrage Association, organized a few
months later, was a delegate body that accepted representatives from all
"recognized" suffrage organizations. Like the old Equal Rights Association, it included men and welcomed many members who did not accept full
suffrage for women.[33]

Thus, the suffrage movement was already split when the Beecher-Tilton
scandal first broke in 1871. Henry Ward Beecher, probably America's
most prominent clergyman, son of Lyman Beecher and brother of Catharine Beecher and Harriet Beecher Stowe, was sued by Theodore Tilton, a
notable journalist and suffrage reformer, for alleged adultery with Tilton's
wife. Beecher had been president of the American Woman Suffrage Association, and the accusations against him inevitably associated the leadership of the more conservative suffragists with scandal, infidelity, and
adultery. Anthony and Stanton took up Elizabeth Tilton's cause, arguing
that under existing law and custom it was always the woman who suffered
most in cases of this nature. For awhile they allied themselves with Victoria
Woodhull, who also supported Mrs. Tilton and who openly advocated free
love.[34] Their stance in the Tilton affair was hardly one which brought
suffrage advocates any friends or supporters from among churchwomen,
for example. Into this void came the woman's temperance movement,
providing a respectable, relatively noncontroversial outlet for woman's
increasing awareness of her capabilities, growing resentment of her inferior status, and desire for widening spheres. While Stanton pressed for
legislation permitting women to divorce inebriate husbands, and Anthony
assisted women fleeing unhappy marriages, and Woodhull repudiated in
theory the sanctity of the marriage relationship itself, Frances Willard
advocated the vote only for the reason that the home could thereby be kept
safe, strong, and inviolate.

However, in openly espousing suffrage, in joining forces with the small
group of women within the WCTU who were active in the suffrage cause,
and in assuming leadership of that group, Willard seemed to conservatives
in the Union to be rocking the boat. Undoubtedly she was taking risks.
Wittenmyer legitimately feared association with the gaudy aggressiveness
of the militant suffragists. In Philadelphia at the 1876 Centennial the
temperance women had behaved with circumspection and decorum, but
on July 4 itself, when the emperor of Brazil graced the platform for the
central ceremonies of the Centennial, Susan B. Anthony had led five

women to the podium, presented the astonished chairman with a Declaration of the Rights of Women, a document he had refused her permission to present, and departed down the aisles scattering broadsides.[35] This performance attracted attention but won little male support for the enfranchisement of women, and endeared itself to no women except a few militants. Despite Willard's move for suffrage that same summer of 1876, she did not lose influence within the temperance movement and in the end strengthened rather than killed the WCTU. Why? Probably that felicitous phrase "home protection" provided the answer. Willard did not demand suffrage as a right, but only as a means of promoting what her supporters saw as moral and proper, the protection of the home from the evils of the liquor traffic.

Willard was reelected corresponding secretary of the WCTU in 1876 and continued to travel widely, organizing new unions and strengthening those already in existence. However, shortly before the fourth annual WCTU convention in Chicago, Willard resigned from that position. She was not yet ready to challenge Wittenmyer, but she could no longer be her close associate. At the same time, suffrage forces were stronger in the Union in 1877 than they had been only a year before. J. Ellen Foster, an attorney and lecturer from Iowa whose fame as a speaker was spreading, nominated Willard for president. Although Willard declined the honor, she received thirty-nine votes to Wittenmyer's sixty; twelve others went to Mrs. S. J. Steele of Wisconsin and to Foster.[36] Wittenmyer came close to receiving less than a majority; she had won this time, but not by much. Despite their rivalry, Wittenmyer and Willard continued to correspond. Apparently Willard tried hard to keep their differences from assuming the dimensions of a personal quarrel. Although Wittenmyer's letters no longer exist, Willard's replies indicate that Wittenmyer continued to counsel more religious emphasis in the movement. On one occasion Willard answered her,

> Let us seek to return to the deepest spiritual phase of our work wherein we have departed from it, but let us not judge one another any more if to any it seems religious to mention *all* the elements of power with which God has invested our cause—even if the ballot be one of them. For me I shall not make a hobby of that, but I shall quietly and frankly speak of it with other weapons when I enumerate the arsenal of such, he has placed in our camp.[37]

A few months later Willard again hoped for mutual tolerance; she wrote,

I beg you to believe that it is the purpose and endeavor of all so
far as I know, to maintain kindly thoughts and friendly personal
relations towards our sisters who think differently from us. . . .
That we should all think alike is impossible but that we should
believe in each other and tolerate each other's views is altogether
practicable.[38]

Willard wanted peace but she also wanted to win, and she had not yet
convinced the national union that endorsement of the ballot for women
was judicious. The Chicago convention in 1877 had reaffirmed the decision of the Newark convention in 1876 in support of petition rather than
even a limited "temperance ballot" to achieve home protection. The Baltimore convention in 1878 would go no further, although it parted company
with Wittenmyer in agreeing that henceforth the columns of the official
publication, *Our Union*, would be open to advocates of the home-
protection ballot. Debate was long and heated. By convention time, five
state unions had joined Willard in endorsing the woman's ballot on matters pertaining to drink. They wished to express their convictions in *Our
Union*. The conservatives were convinced that such expression would
prevent further Union growth in the South, where small beginnings were
being made, and would result in two-thirds of the nation's churches being
closed to the WCTU. As the argument waxed warm, the delegates on one
occasion prayed for guidance. They were roundly scolded on another by
Dwight Moody, a well-known evangelist who was on hand to give an
invitational address, for bringing controversy into the convention. Moody
suggested they save drunkards rather than argue about extraneous issues.
Willard was unsuccessful in promoting official support from the convention for the woman's ballot, but she did obtain the right of open advocacy
in *Our Union* for its adherents, a clear defeat for Wittenmyer and the
conservatives of the East. Of the eastern states, only Massachusetts was in
league with the midwestern radicals. Wittenmyer kept the presidency for
another year but defeated Willard by only ten votes, and the convention
refused to make her election unanimous.[39]

Suffrage sentiment was gaining, but it was clear by the time of the
Baltimore convention that adoption of the home-protection ballot as
national policy by the WCTU was dependent on changing the method of
representation in the national convention. Allocating delegates to states on
the basis of the size of their federal congressional representation rather
than the number of WCTU members for whom dues were paid to the

national Union, gave the conservative and populous East a strength in convention disproportionate to its actual membership. Unions were strong in the West, but they could not translate that strength into convention votes. J. Ellen Foster of Iowa gave notice in 1878 that she would ask for an amendment on representation at the next annual meeting.[40]

On November 3, 1879, the sixth annual convention of the Woman's Christian Temperance Union convened at the First Baptist Church in Indianapolis. There was a huge one-word sign PROHIBITION hanging from the balcony, and Annie Wittenmyer, who had once been reluctant, urged national prohibition in her presidential address.[41] Wittenmyer was clearly committed to national legislative means. However, the chief issue of the 1879 convention was not prohibition, which now had unanimous support, but the presidency, suffrage, and the auxilliary issue of representation. Representation came first to the floor, and the forces for change were led by J. Ellen Foster. The executive committee narrowly supported the new plan, a delegate for every three hundred dues-paying members. Although Wittenmyer opposed it, the plan passed.[42] But the measure adopted by the convention was subject to ratification by the states and was not implemented until 1881. Election of officers interrupted the debate over representation. Willard defeated Wittenmyer, 99 to 40. That fight was over. Wittenmyer accepted defeat gracefully and moved that the election of Willard be made unanimous. Willard responded that she hoped she would not "misuse the confidence nor disappoint the hopes" of her supporters.[43]

Scholars have seen Willard's election in 1879 as changing the Woman's Christian Temperance Union from a temperance praying society to an activist organization.[44] This assessment is inaccurate and unfair, not only to Willard and her supporters, who shaped the movement in a broader image from the beginning, but also to Wittenmyer and the conservatives who never saw woman's temperance limited to such narrow goals. Overtones of political action and assertion of women's rights were present in this movement as early as the Crusade itself. The basic ideology of the Crusade maintained that women had a right to take action, including political action, to close down saloons because they adversely affected their own lives. The right of petition had been used repeatedly. Chicago Crusaders had used it to agitate for Sunday closing of saloons in 1874.[45] Unions had continued to use it. They had also supported political candidates. The

Kansas WCTU, for example, actively campaigned for John St. John for governor of Kansas in 1878 as the candidate firmly committed to prohibition. In one state after another before 1879, WCTU local and state unions had taken essentially political positions and engaged in political activity, albeit in a temperance framework. Wittenmyer herself had lobbied in Congress for the temperance cause. Willard's election in 1879 did indeed have enormous consequences for the WCTU, but there was no clean break, no abrupt watershed, between the presidencies of Wittenmyer and Willard. Willard had already put her stamp on the Union in the 1870s. On the other hand, as president she did not convince the Union to adopt her more radical programs immediately. A change in presidents did not disrupt the basic continuity of WCTU policy, because in the last analysis WCTU policy reflected membership commitment.

Much of this continuity derives from the stability of the WCTU's leadership. Frances Willard was a national officer from 1874 until her death in 1898, with the exception of a few months in 1877 and 1878. For nineteen years she was the Union's president. She led the Union from the beginning, a leadership she first shared with Wittenmyer, but one in which her voice was always loud and clear. Other officers also had long tenures. Caroline Buell served as corresponding secretary from 1880 to 1893, Mary Woodbridge as recording secretary from 1878 to 1893, Lillian Stevens as assistant recording secretary from 1882 to 1893, and Esther Pugh as treasurer from 1878 to 1893. All had been among the leaders from the beginning and all but Stevens had participated in the Crusade. Also Anna Gordon, at Willard's side as her personal secretary from 1877 to 1898, was in many ways increasingly able to exercise more control over the Union's destinies than anyone except Willard herself.

This continuity of leadership insured efficient implementation of program goals, a rank and file that knew its leaders and frequently had some personal contact with them, and a national visibility that a constantly changing leadership could never have achieved. The same officers, especially Willard as both corresponding secretary and president, spoke for the Union for nearly a generation. They were as well known as an articulate veteran congressman. They never had to fight anonymity. The Union never adopted the practice of electing national officers on a partly honorary basis, which would have involved frequent changes of office and would thus have left administrative control and continuity in the hands of an executive secretary and a supporting bureaucracy. The WCTU eventually paid its officers, but real control of both policy-making and implementation was in the hands of women elected and reelected by the membership. In this the WCTU followed a pattern typical of American labor unions rather than philanthropic or reform societies, or even professional organizations.

Although Willard's election to the presidency has sometimes been viewed as the triumph of the radical West, two of her fellow officers were New Englanders. Lillian Stevens was from Portland, Maine. She had been one of the chief colleagues of the Maine prohibitionist Neal Dow, and was to be president of the Maine Union into the twentieth century. Caroline Buell was born in Connecticut. Her husband was killed in the Civil War, and for the first years of her service to the national Union she worked out of Bible House in New York, later moving to Chicago. Although Mary Woodbridge was born in New England, she moved to Ohio at seventeen, when she married a Cleveland merchant. Esther Pugh was also an Ohioan, from Cincinnati, where her father was an editor and publisher; eventually she moved to headquarters in Chicago. Anna Gordon was from Massachusetts (her father was a Boston bank cashier), but she lived much of her adult life in Evanston, Illinois.

Willard met Gordon, then a young woman of twenty-four, while working with Dwight Moody in 1877 in Boston, and Gordon became her traveling companion and secretary. Gordon was a talented organist, and her musical ability complemented Willard's forensic skills. Gordon was eventually to become a capable speaker and organizer herself and was especially successful working with children. Modest, self-effacing, and extremely efficient, she relieved Willard of all the details of scheduling and travel, wrote many of her letters, even to her mother, and performed a myriad of personal tasks. Her advice was also sought and taken. Gordon was as important as Willard in holding the organization together.

All the officers were upper middle-class and financially secure, except Willard and perhaps Buell.[46] Only two, Stevens and Woodbridge, had living husbands and therefore major domestic responsibilities. However, Stevens had but one daughter and was able to hire a governess to assist in her care. Woodbridge had three children, but as the wife of a prosperous merchant she could afford domestic help. The national officers were fully as representative of evangelical Protestantism as the Union itself. Willard was a Methodist, Buell was the daughter of a Methodist clergyman, and Gordon, who was raised a Congregationalist, had joined the Methodist

Anna A. Gordon, Willard's longtime secretary and confidant.
Courtesy the Michigan Historical Collections of the Bentley Historical Library,
University of Michigan, Ann Arbor.

church before she met Willard; Woodbridge was a Congregationalist, Pugh a Quaker, and Stevens a Universalist.

Was Willard's victory a victory of her ideas or of her personality? Certainly the Union was not yet ready to endorse all her positions, but the rank and file, most of whom had heard her on lecture tours, found her fascinating and irresistible, and idealized her. For the next nineteen years they usually accepted her leadership, although sometimes with reluctance and clearly voiced misgivings. This type of adored, idealized figure has been referred to as the "woman as sage" or "prophetess," that is, the cult heroine in contrast to the "woman as expert" (for example, Florence Kelley, the organizer of the Consumer's League, who never captured popular imagination in the same way).[47] Jane Addams, who replaced Willard as chief heroine at the end of the century, was another "prophetess." One historian has described this type of woman as "woman as saint" and believes that Willard, Addams, and Eleanor Roosevelt played the role in succession. All three stressed feminine intuition and advocated womanly techniques for changing society, and all three accepted the public image of self-sacrifice that grew up around them.[48]

Willard's face was familiar to hundreds of thousands, her picture was displayed in countless homes, and she was the subject of dozens of articles in periodicals. Buildings and streets were named after her. A male contemporary described her as leading the WCTU "with the valor of Alexander, the sagacity of Fabius, the patience and piety of Washington."[49] One of her colleagues, Zerelda Wallace, rhapsodized, "At one of our Conventions I introduced our beloved sister as our Moses; at another as our Joshua; and today I introduce her as our John the Baptist, who is going to declare a new dispensation for womanhood."[50] By the 1890s Willard responded unabashed to being called "Saint Frances," and even earlier acknowledged her hankering after sainthood. What qualities in Willard inspired this deep devotion?

Frances Willard at thirty-nine was not beautiful, but she was a singularly attractive woman. Her hair was described sometimes as blond, sometimes auburn, and sometimes light brown; her eyes were a bright light blue and were clearly visible through the rimmed pince-nez spectacles that she always wore, even in formal photographs. She had a slight, elegant figure, and she dressed modestly but well, in a black or brown velvet or silk dress, simply made with a blue ribbon or a touch of white or ivory lace at the throat, and a tasteful bonnet that she often removed when she spoke.[51] Her professional clothes were frequently made for her by a dressmaker who worked in the Boston suburb where Gordon's parents lived.

Like so many women who flocked to the temperance cause in the 1870s, Willard possessed a marked talent for public speaking. Performing on the public platform became a way of life for her, and she enjoyed it from the beginning. Willard and many other temperance women would have made superb actresses: they could play to an audience; they instinctively knew how to use their voices in large halls before the era of amplification; they knew how to carry themselves and how to set the stage and dress for the part they would play. Willard had made her debut as a speaker in 1871, entertaining Methodist meetings with accounts of her European travels. The women of the Chicago Crusade asked her to speak for them in the spring of 1874. At the Clark Street Church in Chicago she faced her first large audience and confessed to being so frightened she did not remember what she said. Obviously she was in full command when she addressed the camp meeting at Old Orchard Beach the following September. The lure of the rapt audience had captured her, and she found ample scope for her platform talents in the temperance movement.

Willard's listeners reported that she had "oratorical abilities of a very high order." Her voice was "oratund [sic] in tone, and yet so flexible as to be full of varying intonations," which could be heard distinctly everywhere even in a large auditorium seating two thousand people.[52] She was "easy and natural in gesture, womanly in voice and manner, able and convincing in argument"; she gesticulated frequently with the forefinger of her left hand, and the gesture had almost a coquettish quality.[53] Unlike other temperance lecturers, Willard spent little time graphically portraying the evils of drink. Instead she emphasized the moral and religious aspects of temperance and the practical cost of the use of liquor, the money and resources that could otherwise have been used for education, food, or some positive purpose. She pointed out the cost of drink-related crime to society, rather than entertaining her audiences with vivid portrayals of advanced delirium tremens. At the same time, her speeches packed an emotional wallop. Newspapers referred to her "burning words," her "magnetic utterances," and the fact that many in her audiences frequently were brought to tears.[54] One editor described her as having an "easy flow of choice, poetic language, now rising to a white heat of fervor, and now falling to a tone of melting pathos and appeal."[55] Like politicians in a grass-roots campaign, she repeated the same speeches over and over. For example, her address on home protection was frequently printed more or less in full in the local papers of the communities where she delivered it, and the speech is identical. She memorized her formal speeches, even her annual reports to the national conventions after she became president, but she also could speak extemporaneously with fluency and was never at a loss for words in a heated debate. She wrote well, if not legibly, and eventually did most of her writing by dictation. In the last decade of her life she kept several secretaries busy simultaneously.

Women liked Willard. Indeed she was more than liked, she was loved, she was adored. Her intense, almost sexual attractiveness to members of her own sex was a major factor in her success. Women competed for her favors and cherished some intimate moment with her as they would the attentions of a male lover. And she was free with these tokens of concern and affection. When Belle Kearney, newly appointed organizer for the infant Mississippi state Union, feeling completely incompetent and inadequate, finished her faltering maiden speech at the state convention, Willard, who was on the platform as the national president, stepped up, embraced her, and welcomed her to the sisterhood.[56] Belle Kearney was of course entranced.

Willard could also convey this sense of intimacy in her writing and from the public platform. She once said to Agnes Slack, a British co-worker, that when she looked at an audience she loved every person in it.[57] She also loved all her readers. She had columns in the *Signal*, the organ of the Illinois WCTU, the *Alliance*, the Ohio newspaper, and *Our Union* before she became president. She continued these after her election, and when the merged *Union Signal* began publication in 1883, she continued to write for it. Her columns took the form of what were essentially personal letters to each and every subscriber. She told them the details of her daily life, both at home and on the road, what her study looked like, what was on her desk, what pictures her mother had on the wall, the culinary virtues of the "hired treasure" in the kitchen. She told them about long, disagreeable train rides, bumpy stagecoach journeys in the West, and the warm hospitality of strangers.[58]

Willard had used and would continue to use her personal appearances, in the boondocks and at conventions, state and national, to keep warm the devotion of the rank and file to the Union cause. She was as skillful at making the most of formal gatherings as she was of private intercourse or

her pen. These annual semiceremonial, semibusiness gatherings were
vitally important in holding the movement together and helping it grow.
The conventions over which she presided were dramatic entertainments of
high order, and their stage settings became increasingly elaborate. The
trend was set in Farwell Hall in Chicago in 1877, when Willard herself was
the designer. The stage approaches were draped with festooned flags. Vines
trailed from pedestals at the sides of the stage, and a profusion of flowers
and green plants rested on every vacant spot on the podium. Speakers and
officers were surrounded by a lush garden, and symbolism was rampant. A
sheaf of flowers and grains, tied with the Union's emblematic white ribbon
of purity and with the initials WCTU intertwined among its stalks, stood in
the center of the stage. The lectern was decorated with a cross of smilax and
tuberoses. The rear wall was hung with more flags arranged as an inverted
arch with a fern cross in the center below a star and the motto For God and
Home and Native Land.[59] Willard gave the welcoming address on behalf of
Chicago that year. She had created an opulent set for her performance.

Elaborate silk banners were designed by the states in the 1880s and used
to mark the seats for their delegations. When the convention was held in
churches, elaborate temporary platforms were sometimes built around the
pulpit to seat officers and notables.[60] By 1894, when the Union celebrated
its twenty-first birthday in Cleveland, the decorations had become so
lavish they were reported in detail in the national press. Doan's Music Hall
was draped in white and gold bunting and smothered in fresh flowers that
were replaced as they faded. Cleveland's business houses were requested to
emulate the convention and decorate their premises in white and gold, the
convention's colors. The convention cost $1,000 that year and tickets for
reserved seats were sold to help pay for the spectacle.[61]

The musical accompaniment at WCTU conventions began simply
enough in 1874; hymns were sung by the women accompanied by a church
organ. Mrs. F. A. Bent's golden cornet was added in 1882, and Mr. Bent
even joined her occasionally. Children were trained to march and sing. At
Louisville in 1882 the House of Refuge choir performed. By 1894 a chorus
of three hundred voices was entertaining the delegates, and the convention's audience had swelled to thousands.[62] Hymn-singing was also used
effectively. Reports of successes, especially financial, were greeted with
"Praise God from Whom All Blessings Flow," and dissension, when
resolved or at least put to a vote, with "Blest Be the Tie That Binds." There
was an air of gala excitement about these conventions, which Willard and

other leaders knew how to use effectively. The leadership of the WCTU did its job well. The drama of the theater and the fervor of a noble cause were artfully combined to intensify the WCTU's appeal.

Willard's womanly charm and pleasant good looks, combined with her manipulative skills and dramatic talents, played a major role in her successful leadership. Like any good politician she was an opportunist. Her emotion-laden public commitment to a noble cause was tempered in private by a realistic eye for the possible, a critical appraisal of the strengths and weaknesses of her cohorts and how they could be used, and a keen grasp of expedient tactics. At the same time, on the public platform she could convey a messianic fervor that seemed to put her above the day-to-day anxieties of institutional politics and personal ambition, although she certainly was not. But she was not alone among the Union's leaders in being able to make use of personal charisma. Caroline Buell and Lillian Stevens shared her good looks and feminine charm. J. Ellen Foster, Zerelda Wallace, and Annie Wittenmyer were powerful orators. In fact most of the delegates to a national convention could occupy a pulpit with credit. Matilda Carse and Foster, among others, were consummate politicians. Willard may have been the queen of temperance, but she was surrounded by an able and talented court; and the rank and file were not reluctant to be led into new paths of womanly assertiveness. She was the leader of a very willing army eager to blaze new trails, as debate on the convention floor, correspondence in the *Union Signal*, and reports from state and local unions clearly show.

By the end of the 1870s the Union had three major assets. First, it possessed a stable and dynamic leadership corps that was to remain in office for most of the century. Second, it had chosen as president the woman who could most successfully combine support for a program of militant, innovative social action with widespread personal acceptance by conservative elements in the larger society, to say nothing of devoted admiration bordering on worship from the membership of the Union itself. Third, its growing membership was assertive, politically active, and gradually broadening its goals, using its devotion to temperance to justify its concern with larger social programs.

To Dare Tell the Good News

THE MECHANICS OF PROSELYTIZING: ORGANIZERS AND PUBLICATIONS

The Woman's Christian Temperance Union over which Frances Willard presided in 1879 was already the largest organization of women in the United States, and probably in the world. Nonetheless, it needed to grow much larger to become an effective lobbying force capable of carrying out the Union's program. This need was met, the "good news" told, and the WCTU's membership quadrupled in the next ten years. Charismatic but stable leadership and a flexible program were central to its spectacular success in the 1880s, but the mechanics of effectively reaching its constituency were also crucial. WCTU organizers carried its message throughout the United States and eventually the whole world. WCTU publications brought the "good news" into tens of thousands of homes.

A strong network of local unions was the WCTU's major asset. Organizing new unions, and keeping old locals functioning well, rested on the shoulders of a taskforce of professional organizers. Willard was the first

The chapter title is from Frances Willard's *Glimpses of Fifty Years*, 347, a diary entry that describes her early organizing efforts: "O God! Can I live near enough to Thee to *dare* tell the good news to Humanity?"

and most important of this group. She had already spent much of her time on the road before she became president, and she continued as the major organizer for her first four years in office. As the Union grew in numbers and resources, she was joined by an increasing body of other women who spent all or part of their time traveling in its interests. However, until 1883, Willard was the WCTU's chief traveling ambassador. Between 1874 and 1883 she spoke in more than a thousand towns at least once, in all cities with populations over ten thousand and most with over five thousand people; she averaged one meeting a day for the ten-year stint, and was home in Evanston only about three weeks in each year.[1]

The WCTU needed Willard's travels to grow; Willard also needed those travels to make a living. She was in no position to subsidize the movement financially, and could not even afford to volunteer her time. No officers of the national organization were paid until 1879, and the president received no salary until 1886. Willard was paid a monthly salary by the Chicago WCTU until she resigned to join Dwight Moody's staff in 1877. After she ended her connection with him she had no income except her lecture fees and free-will offerings. She and her sister-in-law attempted to edit and publish her brother's newspaper, the *Chicago Post and Mail,* for a few months after his death in 1878, but this was not a profitable venture. Essentially, from early 1877 until a salary was provided her as president, nearly ten years later, she was dependent on speaking at public meetings for a living. Her only source of income was the collections taken at meetings where she spoke. The Union's necessity was also hers.

It was not an easy life. During her first year as president Willard traveled in twenty-three states.[2] She spoke and organized in New England, the Middle Atlantic states, and the Old Northwest. She also made her way to Iowa, Kansas, Nebraska, Missouri, Colorado, and Wyoming. To save money she stayed most of the time in private homes as a nonpaying guest. Sometimes her quarters were comfortable, even opulent; frequently they were not. At Council Bluffs, Iowa, she expected to stay at the home of the Baptist minister. She and Cynthia Hanchett, another organizer who was traveling with her, arrived on a Saturday morning, were not met at the station, and made their way to the parsonage by omnibus, only to find their hostess not at home. The two women were shown upstairs to a very cold room that "was spooky enough to scare the bravest hearts into fits." They had a cornhusk bed to sleep on, and rough brown kitchen towels and a wash basin for their ablutions, and were sent to dinner elsewhere. Breakfast was wheat pancakes, doughnuts, and coffee (Willard preferred steak and eggs). Willard spoke next morning at the Methodist church for a collection of eight dollars, and that evening addressed a WCTU meeting at the Congregational church. Dinner Sunday was potatoes, eggs, and apple pie, and there was no supper. Monday morning they left for Omaha, where they had a relatively pleasant place to stay. But at Lincoln they stayed in a very small house and slept downstairs alone with three dogs, and Hanchett wrote to Willard's mother that "the dust and wind are frightful."[3] However, when they reached Cheyenne, Wyoming, on the same trip, they were met by the governor's carriage, served an elegant tea on lovely china, entertained at a seven-course dinner with a dozen guests, and enjoyed the awesome view of the Rockies from their bedroom.[4] Overall, that Western tour was a "hard trip." They had visited nineteen cities and towns and Willard had spoken thirty-eight times.[5] Meanwhile Willard worried about money. She reported to her mother that when Hanchett joined her on the train she brought so ample a lunch basket that they were able to make three meals of it, which at seventy-five cents apiece was quite a saving.[6] Collections were meager. They had begged passes to cover their train fare and finally made a killing in Denver, where the collection netted sixty dollars. Willard jubilantly wrote her mother to buy an oil stove, a new gate, or anything else she needed.[7]

This relative affluence of late spring dwindled quickly to penury by October, when Willard managed to send her mother a small sum but complained she was financially strapped. It was convention time, and she was attending state WCTU conventions, after which she planned to go on to the national convention, and conventions paid less well than regular engagements.[8] Even when physically exhausted, Willard continued her one-night stands. Scheduling was done with pressing financial obligations in mind. In November 1881 Anna Gordon wrote Willard's mother asking just how much cash would be needed to clear up the bills in Evanston, and just how soon it must be paid and to whom, so that she could plan their engagements with that in mind.[9] Until the national organization put her on a straight salary in 1886, Willard always considered money contributed to her personally as subject to any use she saw fit to make of it, including supporting her mother and paying household bills.

While Willard was the first national organizer, Massachusetts was the first state (in 1876) to put an organizer in the field, copying the methods used successfully by the Woman's Foreign Missionary Society.[10] But in her first annual presidential address, Willard began to stress the need for national organizers, suggesting with typical tact that the Union look to spinsters, young unmarried women, and women with grown children for this work, rather than mothers needed in their homes.[11] A decade after Willard's election, there were eleven official organizers and evangelists traveling in various parts of the country and the world, organizing new unions, strengthening the old, and reviving the moribund. By 1895 there were twenty-nine.

Usually Willard traveled with Anna Gordon. Gordon was occasionally ill or had commitments to her family, and Willard then arranged for another traveling companion, often a local person with useful connections. She rarely traveled alone, although some of the other WCTU organizers did. When Pullman accommodations were available, Willard used them— and sometimes shared them with those less fortunate: "Sat up until 2 o'clock last night after talking all day in the convention and took a little 8 yr. old waif of a girl into my berth, who less considerate than my Nanny, rolled herself into a ball and my knees projected over the edge all night long."[12] One berth for two women traveling together was normal, and bedrooms and beds were shared in private homes and hotels, an arrangement that had its advantages when the sleeping quarters were unheated. But trains did not always have sleeping cars, and when there were no passenger trains, organizers rode freights. Ten hours in a slow, lurching freight train caboose with no food or drink except what one carried was not a refreshing experience.[13] They took stages when there were no railroads. Mary Shields, organizing in Arizona Territory in the winter of 1883–84, reported arriving by train at Prescott at 4:00 A.M. An army ambulance had been sent to meet her. They drove fifty-seven miles with a team of six mules, bumping along wretched roads from before daylight until they reached Whipple Barracks well after dark.[14] Willard tended to stick to the main routes, but other organizers went to places she avoided, the malarial lowlands of Arkansas, for example, and they sometimes pointedly remarked that better-known lecturers tended to visit and revisit the same cities.[15]

Willard and Gordon always worked on trains. It was in jerking railroad cars that most of the correspondence was answered, the speeches prepared, and the columns written for WCTU publications. This contrasted with the working habits of Susan B. Anthony, who never worked on trains—she had learned to curl up in her shawl or cloak and relax on the cars. Anthony said she could not speak without rest, and warned Willard on a visit Willard made to Anthony's home that she would burn out if she kept to her frantic pace.[16] (Perhaps Willard should have followed Anthony's advice; Anthony lived to be eighty-six and Willard died at fifty-nine.) Willard was not the only WCTU official to weary herself traveling. Lucy Kimball was exhausted after a campaign where she spoke seventy times in two months, often six or seven times a day on Sunday.[17] Sallie Chapin found the hand-shaking an ordeal; her hand was crushed after one long session, and the pain was not ameliorated by having a baby and a colt named after her.[18] In the early 1880s Willard was on the road almost constantly. During the winter of 1881–82, she managed a week at home for Christmas and a week's rest at the home of Hannah Whitall Smith, the Quaker feminist, near Philadelphia after the convention, but otherwise she spent all her time lecturing and traveling.

One of Willard's most ambitious sorties, and one desperately needed for the strength of the Union, was her successful trip into the South in the spring of 1881. She spent fourteen weeks visiting every southern state and the Indian Territory and spoke in over fifty cities. Her lecture tour was a great personal success—all the more so, as one Richmond gentleman remarked, because she was "a woman, a Northern woman, and a temperance woman."[19] She was making public appearances and speaking from public platforms, and she was accepted well. Few of the people who heard her had ever listened to a woman speak in public before. Nonetheless, the churches of most Protestant denominations were open to her, hotels did not present bills, railways provided transportation at no cost, southern homes proffered hospitality, and even the press was generally sympathetic. Bishops, ministers, judges, and senators sat with her on the platform and introduced her. Her femininity, good looks, and ladylike demeanor helped. The *South Carolina Baptist Courier* described her as wearing a tasteful black suit and bonnet, using few gestures, and devoid of posturing, and praised her address as "a literary gem."[20] The *Montgomery Advertiser and Mail* reported, "Her manner is easy, her language chaste," and added that her address "was one continued flow of eloquence and learning, and engaged the most attention from first to last."[21] In the interest of public relations she took no fees or collections on this trip, although a few people made cash gifts for the work, and the party incurred few living expenses. This "no dunning" policy did not always make life easy. In Atlanta, she was entertained in local residences and temperance women gave her fifteen dollars, but that was two dollars less than the trainfare to get there. She warned Gordon, "We must work up the pass business or be flat."[22] She was receiving no support from national headquarters, and going south represented a financial sacrifice. She could have asked and received generous fees elsewhere.

Willard was accompanied by Gordon for much of the journey, and also by Georgia Hulse McLeod of Baltimore, who was able to smooth Willard's way in southern social circles.[23] Her visit was given the status of an official goodwill tour. She was granted an interview in Washington with newly inaugurated President James Garfield just before she set off. He approved of the enterprise, hoping it would assist in the full reconciliation of the South and urging her to do her best "to unite the two sections with sweet ties of sympathy and mutual help in philanthropic work."[24] Certainly, to judge by Willard's glowing reports of the hospitality with which she was received, the South seems to have viewed Willard's visit as a healing mission, as doing much to dissipate what many felt was lingering northern enmity. She was sent a basket of flowers, on one occasion, with the basket handle wound with blue and gray ribbon, and a note of gratitude for her "brave words, in defense of the harmony we so eminently desire."[25] She referred to her southern audiences as being like "a band of brothers and sisters" and commented that when she spoke at the church where the first secession convention had been held, she was introduced by an officer who had fired on Fort Sumter, and she was accompanied by Sallie Chapin, the friend of Robert E. Lee, and Georgia McLeod, whose son had lost an arm in the service of the Confederacy.[26]

Willard's successful southern tour was widely reported in the northern press. The warmth with which she was received and the friendly hospitality offered her was seen as putting the lie to the allegation that the South was strongly hostile to northerners in its midst. Probably her tour was of minor importance in healing the rift that decades of strife had caused, but her personal stance was certainly conciliatory. She believed healing had taken place, that the sections could work together well in a common cause, that the white South had its virtues as well as its vices and was ready to put sectional antagonisms aside. The political allegiance of most WCTU members in the North was strongly Republican. As they moved into the South they encountered white women whose political allegiances were solidly Democratic. They saw these southern Democrats as very different from the northern urban members of that party, and they welcomed them as sharing their own dedication to temperance and puritan virtues, unlike their northern counterparts in the urban political machines.

Willard spoke to black audiences on occasion. In Georgia she addressed two large audiences of black students at Atlanta and Clark universities and also spoke at a Negro high school.[27] These appearances seem not to have changed the nature of her reception by whites. Willard came from a staunchly antislavery Republican background. She had not been reared to view southern white Democracy with sympathy, but she personally conquered her prejudices on this tour.

Willard went south again in the winter of 1882, accompanied by Anna Gordon. They had somewhat less flattering things to say about many of the places they visited on that trip, probably because they moved further into the hinterland. Gordon wrote Willard's mother from Jackson, Mississippi, that this was a "very strange land," with pigs and "little darkies" equally at home on the main street. Mississippi she saw as "the farthest back of all the Southern states" save Florida and remarked, "they are *so* slow."[28] Again Willard worried about money, sending her mother part of her meager income, which was almost always gifts from individuals. In Texas she was cut off by floods, her engagements were canceled, and she found herself without funds.[29] But there were positive experiences as well. She met and was fascinated by Mrs. Jefferson Davis, with whom she began a correspondence; and she also on occasion saw the results of the previous spring's work. The Louisville Union had achieved great success and was ready to entertain a national convention.[30]

Willard again made a southern tour in 1883, when she was followed by another organizer, Mary Wadsworth, who did much of the legwork in establishing new unions.[31] In five months in 1882 she spoke in sixty-six cities and towns in fourteen states. Willard made no more extensive journeys in the South, but she made shorter junkets. In the spring of 1886 she spent two weeks in Kentucky, visiting ten towns and cities in thirteen days, and was pleased that 60 out of 118 counties had petitioned for local option.[32] She made her last southern trip in 1896.

Willard was not the only or the first WCTU lecturer to go south. In 1879 Eliza Stewart, who had joined the temperance movement in the early days of the Crusade, had been appointed chairman of southern work and had quietly visited Kentucky, Tennessee, and Georgia, traveled some six hundred miles, and assisted in the formation of both white and black unions, of which about five survived the first year.[33] In 1883 J. Ellen Foster spoke in twenty-three cities in eleven states, traveling from Maryland to Florida and through Georgia to Tennessee. Foster seems to have been less cordially received than Willard. She was accompanied by her husband, but even so, Foster reported that few ministers gave them any encouragement, that Methodist bishops were conspicuous by their absence from the platforms she occupied, and that the clergy's coolness probably resulted from their fear that any temperance woman from the North was also an advocate of female suffrage—as Foster indeed was.[34] The ordeal became too much for Foster at one point and she took to her bed and was forced to cancel her engagements for a month.[35]

The Louisville convention of 1882 brought within the borders of the Southland the WCTU tradition of filling local pulpits on convention Sunday with temperance women preachers. Even the Lutheran church heard a sermon from a member of the WCTU. The local press was skeptical and suggested that "the style of oratory generally indulged in does not seem calculated to move a mixed audience, including practical business men. Perhaps when addressed to audiences of women, who are sooner impelled by sentiment, than by broad and practical considerations, a large amount of good for the temperance cause might result."[36] In most cases, it was the first time anyone had heard women speak in public, much less from a pulpit, and the churches were filled to overflowing. Nevertheless, it was not until 1886 that the South Carolina state convention was allowed to meet in a church, when the Methodist church at Newberry finally received them.[37]

Eventually much of the southern work was taken over by southern women, and the "foreign missionary" attitude waned in northern Union circles. Sallie Chapin of Charleston, South Carolina, who had joined the WCTU at one of the Ocean Grove camp meetings, became the most important single force in the Union's growing success in the South. Chapin, of Huguenot ancestry, the widow of a prominent Charleston merchant, had first tasted public service in the Confederacy's Soldiers' Relief Society during the war. She was the daughter of a Methodist clergyman, had attended one of the best ladies' academies in South Carolina, and had written a novel. After the war she was president of the Ladies' Christian Association and taught Sunday school, including a class of black children, and by 1881, she was lecturing and speaking frequently as a WCTU organizer.[38] When the WCTU met in Louisville in 1882 for its

A temperance poster from the South.

Courtesy the Michigan Historical Collections of the Bentley Historical Library, University of Michigan, Ann Arbor.

national convention, the *Cincinnati Commercial* described her as a woman of "strongly marked features," dressed in dignified "plain black stuff," with a well-modulated voice and a southern love for imagery. Her speech was "almost a poem."[39]

Chapin, assisted by Georgia McLeod, was constantly on the road in the 1880s. At the 1885 convention she reported traveling 16,775 miles and visiting every southern state the previous year, allowing herself only ten days' holiday to attend a convocation sponsored by Dwight Moody. She also actively lobbied with legislators for scientific temperance education and local option. She was as assiduous in her work with the black unions as with the white.[40] Chapin continued to champion the cause in the South and was superintendent of the Department of Southern Work until 1889, when southern delegates suggested the department be abolished since the South was no longer a missionary field.[41]

Chapin, Willard, and those who joined them in bringing southern women into the WCTU were engaged in an innovative effort. Southern women had never before participated in a national movement. They were not part of the antebellum reform campaigns. They did not, of course, join the antislavery movement (unless, as did a few militant Quakers, they removed themselves to the North), and other reformist causes—prison reform, communitarianism, education for women, and even temperance— had little impact in the slave states. The missionary-society movement seems to have introduced southern women to organization. They joined the women's missionary societies first and moved into the WCTU from there; but the missionary societies themselves did not develop in the South until the late 1870s.[42] Missions thus gave the new southern temperance women their only previous experience with organizing. Southern women had no experience in nondenominational reform organizations; they had never spoken in public; they had never petitioned a legislative body. They came into the WCTU diffidently, and with reservations. Organizers for the WCTU were referred to as "foreigners" at first.[43]

Southern unions were to remain a conservative element within the parent group for decades. They did not want the ballot, and they were fearful of allying themselves with the broad social aims of the Prohibition party. Southern unions at first found it more congenial to send nosegays and Bible verses to aid jail and prison inmates than to work for model reformatories or the employment of police matrons. But they joined the Union and participated in and hosted its national conventions. They learned how to hold meetings and campaign for a cause, and by the late 1880s women were quite generally accepted as platform speakers in the South. The WCTU had much to do with putting southern women into the mainstream of American life. Belle Kearney, the Mississippi feminist, pointed with pride in 1891 to the number of southern women now attending colleges and universities and reported that it was no longer considered a disgrace for a southern woman to earn her own living. She credited the WCTU with changing attitudes and making "a different world for southern girls."[44]

Not only was participation of southern women in a militant reformist crusade an innovation, but the WCTU, in bringing North and South together again in a voluntary association, was pioneering. The Protestant churches were still apart. The schisms over slavery were not yet healed, and indeed have not yet healed completely today. The Southern Baptists left the Baptist Convention in 1843, and they have maintained a separate organization ever since. The Methodist Church South set up a separate organization in 1844, and the Methodists did not reunite until 1939. The Presbyterians avoided outright schism until the Civil War itself, but like the Baptists they have not reunited. When the WCTU began organizing the South, southerners and northerners had not worked side by side in religious voluntary associations for nearly two generations. Making the WCTU truly national in scope was an accomplishment of major significance, and its implications were not lost on the participants. The platform at Louisville was adorned by a floral shield in which a symbolic snow-white dove joined the motto Sobriety in a tangle of smilax, and one of the convention's official welcomers, Colonel George Bain, stated unequivocally that "Miss Willard in the South and Mrs. Chapin in the North, have done more to bring together the divided sections, than all the politicians who have ever gone to Washington."[45]

The successful integration into a single national organization of women from all sections of the country including the South had another effect. The WCTU was organized in the South just after Reconstruction and before the Populist revolt of the 1890s sent Jim Crow off on his more virulent rampages. Separation of the races had not yet reached its ultimate absurdity. The timing was right, and the WCTU was never an exclusively white organization, even in the Gulf states, although it was by and large a segregated one. Even if southern blacks and whites were not members of the same local unions (nor were they frequently so in the North, for that matter), organization of black women proceeded fairly equally alongside that of white women in the South. Black and white southern local unions were affiliated in the 1880s with the same state and national bodies, and addressed by the same missionary speakers. Willard was heard by audiences from both races on her southern tours, and southern women like Sallie Chapin were active in organizing their black sisters. While this degree of oneness seems surprising, it must be remembered that only relatively radical and emancipated southern white women were affiliated with the Union in the 1880s, when most southerners, male and female, still found participation in public affairs by women distasteful, if not shocking.

The WCTU also organized black women in the North, although attention to this goal was sporadic. In the South, the organizing of black unions was done in the 1880s by white workers, while in the northern states, black women were encouraged to do the work. In New Jersey and Connecticut some unions were integrated; in Maryland and New York they were not.[46] Integration did not always proceed smoothly; the Leavenworth Union became embroiled in controversy between members who wanted its Main Street headquarters open to white and black alike and those who feared the WCTU would become unpopular "if colored people are seen going in and out freely."[47] Much of the WCTU's work with blacks was with children, and there were never many blacks in the Union. There was a single black delegate to the 1881 national convention; she was called to the platform and introduced,[48] but even that much integration was rare in Washington in 1881. The Indiana Union had a black woman as chairman of its Department of Colored Work in 1884. She had a large family that she supported by doing laundry, but she managed to contribute time to the WCTU as well. Indianapolis had four black unions that year and had succeeded in replacing the original white officers with a completely black leadership roster.[49] The Superintendent of Colored Work lamented at the 1886 convention that the black unions were disappearing, but in 1887 she reported a most encouraging year and an increase in enthusiasm. Black churches and preachers were cooperative, although liquor interests frequently threatened that husbands and brothers of women who joined would be fired.

Growing Jim Crowism had its effects on the WCTU in the 1890s. State unions in the South were no longer integrated. Eight southern states organized black unions on the state level. They were usually designated as State WCTU No. 2 rather than as "colored" unions, because, as the president of North Carolina's No. 2 wrote, "[We do not want] to exclude any white sisters who might wish to work with us. . . . We believe all men are created equal."[50] Lucy Simpson Thurman, a black woman from Michigan, was national Superintendent of Colored Work in the 1890s, a feminist who reported that she had "always favored the organization of unions among the colored women for it will be to them just what it has been to our white sisters, the greatest training school for the development of women."[51] Thurman worked hard as an organizer among blacks in the 1890s, but her efforts were poorly supported financially. It was on her motion that the Department of Colored Work, allowed to lapse in 1890, was reinstated in 1893; the discussion was spirited but the motion carried unanimously.[52] Black women appreciated the WCTU's limited acceptance. The Michigan State Federation of Colored Women commended the WCTU at their 1900 state convention because "they have shown the absence of prejudice against us by appointing such women of the race as Lucy Thurman . . . and others to positions of trust."[53] A single black woman, the wife of a Baptist minister, was a member of a local Union in Ann Arbor, Michigan in 1894.[54] This shows that an occasional black was acceptable in heavily white northern unions as late as the mid-1890s, a quite impressive level of tolerance for the time.

However, relative integration did not head off criticism of the WCTU's equivocal racial policies. Interestingly, the strongest challenge to the Union's treatment of blacks came from abroad. It was spearheaded by a British antilynching society that launched an attack in the 1890s in the periodical *Fraternity*, accusing the WCTU not only of segregation but of being an apologist for lynching. Willard replied that the Union favored "sympathy between all races, classes, creeds and communities," but that individual unions always had local autonomy. In practice this meant that in the South black women were organized separately (as were Scandinavian immigrants in the North), not just because of segregation but also because black women preferred their own organizations. She also pointed out that from the beginning, black women had been "among the superintendents and organizers of the WCTU." Of course, the only black superintendent was the Superintendent of Colored Work, and the only black organizers worked solely among their own people. Willard also claimed with justification that the WCTU was one of the first national organizations to go on record as opposing lynching. The editor of *Fraternity* did not accept Willard's "autonomy excuse" or the Scandinavian parallel. He contended that while the WCTU might condemn lynching, it also apologized for it, and no one denied that the WCTU recognized the color line in the Southern states. Frederick Douglass, just before his death, and William Lloyd Garrison were among the antislavery leaders who came to the WCTU's defense against *Fraternity*'s charges. The severity of the British attack reflects the more radical nature of the British temperance movement, and its closer alliance with working-class and socialist elements. Temperance in America was much more middle-class.[55]

The South and the black community were not the only missionary fields. In 1883 Willard, accompanied by Anna Gordon, made a "round-up," as she called it, of the western states. Although unions already existed in California, their trip was the first major organizing effort in the West. That spring, they traveled over 2,200 miles in California and Nevada in sixty-five days, organizing eighteen new unions and adding about a thousand new members. Willard attracted huge crowds wherever she spoke and was almost buried in blossoms. Floral tributes, crosses, harps, baskets, lyres, pyramids, made her platform a bower at every meeting.[56] They also traveled in New Mexico, Oregon, Montana, and Utah that same spring and summer. Organizers were later appointed to work in the West, especially in Utah, where the Union found much to deplore about the condition of Mormon women. The first organizer in Utah was authorized by the 1886 convention; Wyoming and Montana received some aid in 1887.[57]

The WCTU also worked with American Indians. At the 1879 convention the first attempt was made to contact the chiefs of the Five Civilized Nations to interest them in temperance, but even from the beginning pressure was put on the federal government to see that liquor laws were enforced on the reservations.[58] It was always an uphill battle. While sale of intoxicating liquor was forbidden, agents (especially those at army posts) interpreted beer and wine as nonintoxicating, and traders sold them freely.[59] On her western tours Willard visited reservations and was received enthusiastically. There seems to have been little or no prejudice in the WCTU against native Americans. Oklahoma sent Jane Stapler, a Cherokee, as a delegate to the national convention in 1890. She was received warmly.[60]

Organization of immigrant groups also became a concern in the 1880s. As early as 1880, in her first presidential address, Willard urged that immigrant groups be approached and organized in their own languages.[61]

Like contemporary efforts in the South and West, this was seen as a missionary commitment to reach unorganized segments of the population. But the task of organizing immigrant women got under way much more slowly than the organization of the South and West, and at first consisted largely of work with Germans. A few states had superintendents by 1882, and two years later twenty-one states and territories were organized.[62] The WCTU looked at immigrants two ways, first as another group of women with special characteristics who needed to be organized into unions, and second, as a disadvantaged group cutting across sex lines, which was in need of basic social services and whose male members especially could be saved from the evils of drink. There were small numbers of foreign-born women in the Union, primarily Scandinavian, German, and Dutch, and their leadership came from within the ethnic communities themselves. By 1886 the German-speaking members had their own newspaper, and several ethnic churches were beginning to cooperate with the temperance movement. The stronger pull, however, was not for organizing foreign women but for saving foreign men, an exercise of the Union's welfare impulse that was not only paternalistic but was frequently accompanied by bigotry.[63] The Germans and northern Europeans were easiest to accept. Sarah Morrison, reporting in 1881, perceived "an abler class from Germany than any other country" but saw in the Irish an "absence of cleanliness, absence of thrift . . . [and] ignorance, idleness and swagger."[64] Sallie Chapin was less charitable about the Germans, describing them as "these men that landed at Castle Garden a few weeks ago—whiskey, beer-drinking Irish and Germans."[65] How women of European ancestry sitting in the convention reacted to her remarks, we do not know.

Acting on a suggestion proposed as early as 1883, the national WCTU authorized the employment of a missionary evangelist to meet all immigrants as they landed in New York, to distribute literature and information.[66] A Swedish woman, Anna Lindahl, was employed the next year. Literature was distributed in sixteen languages, and the immigration authorities praised her work.[67] But while the WCTU was committed to working with foreigners, it did not in most cases accept immigrants as equals. Willard and many other members tried to offset this ambivalence and stifle nativism and bigotry. Willard was particularly adamant in her condemnation of persecution of the Chinese in the 1880s, but ethnic slurs crept in nonetheless. The WCTU could not really rise above its white Protestant middle-class origins.

In the 1890s, when nativism became more widespread, the WCTU's lip service to tolerance became more transparent. By then the *Union Signal* was using its columns to associate the saloonkeeper and the alien, pointing out that 87 percent of saloonkeepers were aliens, that in sixteen states men voted before they were naturalized, and that the alien vote and saloon power colluded to control municipal elections. The *Signal* saw foreigners as the "strength and bulwark of the liquor power," and the president of the Nebraska Union complained that "our state is in the hands of a foreign mob."[68] The 1892 convention memorialized Congress for stricter immigration laws, although it did "deprecate invidious distinction against any one nationality, as embodied in the Chinese Exclusion Act."[69] Willard's previous tolerance disappeared. In her last address to a national convention she asked that Congress "enact a stringent immigration law prohibiting the influx into our land of more of the scum of the Old World, until we have educated those who are here."[70]

Nativism in the United States has usually been accompanied by anti-Catholicism, and there was anti-Catholicism in the WCTU. Mary Livermore, president of the Massachusetts Union, believed that "no Catholic should hold office in our country whose political allegiance is to the Pope, first. It is time there was agitation."[71] Catholic women, although officially welcome in the WCTU, probably felt uncomfortable with its militant Protestantism. They had their own temperance societies, which were first encouraged by the Catholic National Total Abstinence Union in 1874, the year in which the WCTU was founded. However, at least one Catholic, Sallie Moore, financial secretary of the Catholic women's society, was also a member of the WCTU.[72]

But Willard consistently embraced ecumenicism. She insisted that the Union welcomed Jew, Gentile, Protestant, and Catholic despite its preponderance of Protestant Christian members.[73] She warmly greeted fraternal delegates from Catholic temperance societies and enthusiastically sent WCTU representatives to their meetings. She did not apologize when Boston's temperance women rebuked her for welcoming Catholics to the platform of the national convention, complaining of "the inroads which Romanists are making in our ranks, preventing freedom of speech and action." She answered she "believed the time for such narrowness was past."[74] In 1895 the convention passed a resolution formally inviting Catholic and Hebrew women to join the WCTU.[75] Willard was supported by the WCTU national leadership. Katherine Stevenson, national corresponding secretary, wrote privately about the fracas, "I think if I had to choose today between joining the A.P.A. [American Protective Association] or the Catholic church, I'd go into the latter."[76] Willard, Anna Gordon, and Julia Ames attended the meetings of the Catholic National Total Abstinence Union in Washington in 1891. Willard addressed the assembly and reported in a letter that "the priests are charming. I never met more genial, lovely, cultured men." Some of her Methodist friends like Charles Parkhurst were shocked, but she persisted.[77]

The South, blacks, and immigrants were not the only objects of the Union's organizing zeal. The United States WCTU also set out to organize the world. In 1884 Mary Clement Leavitt, who had been organizing on the West Coast, embarked for the Sandwich Islands with thirty-five dollars in her pocket and the firm intention to pursue her way around the world, organizing unions as she went. She organized a union in Honolulu in June 1885, which generously sent her on to Auckland. She organized eleven unions in New Zealand before she sailed to Australia, where nine unions were formed.[78] And so it went—Japan, China, Siam, Burma, India; Leavitt traveled 39,642 miles in three years.[79] She remained overseas until 1891. By that time she had traveled 100,000 miles in 43 countries, worked with 229 interpreters in 47 languages, held 1,600 meetings, and organized 130 temperance societies. She spent only $8,000 on this great pilgrimage, most of which she raised herself along the way. Only $1,600 had come from her American sponsors.[80] After 1888 she was joined in the work by other international organizers, but she continued to travel mostly alone. When her journey was finished, Leavitt probably knew the world as no other American woman of her time, and she had shared this knowledge with the members of the WCTU in the United States through the columns of the *Union Signal* and her vivid reports to national conventions. When she returned to the United States, reporters flocked to her daughter's home in Arlington, Massachusetts, where she was staying. Leading dailies devoted considerable space to feature stories on her work and travels. The woman's temperance movement, especially in Hawaii, the Antipodes, Japan, and India, and perhaps Africa, stemmed largely from Leavitt's pioneering efforts. The movement in the British Isles and northern Europe had other antecedents, although Leavitt spent most of a year in Britain and on the Continent and continued her organizing there. Not even Willard could match Leavitt's feat as an organizer.

Willard reduced the amount of time she herself spent on the road beginning in 1884. She had traveled through all forty-eight states and territories during the Crusade decennial year, and now wanted time at home with her eighty-year-old mother. She continued to speak but limited the number of her engagements and handled much of her work through correspondence.[81] After 1886, when Willard began receiving a salary, there was no financial incentive to drive her to the hustings. Other organizers were in the field by this time, and the national Union began to pay organizers a salary in 1885.[82] In 1886 there were six national organizers on the road. Mary Byron Reese, who was assigned to Washington and Oregon, traveled over six thousand miles, much of it by wagon. Henrietta Moore, whose territory included most of the United States east of the Mississippi, logged nearly fourteen thousand miles. They made hundreds of set speeches, attended state and district conventions, talked to Sunday schools, conducted evening church services, and organized 312 new unions.[83] The national Union had nineteen national and world organizers at work in 1898.[84]

The WCTU had also founded a lecture bureau in 1874 at Willard's suggestion, but it was always a shoestring operation. Presumably its full-time director (who was paid sixty dollars per month) was supported by a percentage of the fees received by the speakers who used its services, but in 1889, fifteen years after it opened, the bureau had receipts of only $610.04, and the WCTU was still subsidizing it heavily.[85] Actually, every organizer was also a lecturer, since she could not otherwise attract an audience. Her lecture, almost always on temperance, was designed to lure a large group before whom a call could be made for a meeting of interested women the next day, when a local would be formally organized. Only a few lecturers of national stature were not organizers, and they were the ones who belonged to the lecture bureau.

The push for organization was at its height in the 1880s. By 1884, its tenth anniversary, the WCTU was organized in every state and territory on the state level. By the 1890s the WCTU network of local unions had penetrated everywhere except rural areas. There were very few unions for farm women or women in small rural villages, and some modestly successful efforts were made to correct this condition in the mid–1890s. However, in 1890 over half the counties in the United States were organized, to say nothing of scattered local unions in many others. This comprehensive pattern of organizing down to the local level, begun by Willard before she became president, continued by her throughout her life, and assiduously pursued by scores of other women on the international, national, and local scene, was the factor that made the WCTU unique among nineteenth-century organizations and provided it with its strength in comparison to the National American Woman Suffrage Association in the 1890s. It was not until 1894 that the suffrage movement began to organize on the local level, and little was accomplished before 1900.

The printed message broadcast by the WCTU underlined and reinforced the organizers, and the Union's publication program in the 1880s and 1890s held the organization together. Most important of these publications was the national house organ, the *Union Signal*, which continues to exist as the official newspaper of the WCTU. The Union had several newspapers when Willard became president, but no single national publication reached the entire membership. Most of these papers were financially weak and limited in circulation. *Our Union*, which claimed to have national coverage, was published only monthly and was in debt, and its subscription list totaled no more than 5,000. The *Signal*, published by the Illinois Union, was probably the strongest newspaper, but it had no connection with the national Union. Willard began as early as 1880 to push for consolidation to create a single strong voice, using the Illinois *Signal* Publishing Company as her vehicle.[86] However, the merger of *Our Union* and the *Signal* was not completed for nearly three years.[87] Several financially shaky state newspapers also decided to enter the merger, and the new, consolidated *Union Signal* began publication in the old *Signal* offices in Chicago on January 1, 1883.[88] At first both a weekly and monthly edition were published, but the monthly was discontinued before the year was out.

By 1884 the *Union Signal* was the most popular temperance journal in the country, with nearly 14,000 subscribers.[89] By 1890 it was the largest women's paper in the world, with circulation pushing 100,000; only one Protestant religious paper, the *Sunday School Times*, had a larger subscription list.[90] Its parent corporation, the Woman's Temperance Publishing Association, was also publishing two periodicals for children, one German-language temperance paper, and an average of a dozen books and two million leaflets a year, and doing a substantial business in job printing. The plant had acquired an impressive array of modern machinery, and the company boasted total receipts of over $180,000.[91] One hundred eleven persons were employed, eighty-nine of them women who filled positions as compositors, proofreaders, and bindery workers as well as performing clerical and editorial jobs.[92] Dividends were a healthy 7 percent and a sinking fund had been established.[93]

Matilda Carse was the entrepreneur who directed this substantial enterprise. President of the Chicago Central Union from 1878 until her death in 1917, she founded the Woman's Temperance Publishing Association, a stock company of women only, in 1880 as a vehicle for publishing the Illinois *Signal* and temperance and reform tracts and books. Upon consolidation, the Association took over publication of the *Union Signal*. Carse was president of the Association until 1898, and the company continued as the publishing arm of the WCTU until it was dissolved in 1903 when the WCTU purchased the *Union Signal* and its juvenile periodicals.

The first editor of the *Union Signal* was Frances Willard's sister-in-law Mary, the widow of Oliver Willard. She was replaced in 1885 by Mary Allen West, a professional journalist who had been president of the Illinois WCTU. After West's death in Japan in 1892, Frances Willard assumed regular editorship, but her relationship to the paper was at most that of delineating broad editorial policy and making frequent contributions to its columns. Most editorial tasks were performed by the managing editors. Originally a man was employed as business manager, but when George Hall, who had successfully guided the pursuit of revenues and profits since 1885, resigned his post, there was strong sentiment in the Union that he be replaced by a woman, and two women, Fanny Rastall and Caroline Grow, were in turn his successors.[94]

From the beginning, the columns of the *Union Signal* combined education, proselytizing, and entertainment. First of all, the paper acted as the major force holding the WCTU together between conventions. State presidents reported on their more successful programs, local unions contributed items, and Willard and other national officers published regular columns that gave the reader a comprehensive view of the activities of the Union and its work across the country. Program goals were explained, implementation described and suggested. The *Signal* is a much richer source of material on the Union in the nineteenth century than official records.

From its first number, the *Union Signal* proselytized for temperance, prohibition, and the home-protection ballot, and these efforts never diminished. But as the years went by, the *Signal* became more and more openly feminist in its allegiance. Home protection was broadened to general support for woman suffrage. Women's accomplishments, regardless of whether they were related to the temperance cause, were consistently given space. The editor commented in 1885, for example, that although as recently as 1880 women had rarely attended the sessions of the American Social Science Association, they presented many of the most cogent papers at the current meetings.[95] The *Signal* was quick to report the election of a woman as president of the Dover, New Hampshire, Street Railway Company and another woman's election as mayor of Argonia, Kansas.[96] In 1889 Willard contributed a series of sketches of prominent women, not necessarily WCTU members or temperance workers, which encouraged a general recognition of women's achievements.[97] Feminism also manifested itself in other ways. An "Index Expurgatorius" suggested no more use of the word *female* unless for necessary distinction of biological sex; no more *man and wife* for *husband and wife*; no more *poetess*, *authoress*, or any *-ess* ending; and no more use of *relict*—"no woman is relict anymore."[98]

The *Union Signal* also campaigned hard in the 1880s and 1890s for a wide spectrum of social causes, frequently far to the left. Edward Bellamy's *Looking Backward* was analyzed and praised on its publication in 1889. Several series of articles on child-labor legislation, prison reform, and the working conditions of women tackled those problems in considerable depth. The desirability of kindergarten and child-care facilities was explored at length. In 1891 the *Signal* ran a series of articles by W. Howatt Gardiner on Christian socialism, and the editor commented that no longer was anyone afraid of the word *socialism* or convinced that it was associated with atheism.[99] In 1892 there was a series on taxation and the poor, which advocated the graduated income tax.[100] The *Union Signal* narrowed its scope substantially in the late 1890s after Willard's death, but from the 1880s through the mid-1890s it can be compared very favorably with suffragist publications in the extent of its commitment to general social reform.[101]

Despite its concern with organizational matters and broad social issues, the *Union Signal* did not neglect household and maternal concerns. Ella Eaton Kellogg, wife of the director of the famous Battle Creek health resort and sister-in-law of the breakfast cereal developer, wrote a column on food, and health columns by women physicians appeared periodically. Until temperance lessons were adopted by the major Sunday-school suppliers, the *Signal* provided a monthly temperance exercise for children. The journal also provided entertainment and general interest features, publishing poems, stories, short dramas, puzzles, and a page for children; letters to the editor appeared from the start, and a regular book-review column began in 1885. Nor was it without its teapot tempests, such as the great mince pie controversy, which raged in its pages in 1884. Did the alcohol evaporate in the baking and leave the pies harmless? Could an acceptable pie be made without cider or brandy? It could! Or perhaps mince pie, with or without cider, was an unhealthful food, and best avoided.

In the 1890s the *Union Signal* occasionally became a tool for specific organizational goals. When the WCTU began to recruit rural members, the journal published an annual "Fair" issue in August, most of its articles designed to interest farmers and their wives, which was distributed free by local unions at county fairs across the country. The 1891 issue contained among other pieces articles on farm law and temperance education in rural schools, an editorial on the state of farm mortgages, and fiction tailored to the rural scene.[102]

The *Union Signal* had few advertisements in 1883 (a doctor, a dressmaker, a dealer in "reform"—i.e., unconfining—clothing, and several music companies advertised in its first issue), but the number of ads increased rapidly until by the 1890s they filled several pages. Books and periodicals, music and musical instruments, household appliances such as sewing machines, washing machines, folding beds and bathtubs, and clothing (especially "reform" corsets and undergarments) were all well represented. Ads for health nostrums were abundant. Tonics, eye waters, catarrh remedies, cures for piles, and painless pregnancy and childbirth systems were all touted in the *Signal*'s pages. The *Signal* was sensitive about inadvertently accepting ads for patent medicines that included alcohol (the old Illinois *Signal* did advertise Lydia Pinkham's alcohol-based tonic in 1881) and admitted that "some fraudulent and unworthy advertisements have inadvertently been accepted," but insisted that they were withdrawn as soon as noticed.[103] Schemes for making money by selling some product at home, greeting cards and chromolithographs to be sold as fund-raising schemes, and a large number of speculative investment proposals, railroads, Dakota and Florida farmlands, and subdivision development were advertised.[104] The WCTU also publicized its own literature in the *Signal*'s pages.

In addition to the *Union Signal* and other publications of the Woman's Temperance Publishing Association, the WCTU also sponsored a department of temperance literature, based in New York, which antedated the Association and distributed tracts and leaflets of the moral suasion school.[105] By the 1890s its work was of little importance. More important was the work of the press superintendent, who was responsible for contributing temperance columns to secular newspapers. As the daily press became more receptive to temperance materials, significant numbers of people could be reached in this way. In 1885, for example, 125 secular Ohio newspapers used temperance columns prepared by the WCTU. The *Signal* undoubtedly contributed more than any other Union publication to the growth spurt of the 1880s, but all aspects of the publication program had some part in the Union's expansion.

By 1890 the WCTU was strong and rich, with 150,000 dues-paying members and a national budget of nearly $30,000, ten times that of 1880. But this was a small part of the Union's actual receipts: local unions reported raising $317,345 in the 1890 fiscal year, and over $50,000 passed through the state treasuries. There were 28,000 young women in the auxiliary YWCTU and 135,000 children in the affiliated Loyal Temperance Legions.[106] The WCTU continued to grow in the 1890s, but its position as the goliath of women's organizations was already solidly assured. What is more, the Union's successful efforts to attract membership had cut across sectional, racial, and ethnic lines. The organizers and publicizers had done their work well.

Woman's Mighty Realm
of Philanthropy

A BROAD PROGRAM OF

CHARITY AND SOCIAL ACTION

No problem was too complicated, no solution too innovative to find a hearing in WCTU councils of the late nineteenth century. Again, as with home protection, Frances Willard provided the pithy slogan—Do Everything—which aptly described the breathtaking sweep of the Union's concerns, but the membership matched her in range of interest. The WCTU of the 1870s had concerned itself primarily with temperance and temperance-related causes. The WCTU of the 1880s and 1890s added most of the social problems of the day to the list of issues it embraced. Willard articulated this change of emphasis in her address to the national convention in 1891, proclaiming, "Woman's mighty realm of philanthropy encroaches each day upon the empire of sin, disease and misery that has so long existed, we thought it must endure forever."[1] That "realm of philanthropy" had indeed begun to encroach upon most of the nation's sins. Social action had replaced prayer as woman's answer to distress. Although the argument can be made that social action to the WCTU often meant charity—as in Willard's "philanthropy"—and the Union's missions and lodging houses for the indigent or its work with young boys plying street trades can

The chapter title is from Frances Willard's 1891 presidential address, transcribed in the *Minutes* of the convention, 93.

certainly be seen in this light, Do Everything also moved the WCTU into legislative halls where it lobbied for institutional change, and in this sense Do Everything was a program of social reform.

In his essay on the temperance movement, Norman Clark has stated that the American family was more threatened than that of any other society in the nineteenth century, first by the westward movement that disrupted continuity of place, then by the mass migration of non-English-speaking peoples, and finally by the insecurities bred by urbanization and industrialization.[2] Clark sees the temperance movement as one response to these dislocations. Certainly the specific responses of the WCTU to the problems arising from the rapid urbanization and industrialization of American society in the last quarter of the nineteenth century would seem to bear him out. The Union's attention to improving the police force, the prison, and the reformatory; its work with and for indigent children; its concern for the working woman; its attention to problems of public health (of which it properly saw alcohol abuse as one), were all designed to find solutions to problems created by burgeoning cities and a rapidly changing economy. The Union literally tried to take on most of society's problems.

The openness of the WCTU contrasted with the line taken by militant suffragists during the same period. Susan B. Anthony was convinced she must stick to a single issue to be effective. Before the Civil War she had advocated a number of causes simultaneously, but she believed she had learned an important lesson when she adopted the short-skirted bloomer costume for a brief period in the 1850s: people looked at her clothes rather than listened to her words. "If I wished my hearers to consider the suffrage question I must not present the temperance, the religious, the dress or any other besides, but must confine myself to suffrage."[3] While Elizabeth Cady Stanton never approved of reducing the woman suffrage movement to a single goal, the broad perspective of the earlier period was abandoned in the last quarter of the nineteenth century. During its first years, from 1868 to 1871, the National Woman Suffrage Association, the militant wing led by Anthony and Stanton, had addressed itself to broad social and economic questions, but it gave up public expression on these issues by 1871 because of the opposition it inspired among women, an opposition that it believed would jeopardize the suffrage goal.[4]

Although neither prohibition nor the vote for women was achieved until these campaigns became single-issue movements, the nineteenth-century WCTU did not conceive the temperance issue narrowly. Instead it approached temperance as part of a complex of related issues that should be dealt with simultaneously. Part of the Union's appeal in the closing decades of the nineteenth century was its eclecticism. The WCTU offered some way for almost every woman to relate to the movement, from encouraging young children to sign the time-honored pledge of abstinence to advocating a new socialist society. The Union's eclecticism may have hurt its usefulness to the temperance cause (prohibition efforts lost ground during the 1890s), but it helped make possible the WCTU's impressive numerical growth and thereby its importance as a vehicle for the woman's movement. Do Everything made the Union strong and gave it depth. It attracted women who pioneered in the professions and business; it provided a channel through which women who were deeply concerned with social problems could find a constituency and a forum. When it reverted to a single-minded temperance stance in the twentieth century, the Union lost many of these women.

Do Everything was operationally possible because of the large measure of organizational local autonomy that the constitution of the WCTU provided from the beginning. Aside from a commitment to teetotaling temperance and a willingness to pay nominal national dues, each local, county, or state union had no nationally authorized duties and could decide for itself what aspects of the program it wished to pursue. A national program was adopted by majority vote of delegates to national conventions, but any union or union member could choose not to implement any part of that program or even deny it tacit support. The reluctant South need not advocate the vote for women. No member was compelled to cease wearing feathered hats or discard her corset-stays to conform to dress reform standards. No local union was forced to emulate Frances Willard's growing ecumenical outreach to the Catholic community. There was a large measure of grass-roots support for most of the national program, but support of its more radical aspects was always thin, especially when a new program task was first adopted. At the same time there was room for militant and radical women to work effectively within the organizational framework. Devotion to the temperance cause was the cement that held the conglomerate together.

In 1882, of the twenty departments (each headed by a superintendent) into which the work of the national union was then organized, only three—the franchise, prisons and jails, and juvenile affairs—were not solely concerned with promoting the temperance cause.[5] The next year the number had risen to nine out of thirty-one, and by 1896 twenty-five departments out of a total of thirty-nine were dealing wholly or in major part with nontemperance issues.[6] In 1889 the WCTU in a single city, Chicago, was sponsoring two day nurseries, two Sunday schools, an industrial school, a mission that sheltered four thousand homeless or destitute women in a twelve-month period, a free medical dispensary that treated over sixteen hundred patients a year, a lodging house for men that had to date provided temporary housing for over fifty thousand men, and a low-cost restaurant.[7] The national convention that same year passed an antivivisection resolution, petitioned Congress to prohibit the manufacture of cigarettes, petitioned the Czar for more humane treatment of Siberian exiles, petitioned state legislatures for free public kindergartens, and agreed to continue work for reformatories for women and the employment of police matrons and women administrators for women's correctional institutions.[8] Small local unions were also engaged in social action projects. For example, the little Harriman, Tennessee, local in 1891 was working to secure athletic facilities for young men and a Saturday half-holiday in factories.[9] The WCTU of Hampden, Massachusetts, established in 1890 a residential vocational school for inebriate and "fallen" women at South Hadley in the pleasant twelve-room house of a union member.[10]

Generally speaking, however, it would seem that state and local unions paid less attention than the national organization to broad social issues. In September and October 1893, at the depth of the financial panic, when the *Union Signal* was devoting much editorial space to economic and social problems, the reports it published from state unions described primarily temperance activities. Five states reported only temperance activity, although one of these reports was from the Illinois Union, where Chicago alone had several nontemperance projects running. A few state unions reported a variety of other projects ranging from home placement of orphaned children to cooperation with the Knights of Labor.[11]

Although some of the original efforts to reform the drunkard continued after the 1870s, the gospel temperance meeting and the jail prayer meeting received less emphasis in the 1880s and 1890s. Concrete practical help took their place. For example, there was increasing concern with inebriate women, a push for both reform and prevention. The WCTU set up programs for meeting young girls coming to the city for the first time, to assist them in finding employment and housing. The Chicago Union sponsored a lodging house for transient women that provided a clean bed in a dormitory and a nightdress for ten cents, and a light breakfast at low rates.[12] Coffee tanks were placed in factories that employed women, in order to discourage the use of gin and beer, the only liquids previously available.[13] Shelters for homeless men and cheap coffeehouses and restaurants that served a well-balanced meal were aimed at helping the drinker resist the temptation of the saloon's free lunch.

Most importantly, by the 1890s the WCTU leadership had moved close to seeing alcoholism as disease rather than sin.[14] In 1891 Willard unexpectedly devoted a large proportion of her annual address to the question of whether drunkenness was a disease or a moral aberration. She argued that it was both: the drunkard was sick and should be treated with all the remedies science could devise, but "the flask in his pocket should also be replaced with a Bible."[15] She went on to say that "a purpose to drink liquors is a sin" but that the "appetite thus formed and forced is a disease," and she advocated locking up the liquor rather than the man, an early plea for the decriminalization of insobriety.[16] By 1893 Willard openly asserted that although many people could use alcohol moderately with no ill effects, prohibition was wise and necessary to protect the few who would become addicted. She continued, in a convoluted argument to explain her position,

> It will always be true that a certain number of people must, for their own sake, let intoxicants entirely alone. . . . If, then, anyone elects to be an abstainer, in order that those who *must* follow that practice shall not be a class by themselves marked as weaklings and of singular ways of life, and also for the reason that it is more absolutely safe to let liquors alone than to use them, he is in a position wholly scientific, ethical and in accordance with the Golden Rule.[17]

The WCTU slowly replaced gospel temperance with the recognition that alcoholism was a serious public health problem. Eventually it was also to see poverty as a cause rather than result of drink.

Prison reform was the first nontemperance issue to attract widespread attention from the WCTU. That attention was originally triggered by the gospel temperance meetings in jails, but in a very few years a department for prison, jail and almshouse work was petitioning for rehabilitative reformatories and police matrons, establishing halfway houses for released women prisoners, and demanding women be appointed to state boards of charities and corrections. A strong element of social feminism had crept into the work. As early as 1882 the national Superintendent of Prison and Police Work commented, "It is a standing rebuke to our civilization that women are arrested and given into the hands of men to be searched and cared for, tried by men, sentenced by men, committed to . . . institutions where only men have access to them."[18] Pressure from the WCTU put four police matrons in Philadelphia station houses by 1885, and increased the number employed by Chicago from ten in 1885 to twenty-one in 1890. By that year, largely through Union efforts, matrons were employed in thirty-six United States cities, the larger cities employing several.[19] Willingness to participate in the work of this WCTU department was almost universal; there were active departments in forty-five states and territories as early as 1889.[20] In most cases pressure was put on state and local governments to improve and reform services, but several unions supported halfway houses themselves. The Arkansas Union paid the salary of a police matron, and almost everywhere unions demanded and stocked prison libraries, which had been almost nonexistent before.[21] Some efforts were frivolous, if touching. The Arkansas Union entertained at a strawberry festival at the state prison in June, complete with buttonhole bouquets and an organ recital.[22]

Prison work was slowest to move beyond the gospel temperance syndrome in the South. The Louisiana Union found it difficult to find recruits for prison work because all the women who became superintendents soon found that their husbands disapproved of their visiting prisons.[23] Nonetheless two Union women, Rebecca Felton of Georgia and Julia Tutweiler of Alabama, led the fight against the convict lease system in the South in the 1880s.[24] The *Union Signal* carried full accounts of the sessions of the National Prison Association and the National Conference of Charities and Corrections, and by 1894 Willard strongly recommended support for policewomen—not matrons but women on the beat.[25] Because of pressure from the Woman's Alliance and the WCTU, the Chicago city council as early as 1889 authorized the commissioner of health to appoint five women to the sanitary police force that inspected tenements and factories.[26] A WCTU member actually served as police chief of El Cajon in San Diego County at the turn of the century.[27]

Another area into which the WCTU moved early was work with children. Again the Union began with temperance-oriented activity, the organization of juvenile unions whose young members signed the pledge and assisted the temperance cause. The juvenile temperance movement had begun in Great Britain in 1830. It was formally organized in 1847 as the Bands of Hope and was open to children under sixteen. Children's temperance clubs were popular because little formal entertainment was available for youngsters, and the excursions, lantern slide shows, and other club-sponsored outings filled this lack. There is no evidence of organized work with children in the United States before the Civil War. The WCTU began juvenile work in the mid-1870s, and the department formed for the purpose reported to the national convention for the first time in 1878. Membership of children's groups varied and was erratically reported since it had no representation in national conventions, but in 1880 Massachusetts reported seventy-six juvenile unions, with over 15,000 members; New York, fifty-nine, with over 7,000 members; and Michigan, sixty-one, with 10,000 members.[28] Many juvenile unions, some later called Loyal Temperance Legions rather than Bands of Hope, were affiliated with Sunday schools, and their exhibitions of marching and song were always favorite entertainments at WCTU conventions. The members of Bands of Hope and Loyal Temperance Legions were not always the sons and daughters of temperance women; the San Diego WCTU organized a Band of Hope in 1889 among derelict children on the waterfront.[29] The Loyal Temperance Legion was strongest in the 1880s. It met strong competition in the 1890s from the United Boys' Brigade, a quasi-militaristic, uniformed marching and drilling organization frequently sponsored by churches, which lured the young away from the gentler temperance cause.[30]

From organizing Sunday-school children the WCTU moved on to work with bootblacks, telegraph messengers, newsboys, and street urchins. Street trades were normally plied in the late nineteenth century by children, an impoverished, abused, scruffy lot, who—with little else to comfort them—were frequently habitual users of alcohol and tobacco. Reading rooms and coffeehouses were provided by the WCTU for their use as well as that of their elders, and food and entertainments were arranged at intervals. For example, the New Orleans WCTU gave a holiday "Robin Dinner" for four hundred news, telegraph and messenger boys, including "about forty young tramps." They fed them on donated ham, turkey, tongue, and chicken and lobster salads, cake, fruit, and coffee. Of course, they invited them to attend their Sunday gospel temperance meetings and sign the pledge. Some forty obliged.[31]

A corollary of work with street boys was the "kitchen garden" program for girls. Beginning in 1882, training schools in the domestic arts, nutrition, food preparation, and simple sewing were initiated in poor neighborhoods, almshouses, and orphanages. Usually this program was the responsibility of the Young Woman's Christian Temperance Unions, known as Y's. By 1883 schools had been started in eight cities. Yonkers had one class for black children. Occasionally the kitchen garden program was designed for middle-class children, as in Louisville, and tuition charged, the proceeds being used to support the work among the poor.[32] The program was discontinued in 1887, but the convention expressed the hope that Y's would continue the work.[33] (The settlement-house movement soon initiated similar training programs.) In the mid-1880s the WCTU began to emphasize industrial training schools for girls rather than weekly classes in the domestic arts. The curriculum was broader, including printing, drawing, telegraphy, typewriting, and stenography, as well as housekeeping skills. Frequently these schools were residential institutions in rural settings, designed to remove the young from urban temptations. They were usually privately supported but occasionally received public funds. The *Union Signal* published frequent items in 1888 on the new industrial schools.[34]

In 1891 the national Union created a department for work with homeless children, which promoted finding foster and permanent homes for orphans and dependent children rather than institutionalizing them. Where possible the department cooperated with state agencies and private institutions. By 1894 the unions of twenty-one states were engaged in the program, and states not participating were those where the need was already being filled by active Children's Aid Societies or Societies for the Prevention of Cruelty to Children.[35] Child abuse was always a concern of temperance women and was seen as proper cause for terminating parental rights. Incidents of child abuse were regularly reported in the *Union Signal* and almost invariably blamed on drunkenness.

One of the WCTU's major social contributions in the 1880s was its enthusiastic promotion of the kindergarten movement. Willard found this cause especially rewarding. She called it the "greatest theme, next to salvation by faith, that can engage a woman's heart and brain."[36] San Francisco's Golden Gate Kindergarten Association founded the first free WCTU kindergarten in 1880, and by 1890 that center alone had over fifteen hundred children enrolled.[37] The Baltimore Union sponsored a free kindergarten, manned by volunteers and a paid teacher and assistant, that clothed and fed fifty children "from homes of wretched poverty," where four-year-olds "who used tobacco" were cleaned up and cured of their bad habits. Twelve additional children, too young for kindergarten, were cared for in a day nursery.[38] The sponsorship of kindergartens was largely an urban movement and was specifically designed for the children of working mothers who would otherwise be forced to leave their children alone in locked rooms. Usually children were served three meals a day and spent twelve hours, from 7:00 A.M. to 7:00 P.M., at the "creche." Ten cents a day was charged mothers who could afford to pay. The San Diego Union, only three years old at the time, established a day nursery for the children of working mothers in 1887, which they expanded by 1890 to a day-care and residential facility for orphans. The older children attended public school and the younger ones a kindergarten class on the premises. Parents who were able paid a nominal fee, the state paid the cost for its wards, and the city supervisors paid for those placed by the city. Part of the time women without resources were accepted with their children. The institution lasted well into the twentieth century and is an example of a WCTU social welfare project on the local level that was both meaningful and permanent.[39] Frequently, training programs for teachers were attached to WCTU kindergartens.[40]

Although some WCTU locals lobbied for public kindergartens as early as the mid-1880s, the national WCTU began to promote kindergartens as part of the public school system in the 1890s.[41] It is incorrect or at most partially right to attribute Willard's support of the kindergarten movement to its usefulness as an appeal through children to solicit women for the temperance cause.[42] The WCTU supported kindergartens as a necessary service for working-class mothers and children. Temperance recruitment was a small part of the motivation.

Many of the WCTU's social service activities were both initiated and most effectively implemented in the Chicago area, the same neighborhood where Jane Addams established Hull House in 1889. The WCTU was not an enthusiastic supporter of Addams's and Ellen Starr's plan when it was first presented to the Chicago establishment in 1888–89.[43] Official WCTU records and publications are silent on Hull House at first, although in 1892 the *Union Signal* praised the Hull House program for training household workers, and urged support for it.[44] Most Chicago reformers were settlement enthusiasts from the beginning, and Hull House has even been called a "fashionable fad."[45] The WCTU may have resented the competition of what it saw as Johnny-come-lately do-gooders. The Hull House program—a kindergarten, recreational activities for street boys, classes in cooking and sewing for young immigrant or impoverished girls, residential and recreational facilities for working girls—were all projects that the WCTU had promoted in the Chicago area and elsewhere for some time. However, Willard was enthusiastically plugging the settlement-house movement by 1895 and urging the WCTU to found its own settlements, saying that the settlement house would replace "the haphazard form of charity accepted in the past."[46] Jane Addams contributed a three-column piece to the *Union Signal* in 1896 outlining the objectives of the movement and suggesting the WCTU operate its own houses. In 1897 Boston's Willard Y Settlement opened its doors.[47]

The WCTU's first approach to the problems of labor offered a simple solution: drunkenness breeds poverty; eliminate drunkenness and the economic problems of the working class will disappear. As late as 1886 Willard stated that the central question of labor reform was not "how to get higher wages," but "how to turn present wages to better account." She believed the labor movement must learn that lesson and that only the WCTU could teach it.[48] The Union's reports and publications emphasized the large average per capita expenditure on drink by the working man.[49] The Union began its practical efforts to aid the working man by asking the new industrial giants to require total abstinence from their employees.[50] Efforts were spotty and confined largely to public transportation companies at first, where a sound case could be made for stringent rules on the basis of safety. But the WCTU also attempted to reach the working man directly. The gospel temperance approach was tried among lumbermen and miners as well as railroad workers in the mid-1880s with at best indifferent success. Lumbermen were most responsive to these missionary efforts, because they provided some small respite from the lonely boredom of the pineries in winter.

The severe depression of the mid-1880s and the attendant economic distress and labor unrest slowly convinced the WCTU that it needed to take a second look at the causes of poverty. In the same presidential address in 1886 that voiced her belief that abstention from liquor could solve the laborer's money problems, Willard endorsed the eight-hour day as a way to reduce unemployment and made her first overtures toward organized labor, expressing sympathy with its methods when it used arbitration, cooperation, and the ballot box. Terence Powderly and the Knights of Labor had won her admiration with their equal rights stance, a membership ban on liquor dealers, and advocacy of temperance.[51] It seems almost as though her statement on poverty and drunkenness was a ritualistic mouthing of long-outgrown convictions, because at her request the 1886 convention authorized her to approach the labor movement formally and changed the name of its relevant department from the Relation of Intemperance to Labor to the Relation of Temperance to Labor. Clearly the Union's design was no longer simply to convert, or coerce through management, but to explore the possibility of a working alliance between the WCTU and organized labor.

The first approach by the WCTU to organized labor had been made in June 1886, when the general officers sent a delegation at Willard's behest to bring greetings to the Knights of Labor convention in Cleveland; Mary Woodbridge carried the message. The Knights were surprised at this overture but received Woodbridge kindly with frequent applause, and Powderly later wrote that it was the first time a representative of another organization had been admitted to their conventions.[52] The 1886 convention endorsed and continued this overture, and Willard composed a letter addressed to the Knights of Labor, trades unions, and other labor organizations, that expressed sympathy with the labor movement, saluted it as an ally, and especially commended its stand on women: equal pay for equal work, admitting women to membership, and support of woman suffrage. But only the Knights among labor groups were endorsing broad feminist aims. Willard went on to commend the Knights' attitude toward the saloon and asked labor's support for compulsory temperance education, sabbath closing of saloons, and an end to the double standard. Powderly responded positively, saying he had read her address with pleasure and would publish it in the Knights' official organ.[53]

Thus began an informal alliance that was to persist for several years. In February 1887 Powderly agreed to distribute through his locals 95,000 petitions for the protection of women. Later that month the Knights cooperated with the WCTU in its lobbying effort on behalf of Senator Henry Blair's bill for federal aid to public elementary schools.[54] Meanwhile Willard was conferring with the leadership of the Knights and addressing labor meetings. In many ways this was a strange partnership, and one that surely would not have existed without Willard's initiative. Most of the rank and file of the WCTU were not radical, and organized labor was viewed with alarm by even the enlightened middle classes in the 1880s. The prominent feminist Lucy Stone watched Willard's approaches to the Knights of Labor "with fear and trembling"; she saw the Knights as extremely disruptive to business and looked with horror at their strikes.[55] The Knights of Labor was certainly perceived as the embodiment of the radical left and in this sense occupied the position as bête noire assumed by the Communist party in a later era. Willard and Powderly were friends, worked well together, and admired one another's ideas, but there is no evidence of a close personal relationship between them. They corresponded infrequently and met seldom.[56] Willard herself hinted in her autobiography at a romantic attachment in her life that she wished revealed only after her death, and some have speculated Powderly was the man, but there is nothing that supports such a view.[57] Their relationship was a professional one between two reformers.

Willard, who was actually inducted into the Knights in 1887, did not lead the WCTU down the labor union path without opposition. By the end of 1887 considerable protest against Willard's romance with the Knights of Labor was developing in the columns of the *Union Signal*. Some questioned fraternal ties with a secret society, others feared the alienation of conservative friends of the WCTU.[58] Willard felt compelled to answer her opponents in her presidential address in the fall of that year, and she mentions her labor union ties briefly in *Glimpses*, where she also provides a transcript of her 1886 open letter to the Knights and other labor organizations. Although there must have been many WCTU members who found organized labor a strange bedfellow, Willard calmed the Union's misgivings by emphasizing the Knights' commitment to temperance and woman suffrage. Religious groups were aghast at the affiliation. The editor of the *Christian Cynosure* chided Willard for associating with Powderly, whom he described as "a faithful son of that Apocalyptic woman called the *Mother of Earth's Abominations*."[59] Nonetheless Anna Sneed Cairns, superintendent of the Department of the Relation of Temperance to Labor, reported the unions of eighteen states were engaged in some variety of cooperative effort with either labor unions or militant farmers' groups, and Cairns herself urged the rank and file to join the Farmers' Alliance or the Knights of Labor.[60] Strikes and violence posed a stumbling block; even Willard found it difficult to condone the Homestead rioters, and the *Union Signal* hedged, avoiding outright support of the strike but condemning the use of Pinkerton men and troops.[61] Officially the WCTU, like the Knights for that matter, was committed to arbitration and conciliation rather than the strike as the way to settle labor disputes.

During the years when it began to establish its tentative alliance with the labor movement, the WCTU also moved toward a radically changed position on poverty and economic distress. Its old assumption that temperance would cure poverty was sharply challenged during the depression winter of 1885. A *Union Signal* editorial described homeless men walking back and forth in railroad tunnels trying to keep warm. Thousands were unemployed in Chicago alone, and thousands of children lived "in homes bare of food and fire." The editor commented, "Is there not justice in the demand that our costly churches shall be opened in such severe winters, for the shelter of the homeless, and the warmth and protection of those who have neither?"[62] In 1886 the WCTU organized its Department for the Prevention of Pauperism, building on the experience of the Association of Organized Charities and using much of its literature.[63] This action represented a formal change of position on poverty. However, through its many programs for the alleviation of alcoholism the Union had long been supporting institutions and services designed to ameliorate the lot of the poor.

In 1889 Willard publicly reversed her stance and attributed intemperance to bad working conditions and long hours, stating that overwork drove men to drink and that poor working conditions sent the factory girl to the saloon at night.[64] The *Union Signal* had paved the way the previous winter by running a long series of articles on the evils of child labor that showed how the use of stimulants flowed naturally from wretchedness and deprivation, and by pursuing an editorial policy that called for the "study of poverty as a cause of intemperance."[65] By the 1890s the vocal elements within the Union were practically unanimous in accepting the view that poverty breeds intemperance. Annie Jackson wrote in the *Union Signal*, "Men and women, overworked, with a state of low vitality and innumerable difficulties to meet, naturally turn toward anything that will afford temporary relief. . . . In the midst of misery, drinking is almost inevitable. Several American manufacturers have testified that with solitary exceptions the men who work the longest are the most given to dissipation."[66]

Meanwhile Frances Willard believed she had found the real solution to poverty. In 1889 she stated in her annual address that "the land and all resources of the earth [must] be held and controlled in some way by the community as a whole."[67] Willard had been converted to Christian socialism. The instrument of her conversion had been Edward Bellamy's *Looking Backward*, which had had a profound effect on several among the WCTU leadership. Zerelda Wallace hailed it as "the greatest book of its kind of the century" and predicted that its power to inspire change would rival that of *Uncle Tom's Cabin*.[68] Willard advocated that fundamental reform of the economic system begin with relief for the unemployed, the five-and-a-half-day week, free technical education, free school lunches, and gradual nationalization or municipal ownership of the railroads, the telegraph, public utilities, and factories.[69] She adopted these views long before her association with the English Fabians, who simply reinforced positions she already held. The economic dislocations that followed the panic of 1893 brought others within the WCTU to espouse her position. The *Union Signal* deplored the concentration of economic power in the hands of a few capitalists and advocated "a change of ownership. [The general benefit of mankind] cannot be expected as long as these great wealth producing interests are in the hands of individuals or private corporations. The only other ownership is, of course, the national government."[70]

While their leaders sought utopia, the rank and file usually embraced more limited objectives. Sabbatarianism was a Union cause from the beginning, although not consistently adhered to. At the 1886 convention a resolution admonishing the membership to eschew Sunday railroad travel failed to pass.[71] But in 1887 seventeen states reported having Superintendents of Sabbath Observance, and the convention petitioned Congress to abolish Sunday mails and army dress parades and inspections and approved the circulation of a Sabbath observation pledge.[72] The Union broke with the suffrage leadership and the Board of Managers (of which Willard was a member) in condemning Sunday opening of the Chicago World's Fair.[73] One link between sabbatarianism and labor support was that the WCTU's commitment to the five-and-a-half-day week was usually based on sabbatarian considerations: to keep the Sabbath properly, workers needed another half day for recreation and personal business.

Health, heredity, and drugs also came in for their share of attention. As early as 1881 Willard was campaigning for whole-wheat bread, because white bread "heats the blood and paves the way for all diseased appetites";

she also predicted that by the end of the century, "the internal use of drugs will be discarded by all intelligent physicians."[74] Departments concerned with hygiene and heredity were formally added to the program in 1883 and quickly adopted on the local level. By 1885 one-fifth of the local unions and twenty-eight states had superintendents under the national leadership of Ella Eaton Kellogg, a health-food advocate and vegetarian.[75] The Department of Heredity was studying eugenics and lobbying for legislation that would limit "the propagation of vagrant and criminal classes."[76] The new Department for the Overthrow of the Tobacco Habit reported for the first time in 1884, citing the health hazards of smoking and suggesting its best chance to make headway was with the young. In 1895 the *Union Signal* was arguing the right to fresh air and advocating smokers be permitted to smoke only in such places and ways as would not interfere "with the rights and freedoms of any other individual."[77] Education on the effects of narcotics, a department of work in which the WCTU is still active, was under way by 1885. The Union was ahead of its time in condemning the indiscriminate use of nostrums and drugs, and some of its earliest reports noted that women were particularly susceptible to addiction to opium, cocaine, and morphine and warned of the danger of babies becoming addicted through their mothers.[78] The use of patent medicines containing alcohol was deplored at the 1884 convention.[79] As part of its health program the WCTU supported a temperance hospital dedicated to treating all diseases without the use of alcohol. Opened in Chicago in 1886, the thirty-five-room hospital had representatives of both homeopathic and allopathic medicine serving on its staff. A nursing school was attached, and women physicians comprised most of its staff.[80]

Dress reform was hailed enthusiastically in principle, if less than widely practiced by its fashionable adherents, and Frances Willard had adopted "emancipation underclothing" by 1881.[81] She perennially agitated for sensible clothing and even called for legislation forbidding "women to mop the streets with trailing dress skirts or to deform their figures by compression of the floating ribs."[82] Antivivisection was added to the Union's causes in the 1890s. Bird feathers adorning women's hats also became one of the Union's abominations.

The Ohio Union requested the national organization to add a department for the promotion of peace in 1885, and in 1887 the Department of Peace and International Arbitration was created. Thirteen states and territories adopted the department within the year. The department opposed military training in schools and colleges, including the Reserve Officer Training Corps in land-grant colleges, provided lecturers on the peace movement, and cooperated with the American Peace Society.[83] Peace as a cause caught on slowly with the rank and file. Mary Woodbridge, one of the department's lecturers, complained that at first only members of the Friends' Meeting understood its principles, but by the 1890s the department had marshaled support for naval disarmament, sent representatives to the Universal Peace Congress in London, and endorsed the Pan-American Congress. Twenty-four states reported peace departments in 1895 and thirty-eight counties were organized in New York state alone.[84]

The social purity department of the WCTU, also called the White Shield–White Cross program, moved through the typical evolutionary cycle. Begun in 1877 as the Committee for Work with Fallen Women, the program at first allied its goals with gospel temperance, with saving the prostitute from her life of sin by converting her to evangelical Christianity and teetotalism. In 1883 the program for rescue of fallen women became the Department for the Suppression of the Social Evil, a change in name that reflected a changing emphasis: the WCTU no longer saw personal conversion as the only way to eliminate prostitution. Legislative measures were considered, and an element of feminism invaded the work. In 1885 the name was changed to the Department of Social Purity, which emphasized positive preventive measures rather than negative suppression. "Houses of refuge," providing temporary shelter for women who wished to leave prostitution, were the obvious implementation of the first phase, and a few such facilities were tried, but the resources of the Union in the 1870s were too meager to accomplish much. However the Manistee, Michigan, Union opened a shelter for prostitutes who wished to escape the brothels of the pineries, and the Colorado Union assisted the inmates of those adjacent to the Leadville mines.[85]

The legislative phase, which continued through the 1890s, was much more successful. The first line of attack was to raise the age of consent. In 1886 the laws of twenty states placed the age of consent at ten years, and one at seven.[86] By 1894 only four states (all in the South) still put consent at ten, and in twenty states legal consent had been raised to sixteen, an accomplishment for which the WCTU could take substantial credit.[87] Twelve states passed legislation raising the age of consent in a single year.[88]

The Union performed this miracle largely by petition; during one campaign in 1888, seventy yards of signatures (15,000 names) were presented to Congress, asking that the age of consent be raised to eighteen in the territories and maritime and admiralty districts of the United States.[89] At the same time, the Union attempted to put an end to the double standard, to obtain legal and social adoption of a single code of morals "to maintain the law of purity as equally binding on men and women."[90] The WCTU opposed licensing and medical inspection of brothels and advocated legislation that made male patronage a felony.[91] Social attitudes were also under attack. A letter to the editor of the *Union Signal* queried if it was right to treat an impure male acquaintance as if nothing were amiss, while society expected an impure woman to be cut and scorned. The *Signal* advised treating them alike, "with kindness and recognition in the daily walks of life," and added that there was no need "to pretend the man had not done wrong, as social usage indicates."[92]

Prevention and education were also part of the social purity program. Travelers' aid in the form of "life-saving stations," places where young girls coming into the city were intercepted and given help and counsel, were established in a number of metropolitan areas.[93] Mothers' meetings designed to teach women how to impart sex education to their children were organized on the local level. Actually, the mothers' meetings were concerned with much more than sex education. In some ways they were forerunners of the Parent-Teacher Association, and brought mothers together to exchange ideas, influence the schools, and learn about child development. Many women who did not belong to the WCTU attended.

The suggestion has been made that by and large temperance women were repelled by the social purity movement.[94] Perhaps this was true in the 1870s, but it seems an unfair representation of the WCTU's position from the mid-1880s on. In 1886 there were 34 social purity departments in states and territories, and 185 district, county, and local unions had superintendents who made formal reports to the national superintendent, a record that compares favorably with any other department.[95] There was, of course, an occasional departure from this general acceptance, especially in the South; in one instance, Willard was asked by the local women not to preach on social purity at a large church service she addressed the Sunday before the Nashville convention in 1887.[96]

One manifestation of the WCTU's increasing attention to feminist issues was its concern with the working woman and the conditions under which she labored. The Union's earliest attention to working women was to praise the skill and achievements of business and professional women. In the early 1890s the Union broadened its attention to include white-collar working women. The *Union Signal* began to focus on women office workers in its editorials, praising the excellence of their service despite low pay, long hours, and poor living conditions in boardinghouses; it berated the churches for paying attention only to the Christian woman who stayed at home, charging that the clergyman "sees but one class (womanhood which remains at home surrounded by sons and daughters), recognizes no other, knows no other. He has not one word to say for the woman living and working alone, because she will not live in idleness and dependence."[97]

As the Columbian Exposition drew near, Willard began to press its Board of Managers, of which she was a member, for an exhibit on the working conditions of women in industry. Her concern was greeted cautiously. Bertha Palmer, the board's chairman, replied that they would need to be very careful in dealing with manufacturers: "If we cause them to think we are going to put them under surveillance and expect to look at their books . . . it may cause them to discharge the women who are working for them so that while we want to get the facts . . . and spread them before the world . . . [we] will have that work done quietly."[98] By 1893 the *Union Signal* was demanding legal protection and better working conditions for women industrial workers and citing especially desperate cases: "It is dreadful to see those girls [mule spinners], stripped almost to the skin, wearing only a kind of loose wrapper, and running like a race-horse from the beginning to the end of the day. . . . The hard slavish work is drawing these girls into the saloons looking scared and ashamed."[99]

In 1892 the *Signal* called attention to the fact that the WCTU showed no concern about the working conditions and training of domestics and criticized the way immigrant girls were treated by their mistresses, presumably including WCTU members, who expected untrained servants to perform perfectly. It stressed the need to "organize self-supporting women, to bring household labor into line with other kinds of labor by making it skilled, and by teaching women who engage in it to stand by each other in prosperity and adversity."[100] The *Signal* admitted the WCTU was doing much less than the settlement houses for domestic employees. Hull House was pushing for regular hours and systemized training among other things, but the *Signal* was cheering on Hull House's efforts and urging WCTU women to cooperate with its programs.

The WCTU's actions on behalf of women industrial workers and domestics were modest at best. But the Union was ahead of the suffrage movement, which did not become interested in the woman factory worker until exposed to the influence of Margaret Dreier Robins after the Women's Trade Union League was organized in 1903.[101]

WCTU women also waged a battle in the 1880s and 1890s to be admitted to full voting membership in the governing bodies of Protestant churches. The fight to speak from most Protestant pulpits had already been won in the North in the 1870s, and victory came easily in the South in the early 1880s, but participation in church governance was another matter. Willard became a symbol of the struggle. She was elected a lay delegate to the General Conference of the Methodist church in 1888. The parties for and against a woman delegate were clearly defined: northern liberals favored seating her, and the opposition's strength centered in the clergy. Willard lost the fight in 1888 and was not seated, but her election had solicited a year of unequaled public discussion of women's relation to the churches.[102] In fact, Isabella Beecher Hooker hoped Willard would not win the fight "because the howl of indignation would be so great it would be a kind of victory."[103] The fight continued in the Methodist church until 1896; women were elected delegates to the General Council in 1891 and 1893 but were not seated. The Methodist Episcopal church was slower than the Free Baptist church to accept women. The Free Baptists had eight women delegates to their General Conference in 1889 and thirteen in 1893.[104] The Southern Baptists, Presbyterians, and Protestant Episcopalians accepted women delegates much later.

The growing movement within the evangelical churches in the early 1890s for the equal status of women certainly resulted at least in part from the heightened social and political awareness that churchwomen had gained through membership in the WCTU. Women were no longer willing to play a subordinate role in the churches once they were accustomed to governing their own affairs in the temperance movement. Clara Hoffman, president of the Missouri Union and recording secretary of the national organization from 1893 to 1906, certainly saw the WCTU as more central than church organizations in widening women's sphere. She contrasted the many activities of the Union, where women were fund-raising, agitating, organizing, lecturing, writing, and lobbying, with the missionary societies, where "multitudes of women in the church have not yet advanced to activity beyond the sewing circle, the June strawberry festival and the December oyster festival to help out the current expenses."[105]

The WCTU first addressed itself to equal rights for women, as it did everything else, from the vantage point of temperance. The need to reform or restrain the drunken husband who abused or abandoned his legally helpless wife and children was the redundant chorus of its publications, public meetings, and prayers in its early years. But as Frances Willard summarized the Union's changed attitudes,

> The Crusaders wrought only for their tempted husbands and fathers, brothers and sons; but behold seventeen years later all this work has tended more toward the liberation of women than it has toward the extinction of the saloon.[106]

Change occurred first in the WCTU's attitude toward women's place within the family. Not only was the wife entitled to a sober husband, but she was entitled to a share of the income of any husband, however exemplary. In "A Word to Husbands" in 1886 the *Union Signal* exhorted,

> Your wife is entitled to a share of your income. It is her income as well as yours. . . . To dole out money grudgingly to your wife is more than ungenerous, it is unjust. The treasury is a common treasury. You and she are, commercially speaking, partners. She has a right to a reasonable portion of your income; to have it regularly; and to have it without hesitation . . . and not to be called on to account for each dollar.[107]

Willard called for putting "a money value" on homemaking chores and for giving this money directly to the wife, to be "hers out of the common income and collectible by law."[108] This campaign continued into the 1890s. The *Signal* also agitated for educating boys in "husbanding" as well as the professions and world of work.[109]

Willard could never bring herself to accept divorce per se, but she came very close as early as 1889 and condemned laws that made the husband the master. She called the wife under the existing civil contract "the completest slave the earth has known."[110] In 1895 the national WCTU convention resolved that "the question on divorce is of equal importance to men and women, and . . . to insure justice, women should have a place and voice in the commissions appointed by the several states to consider the divorce law."[111] Willard believed women had a right to refuse sex in marriage, that enforced motherhood was a crime, and that there should be no accidental children or forced pregnancies.[112] This was more than tacit acceptance of the fact that women, as the nineteenth century progressed, exercised more control over their own bodies within the marriage relationship. It had within it a strong plea for equal rights, perhaps even unilateral rights for women that superseded those of men.[113] A woman's legal right to her children was an issue that the WCTU continually championed. The Minnesota WCTU fought hard against a statute passed by the legislature in 1889 that made the father sole guardian of his minor children and permitted him "to will away his children" even before they were born.[114] Willard distressingly pointed out that in thirty-six states in 1890, the married mother was not the legal "owner" of her child.[115] These concerns naturally reinforced the Union's equal-rights position. The *Union Signal* published in 1890 a long, carefully reasoned article by Laura Clay citing scripture to prove that God intended equal rights for man and woman rather than the widely accepted dual spheres.[116] Officially the Union never quite repudiated the idea of spheres, although it always espoused the enlargement of women's sphere.[117] However, by the 1890s the new woman had been accepted in practice by many in the WCTU. Anna Sneed Cairns, superintendent of the Department of the Relation of Temperance to Labor, put it this way: "We are trying to type for the world a new kind of womanhood, with brains large enough to understand the misery of the world, and with a heart as large as the brain, that can feel not only in our own dear circle of home, but for all humanity, and calls nothing human foreign to ourselves."[118]

For the women of the Union as well as many others, their new sense of identity found focus in the Columbian Exposition of 1893. The Woman's Building for the Exposition had its own Board of Managers, on which the WCTU was represented. This board ran its own programs as well as participating in the deliberations of all the congresses. At the dedication of the building, the *Union Signal* wrote,

> The noble women of all lands must have felt an electric thrill of sympathy with these representative women of the world who assisted to register an event in history as new as the creation—the consecration of a building, planned and decorated by women, to the arts, industries and literature of women; and greater still to chronicle the first setting of its women by a government, in a great national enterprise, in a position independent of and coordinate with the men of the nation.[119]

The Union also rejoiced in the tardy public recognition of Susan B. Anthony. She was the true heroine of the Exposition, which paid her full homage in contrast to the public rebuff she had experienced at the Philadelphia Centennial celebrations in 1876.[120]

Willard's Do Everything policy, "that woman's mighty realm of philanthropy," began with a strong emphasis on temperance and temperance-related causes and ended with the Union leadership's commitment to revolutionary changes in the structure and organization of the economic system, a commitment less widely shared by the membership. Nonetheless, Do Everything embodied strong feminist goals that found general acceptance at all levels. Do Everything may have begun in some measure as domestic feminism. Its rhetoric was aimed at establishing woman's position in the home, but Do Everything from the beginning emphasized pragmatic or social feminism. It aimed at solving specific societal problems. Certainly the Union ended the century with a large proportion of its membership committed to militant feminism, equal rights, and full participation in the political process. In this sense the Union was the cutting edge of the feminist cause in the nineteenth century. Broad social reform was equated with feminism more strongly and clearly in the Union than anywhere else. William O'Neill has suggested that nineteenth and early twentieth-century feminists made a mistake in emphasizing the ballot rather than joining the Socialist party. He believes that the greatest weakness of the feminist movement, and the reason the victory of the suffragists in 1919 did not initiate a new era for women or result in their achieving full social and economic equality, was the result of the feminists' inability to appreciate how the larger organization of society would hamstring the achievement of its objectives.[121] Of all major women's organizations, the nineteenth-century WCTU came closest to advocating sweeping societal reform. But for a variety of reasons, despite its limited goals, the suffrage movement rather than the Union was to lead women to nominal political power and the vote.

From Home Protection
to Gospel Socialism

THE PRACTICE OF POLITICS

Although the WCTU never became a political party, the Union was thoroughly politicized in the 1880s and 1890s. It openly allied itself with a political party, came close to merging with the Prohibition party, and used every available political device to implement its program. Some of this politicization resulted from Willard's urging and her skillful manipulation of a constituency that was overall more conservative and cautious than she. As early as 1883 Willard knew where she was going and where she wanted to take the Union in the political sphere. She was committed to a legislative solution on the federal level for the temperance problem; she was convinced national prohibition could be achieved only by political action in which women fully joined because they had succeeded in getting the ballot; she saw the Prohibition party as the only vehicle through which constitutional prohibition could be achieved and which would accept women as equals in working for that goal.

However, Willard was not the only force that politicized the WCTU, and her political goals were never its only political aims. The Union's most successful excursions into politics occurred on the state and local level: the dozens of local-option campaigns in which it participated, the battles for

The origin of the phrase "home protection" was explored in chapter 4. Frances Willard entitled one section of her 1893 presidential address "Gospel Socialism" (transcribed in the *Minutes* of the convention, 104). Its first sentence reads, "In every Christian there is a socialist; and in every socialist a Christian."

legislative or constitutional prohibition in the states, the fight for temperance education in the public schools, to say nothing of woman suffrage campaigns in the states.

On the national level, however, the WCTU's excursions into politics proved the most controversial and internally disruptive aspect of its program and became as well the arena in which Willard most clearly used her influence to lead, sometimes maneuver, a reluctant rank and file toward accepting her goals. On two major political questions, the national Union's commitment to woman suffrage and its alignment with the Prohibition party, Willard decided on a course of action and eventually pulled most of the membership with her. She failed on two others, her attempt to create a broad reform coalition in the 1890s embracing Populism and the Prohibition party, and her abortive attempt to lead the Union to embrace socialism. She failed in one case because she could not find the outside constituency to establish a wide reform coalition. In the second case she failed because although she was not alone in the Union in embracing socialism, the membership, Protestant and in most cases middle-class, did not envision overturning the world in which it lived. The Union's progress into politics in the 1880s and 1890s raises perhaps more persistently than any other issue the recurring question of where Willard's influence ended and the membership's goals took over in shaping WCTU policy and programs. Willard was a strong-minded woman with conscious and articulated goals, but she never acted alone; others in the membership, at one level or another, always shared her views and frequently did more than she to implement them. At the same time, the rank and file, on their own, enthusiastically and successfully pursued political goals more modest in scope, but which nonetheless provided thousands of women with experience and expertise in manipulating the political process.

Political action was a weapon used by the WCTU from the beginning, even though it did not endorse the woman's ballot until 1881. Willard had of course urged WCTU support of woman suffrage in 1876 when she made her home-protection speech to the Newark convention, but after 1879 she could proselytize more effectively in her role as president and use her annual address as the vehicle for her appeal to the Union. In 1880 she asked the WCTU to put its strength behind the creation of "an army of voters which absenteeism will not decimate and money cannot buy" and which would bring prohibition to the United States.[1] The membership was not ready to support woman suffrage in 1880, but the same convention that subscribed to the Do Everything policy in 1881 went on record for the ballot, favoring "Home Protection where Home Protection is the strongest rallying cry; Equal Franchise, where the votes of women joined to those of men can alone give stability to temperance legislation."[2] It had taken Frances Willard two terms as president to secure membership approval of the home-protection ballot. Once the WCTU officially adopted this position, Wittenmyer and a dozen or so antisuffragists withdrew from the Union.

After the 1881 convention, there were continual rumors that the WCTU had unequivocally joined the suffragists. The combination of the home-protection resolution and the fact that Susan B. Anthony had been on hand and been introduced from the platform of the convention was seen by the press as overwhelming evidence of conjunction. But the Union tried hard in the early years to dissociate itself from the suffragists. WCTU literature was explicit in pointing out the difference between its appeal and that of suffragist organizations: "The W.C.T.U. seeks the ballot for no selfish ends. Asking for it only in the interest of the home, which has been and is woman's divinely appointed province, there is no clamor for 'rights,' only a prayerful, persistent plea for the opportunities of Duty."[3]

The national convention of 1881 had certainly endorsed woman suffrage, but there was always room for equivocation and nonparticipation in any course the Union followed. As late as 1893 only Texas of the southern unions engaged in any franchise work, and among the northern states the Connecticut Union was still nonparticipating.[4] Only five state unions were committed to full suffrage before 1885, the year Zerelda Wallace saw true consensus on the woman's ballot beginning to develop. Each succeeding year support became a little stronger within the Union. At the same time, emphasis on the home-protection aspect of the ballot reduced criticism from outside. Mary Leavitt's report for the franchise department in 1883 stated her belief that clergymen were beginning to be sympathetic, although frequently unwilling to let their sympathies be known.[5] What support the suffrage cause developed in the Protestant churches in the 1880s and 1890s was largely due to the Union's influence. Churches liberalized their position on woman suffrage because they had been converted to prohibition by the WCTU and they saw the woman's ballot as the only way to achieve this goal.[6] Only through WCTU pressure and influence did the Republican party in the West become interested in woman suffrage at all.[7] This interest was directly related to the the WCTU's growing political clout, a function of its rapidly increasing size and organizational power. The main strength of the WCTU was its local organization, which extended into almost every county in the United States. No other grassroots organization existed to promote the woman's ballot. In many states there were so few members of suffrage organizations that the real work for the suffrage cause was almost entirely done by the WCTU. The Iowa Union campaigned hard for the ballot during the 1883–84 legislative session.[8] The Illinois WCTU sent petitions with nearly thirty thousand signatures to the general assembly in 1883–84 asking that the word *male* be stricken from the electoral section of the state constitution.[9] The Washington territorial Union secured thirty thousand signatures for a woman suffrage petition presented to the state's constitutional convention in 1889.[10] The WCTU had made woman suffrage respectable in many white Protestant middle-class circles by the late 1890s.

The Union itself had moved far beyond the home-protection argument by that time. The *Union Signal* editorialized, "Men have no more moral or natural right to ordain that women shall not vote, than women have to disfranchise men," and went on to quote the arguments on natural justice that Wendell Phillips had used earlier in support of slave emancipation.[11] In her 1892 presidential address Willard stated the natural rights argument clearly:

> The more I reflect on the world, and the way its affairs are managed, the more I see that the right to vote in a democratic age is an acknowledgment by the States of the right of the citizen to have an opinion and a right to tender it for the guidance of her fellow citizens. . . . The voteless adult is nowhere, whose rights, whose individuality, whose common nature, even, are all held by suffrance, permitted rather than recognized, and as a consequence minimized beyond endurance.[12]

This is far from the expediency of home protection. By 1894, there was no doubt of the WCTU's official commitment to the natural-rights argument as justification for the woman's ballot. The national convention adopted a resolution on suffrage that asserted that "women are wronged who are governed without their consent."[13] Some unions moved to the natural-rights argument much earlier. At its first state convention Arizona adopted a resolution stating that "the exclusion of woman from the possession and exercise of her natural rights has been calamitous to the whole human race . . . [and] the votes of woman are imperatively needed to promote temperance, purity and peace, to give woman greater self-reliance, self-respect and personal independence, and to secure to her a fair day's wages for a fair day's work."[14]

Although the Union rank and file were frequently uneasy about suffrage activities in the early years, by the 1890s the reverse was true. The Union's support of suffrage caused the brewers and other liquor interests to see prohibition as a possible result of the woman's ballot. They began to oppose suffrage with all their considerable money and political influence, and the suffrage forces grew afraid that any alliance with temperance groups would defeat their own cause.[15] Their fears were realistic. Washington territory granted women the vote in 1887. These new women voters helped to pass a prohibition amendment, and a case was brought —strongly supported by the brewers and distillers—that resulted in the Supreme Court's declaring the woman's ballot unconstitutional. In a second election in 1889 prohibition failed, and part of the opposition came from prosuffrage forces.[16] Temperance was seen as too great a danger to the woman's ballot to command active support from suffragists.

Although the relationship was not always harmonious, the WCTU and the organized suffrage movement were closely interconnected in the last quarter of the nineteenth century. There was some overlap in leadership, and many suffragists were also temperance advocates—for example, Anna Howard Shaw and Mary Livermore were highly visible in both organizations. There was occasional uneasy cooperation, as in the South Dakota suffrage campaign of 1890, when Susan B. Anthony and Henry Blackwell eagerly courted the overt support of the WCTU on both the state and local level.[17] In 1894 the National American Woman Suffrage Association requested the WCTU's cooperation in suffrage campaigns, and the request was granted.[18] Willard moved the WCTU national convention in 1896 from California to St. Louis at the behest of Anthony, who feared that the WCTU's support of suffrage and the attention that a national convention would bring could hurt the chances for a favorable vote on California's proposed suffrage amendment.[19] The suffragists did not return the courtesy, but instead asked WCTU members working in the campaign to remove their white ribbons and remain silent on prohibition. The WCTU denounced this stricture as "an indignity to the position we have taken from the beginning,"[20] but more indignities followed. In 1899, Carrie Chapman Catt, then president of the National American Woman Suffrage Association, proposed that the WCTU no longer "initiate any suffrage legislation" and leave suffrage campaigns to the Association. This proposal was unequivocally rejected.[21] Nonetheless, much mutual respect and sisterly affection was frequently expressed on both sides. When the WCTU convention met in Boston in 1891, the *Woman's Journal* offered the hospitality of its parlors to WCTU delegates "for resting between the sessions, depositing bundles and meeting friends."[22] Willard died during the annual meeting of the National American Woman Suffrage Association in 1898. The published proceedings of the convention, in page after page of eulogies, attest to the place Willard held in the suffragists' esteem and affection. Anthony and Willard were close friends and lifelong correspondents, and in their scrapbooks each kept a faithful record of the accomplishments and activities of the other.

In the 1890s suffrage leaders joined the nativist upsurge and began calling attention to what they saw as the enfranchisement of ignorant male foreigners while women were denied the ballot.[23] Carrie Chapman Catt and Anna Howard Shaw were both fulminating against the humiliation suffered by American women, by which they meant native-born white middle-class women, at being ruled by all races and nationalities. Elizabeth Cady Stanton came out in support of educational qualifications for voting, and many suffragists argued that only the votes of women would enable white Protestant native Americans to outvote new immigrants in the North and blacks in the South.[24] Women in the WCTU were not immune to this growing nativism and racism, and the Union's campaign for the franchise began to raise the specter of the ignorant immigrant and black vote. Willard in her maiden speech on suffrage in 1876 had seen women balancing "the infidel foreign population of our country,"[25] but she abandoned her nativist stance almost immediately, and the WCTU did not make educational qualifications a part of its suffrage resolution until 1895, when the convention modified its previously unequivocal call for woman suffrage by the phrase "and we believe in an educational limit for both sexes."[26]

However, this position was not reached without opposition. Susan Fessenden unreservedly argued against educational qualifications in the *Union Signal* in 1890.[27] As late as 1895 Sophie Grubb was protesting all the talk of "the illiterate foreign vote" and pointing out that in the Kansas election on the suffrage question in 1894, districts with large foreign-born populations supported enfranchisement of women much more strongly than native American centers such as Topeka.[28] Willard hedged. In her 1891 presidential address she pointed out that immigrants could vote six months or less after landing, while "devoted, intelligent and patriotic women" could not, adding, "I do not see any way out for this country, which cannot very well go back on its position as to manhood suffrage except to improve the quality of the voting by admitting intelligent women, and barring out the ignorant women, thus putting a premium upon knowledge and character as conditions of the voter." She seemed to be accepting retention of universal manhood suffrage but adding a qualified woman's suffrage. She went on to say this selection would be "done in no spirit of unfriendliness" but only to give the debarred classes the highest possible motive for improving their minds.[29]

By the early 1880s Willard had succeeded in achieving the Union's endorsement of two aspects of her political program, the support of both woman suffrage and federal prohibition by constitutional amendment. She had yet to generate enthusiasm among the membership for an alliance with the Prohibition party, and the struggle over outright partisan commitment involved the Union in one of its major internal conflicts. The upshot of Willard's decision to lead the WCTU into the Prohibition party was a rupture within the leadership and rank and file of the Union that proved more divisive than the differences over the woman's ballot. Although the battle lines were not fully delineated until the fall of 1884, Willard was consciously or unconsciously already planning her strategy in 1880 and 1881. The struggle did not end until 1889, when the faction opposed to party affiliation withdrew from the Union. As in the suffrage fight, Willard both won the battle and emerged heading a stronger organization with broader influence. For the short term, her policy was clearly successful. The long-term effects on both the Union and the temperance cause are much more equivocal.

The national Prohibition party, which Willard began to see as the appropriate political ally of the WCTU about the time of her election as president, had been organized in 1869 by a group of Good Templars in Oswego, New York. Like the Templars, it accepted women as members from the beginning; thirty women were delegates to its first convention, which endorsed woman suffrage as well as prohibition. While its political impact was negligible nationally in the 1870s, it posed a potential threat to the Republicans, who occasionally found themselves in jeopardy from the

Prohibition party on the local level. In 1873 Ohio Republicans lost the election by less than a thousand votes, a loss they could properly blame on their temperance rivals.[30]

Willard's account in her autobiography of her movement toward the Prohibition party is largely romantic fiction. She reports her usual conversion experience, in this instance at Saratoga in 1881—a sleepless night, much soul-searching, a sudden conviction that she must "take sides for the Prohibition party"—and a reaffirmation two months later at Lake Bluff, Illinois, inspired by the untutored sentiments of a reformed drunkard.[31] More important by far than this encounter was the fact that Prohibition party leaders John St. John, John Finch, and George Bain were present at the Lake Bluff meeting, eager to encourage her new allegiance. Actually, Willard had for all practical purposes endorsed the party in her first presidential address the previous fall, but protected herself with her usual equivocations to reassure the membership: "Though we have not taken sides as yet in politics, we cannot be insensible to the consideration shown us in the platform of the Prohibition Party—a prophecy of that chivalry of justice which shall afford us a still wider recognition."[32] But the Union was unready and Willard acted on her own, repeating her typical pattern of leadership on those issues where rank-and-file support was weak. She took a strong position and gradually brought the membership along. She made a vigorous plea for a Prohibition party connection at the 1881 convention, but again the Union was unwilling to follow.

Rather than forthrightly joining the Prohibition party as an individual in the hope she could bring the Union with her, Willard pursued her goal obliquely. She began organizing home-protection clubs, frankly political but autonomous units of WCTU women. These clubs were designed to provide a nucleus of strength that she could eventually bring with her into the Prohibition party and use for bargaining purposes there, while they also furnished a vehicle through which those forces in the Union already committed to a party connection could work. Both the home-protection clubs and the Prohibition party met in August 1882 in national convention in Chicago, and they predictably fused into the Prohibition Home Protection party. But this action was still without national WCTU endorsement, although the Illinois Union had endorsed the Prohibition Home Protection party. At the 1882 convention, despite Willard's impassioned declaration that "the Prohibition Home Protection Party stands forth as a woman's answered prayer," she saw that "the convention was reluctant to make this new departure."[33] She was ready to compromise, however, as she had with the home-protection ballot, and the convention resolved "to influence the best men in all communities to commit themselves to that party, by whatever name called, that shall give to them the best embodiment of prohibition principles, and will most surely protect our homes!"[34] The Union had not endorsed it by name, but almost everywhere only the Prohibition party could meet these criteria.

Iowa was an exception. The Iowa Republican party was committed to both statutory and constitutional prohibition. It had tempered its radical position by insisting that this was not a commitment of principle but only a matter of policy in response to the wishes of a majority of Iowa's voters. But this was enough to cause trouble in the Union. J. Ellen Foster, national Superintendent of Legislation, a delegate to the first WCTU convention, and an early supporter of Willard in her power struggle with Wittenmyer, was an ardent Republican and had worked hard, long, and successfully to bring the Iowa Republicans under the temperance standard. She could not accept WCTU alignment with the Prohibition party, which usually drew what votes it got at the expense of Republican strength, and if Willard was determined to have the WCTU firmly in the Prohibition Party camp, she was equally determined to prevent it—especially since a presidential election was less than two years away. It was a confrontation neither would personally have chosen. Both were brilliant, strong-minded women; they had worked well together and cherished a friendship based on deep affection as well as common goals. When their differences first showed signs of irreconcilability and sharp words were exchanged, Foster still could write to Willard, "I wonder that you should call a questioning and a free conversation as to methods and plan of work 'an arraignment.' . . . I never have in thought or deed arraigned my friend Frances E. Willard because of her official acts." Instead she had loved Willard "as I have never loved any other woman."[35] But affection and mutual respect were not enough to heal the rupture. Although the Union did not endorse the Prohibition party by name until 1885, its actual attachment to the party became stronger every year. Willard used the columns of the *Union Signal* to help her cause, and Foster countered by enlisting a substantial following and catching the ear of the public press, which took the Republicans more seriously than the Prohibitionists.

By the summer of 1884 the battle was fully engaged. In some ways Willard fought unfairly. While the convention had not endorsed the Prohibition party by name, the *Union Signal* did, and it also was not above quoting Foster out of context and exhuming her every public statement since the 1870s to accuse her of inconsistency.[36] Foster used letters to the editor as effectively as she could. Willard stood off to one side, viewing the furor she had created with sweet reasonableness, and protesting in the *Signal*'s columns that she was only following the orders of the Detroit convention of 1883, which had asked for nonpartisan prohibition conventions in every state before the party conventions of 1884 and committed the Union to an effort to influence electors to declare they would vote for no party that did not favor prohibition.[37] On the national level only the Prohibition party supported prohibition; therefore, Willard reasoned, the national WCTU could support only the Prohibition party. State unions could do otherwise on the state level if prohibition had been aided by a major party in their constituency.

When the national convention convened in St. Louis in 1884, the show of sisterly solidarity that marked the opening session was deceiving. Willard was reelected easily enough, although Foster received ten of the opposing fourteen votes. Foster herself moved that the election be unanimous.[38] In her presidential address, which preceded the vote on the controversial endorsement resolution, Willard described and justified the move that led to outright Prohibition party support as an inevitable outgrowth of the Detroit resolution. She again stressed the need for united allegiance: "As a national society we could not act in view of Republican efforts for prohibition in isolated states, as Iowa and Kansas, nor yet in view of Democratic, as in Maryland or Tennessee, but we had to act from a national point of view."[39] After all, the Prohibition party had accepted the Union's memorial, which the other national conventions had refused. The transcript of the lengthy debate that followed the introduction of the endorsement resolution occupied fourteen columns of the *Union Signal*. Although the resolution was introduced in the morning, Foster did not speak until afternoon. She said she opposed the resolution because it was ambiguous—which it was—and argued that while it purported not to bind the membership, and any individual or local union could determine its own position, the national officers and the *Signal* in effect did speak for the membership, and she was convinced nonpartisanship was as essential as nonsectarianism for the Union to thrive. She favored partisan behavior by individuals, but not by the Union as a whole, and she defended herself ably against questions from the floor.[40] But by this time the membership was in favor of endorsement, and the resolution carried 182 to 52.

Local unions, and of course Willard and the national Union, campaigned hard in the few days remaining before the election. Hannah Whitall Smith and the members of the Germantown, Pennsylvania, local stood in the rain all election day passing out Prohibition party tickets.[41] The *Union Signal* scoffed at the charge that the WCTU was now a political party. Did the fact that the Chicago Congregational Ministers' Association had passed a resolution supporting Republican candidate James G. Blaine make them a political party?[42] However, after the election the WCTU agreed with the Prohibition party's claim that it had defeated Blaine. In several key states, New York especially, the Prohibition tally probably made Grover Cleveland's victory possible, and the *Signal* predicted that the Republican party would be forced to prove its attachment to temperance if it wished to regain power.[43]

Foster resigned as Superintendent of Legislation but continued as chairman of the Committee on Constitutional Revision. She and her following (largely from Iowa and Pennsylvania) continued for five years to fight within the Union for nonpartisanship. Their well-organized, carefully reasoned arguments were presented at each convention, where they also gave notice each year that they would continue to try for an amendment to the WCTU constitution that would ban party endorsements. Meanwhile support for Foster within the Union was dwindling, and by 1887 only seventeen members signed the annual protest against party endorsement.[44] Impatience with the dissenters' legalistic tactics also increased, and many had grown weary of the repeated arguing; the 1886 convention agreed to eliminate debate on resolutions dealing with political endorsements.[45] But in 1888 Foster again forced unlimited debate. Anna Gordon called it the hardest convention yet, with the whole matter opened up for the convention "to discuss and cuss all it wants to."[46] Personal relationships eroded. Foster accused Willard of unethical tactics and violations of parliamentary procedure, although they had appeared on the same platform at a large temperance mass meeting in the spring.[47]

Both Foster and Willard were politically active during this period. Foster figured prominently in Republican councils. She appeared before the Republican platform committee, arguing eloquently for a strong temperance plank, but at the same time declared her loyalty to the party was not dependent on the action it took. Her efforts were partially successful. In 1884 the Republicans had ignored the WCTU delegation of which Foster was a member when they came asking for endorsement of the temperance cause. In 1888 they were received courteously and given time to present their position before the platform committee and the national convention. The floor of the convention adopted a mild protemperance statement: "The concern of all good government is the virtue and sobriety of the people and the purity of the home. The Republican party cordially sympathizes with all wise and well-directed efforts for the production of temperance." The *Union Signal* scoffed, but Foster declared she was "proud of the party's record."[48]

Meanwhile Willard was playing a sizable role in Prohibition party councils. She attended the 1884 convention with several temperance stalwarts, including Mary Lathrap, Martha McClellan Brown, Mary Burt, and Caroline Buell. She was the heroine, the "prophetess" of the meetings, lionized, flattered, and cherished. She not only presented her own resolution (the same one she had brought unsuccessfully to the Republican and Democratic conventions) but was invited to sit on the platform and to give a major nominating speech for John St. John, an old friend who was to be the party's candidate that year.[49] Suffragists Mary Livermore, Elizabeth Cady Stanton, and Susan B. Anthony were supporting the Republicans, but in her support of the Prohibition party, Willard personified the WCTU with its superior numbers and popular influence. No wonder the Prohibitionists appreciated her presence. At the 1888 convention she was asked to make a major address, served on the resolutions committee, and was instrumental in fighting off an attempt to abandon the party's commitment to equal suffrage. She also went on the campaign trail. Her appearance at a mass rally in Minneapolis was marked by the largest parade that city had ever seen. She was driven to the hall in a carriage covered with white roses for the Prohibition party and white ribbons for the WCTU.[50] The columns of the *Union Signal* read like campaign tracts that summer and fall. In a single issue seven and a half columns were devoted to an enthusiastic account of the Prohibition party convention, and there was also a two-column biography of its presidential candidate.[51]

Union membership continued to increase, growing 69 percent between 1885 and 1890. Willard repeated the success she achieved when she led the Union down the dangerous suffrage path. Support of a political party, despite the internal bickering and rancor it elicited, seems to have strengthened rather than hurt the Union. In many ways it was probably easier for its members to commit themselves to a political party than to woman suffrage. Women were accustomed to political allegiance even if they could not vote, and most northern members before 1884 thought of themselves as supporters of the Republican party, while the southerners considered themselves Democrats. Women were able to be good party loyalists without voting. Asking for the vote represented a more radical stance, an innovative action. One by one the state unions endorsed the national Union's stand on the Prohibition party, and by 1888 all state unions had come into the fold except Iowa. Even elder stateswomen become Prohibition party enthusiasts. Eliza Stewart, one of the first Crusaders, attended the 1884 Prohibition party convention.[52] Eliza Thompson, who had led the Hillsboro Crusade, reported, "The Judge [her husband] is still an old 'Temperance Republican,' and I am a Prohibitionist White Ribboner. . . . If I had a vote he knows it would go where there could *be no mistake*." Her loyalty did not waver during the 1888 presidential campaign: "The Judge is loyal to you [Willard]—but more so to the Republican Party, I reckon, these Harrison Times!—We are one, and yet twain."[53] Church support of the WCTU seems not to have been damaged by partisan allegiance. The United Presbyterian church, traditionally cool to women activists, formally expressed general approval of the Union's work in 1885.[54]

In 1889 J. Ellen Foster led the small remnant that still resisted Prohibition party allegiance out of the national convention and the WCTU. She received only eleven votes for president that year, although her rank-and-file support was probably greater than her delegate strength indicated.[55] The official Iowa delegation went with her, but woman's temperance forces in Iowa were badly split, and many Iowans (125 out of 250 local unions) did not share her enthusiasm for the Republican party and stayed loyal to the national Union. Foster's splinter group organized as the Non-Partisan Woman's Christian Temperance Union, which annoyed the WCTU regulars. Willard was still reiterating the national WCTU's basic nonpartisanship and insisting that when the Republicans and Democrats embraced prohibition, they too would receive the Union's support. The Non-Partisan WCTU never achieved sufficient strength to challenge the parent union seriously. At its height in 1890, only eleven states were represented at its Cleveland convention, and it could count less than one hundred local unions outside Iowa (the WCTU numbered over ten thousand locals at the time). The press considered the nonpartisans a Republican movement from the beginning, as did the Democrats of the southern WCTU, who gave it no support despite its conservative platform.[56]

Although the long struggle over partisan commitment did not sap the

Union's strength, the resulting wounds did not add to the organization's reputation for dignity. Zerelda Wallace wrote Willard, "What a spectacle we presented before that great audience [the 1888 convention]. I was never so humiliated in the person of womanhood in my life. I hope I may never be so again. I hope so much from woman."[57] The row did provide opportunities for the press to ridicule the movement. If temperance ladies could not agree among themselves, why should they command a hearing from the larger body politic?

Logic and consistency were on Foster's side. The Union could not be nonpartisan and endorse a political party, no matter if it was merely called "lending influence." As Foster said in her apologia, *The Truth in the Case*, Willard "arrives at certain conclusions in her own mind about what our society should do and what positions it should take. She has wonderful skill in knowing what not to say as well as what to say to get a new departure accepted. She 'insinuates a doctrine.' "[58] Foster's comments were appropriate. Willard was all too ready to insinuate a doctrine. As Mary Aldrich pointed out in the same publication, resolutions were frequently vague when first introduced, but "the president follows with specific action based on the general resolution. Eventually the resolution becomes strong and unequivocal." Aldrich cited the example of suffrage: support for suffrage began with a modest and vague statement from the convention about home protection, which Willard soon shifted in her own mind to full support for the woman's ballot. Aldrich also accused Willard of seeing authorizations from the Executive Committee (the national officers and state presidents) that were not always there.[59]

Willard was indeed an autocrat; once convinced of her own wisdom she tolerated little opposition. But the hand of the despot was always gloved in silk. She was kindly, Christian, and charitable toward her enemies. She never wielded her gavel in acrimony or publicly criticized those who disagreed with her. She did not need to stoop to rancor or ridicule. Not only did Willard possess a remarkable charisma, but she also presided over stacked conventions. In the 1880s and 1890s nearly half the delegates were ex-officio, and most of these owed their positions and influence to Willard. She appointed department superintendents and, in practice, all other officers, subject only to convention veto.

Whatever her intentions, Willard was logically in the wrong in her disagreement with Foster, and the means she used to achieve her ends were devious at best. However, the motives of both protagonists, whether they knew it or not, were equally self-serving. Willard received attention, influence, even deference from the Prohibition party in return for her support. She enjoyed playing on the larger stage. Foster also had her reasons for not betraying the Republican party, and she enjoyed the attention her support brought her from the national Republican leadership. Presumably no one would have minded if Foster had stayed in the Union, continued to support the Republican party, and exercised her right of dissent from national policy. But that she could not do, because like Willard she was convinced of her own importance and righteousness.

The respective wisdom of their two positions is unclear. By 1894 the Union had moved away from alignment with the Prohibition party. In that sense the WCTU and Willard admitted the partnership had been a mistake. Willard looked elsewhere for political influence as early as 1889. Prohibition party influence had peaked in 1884, when it very probably cost the Republicans the presidential election. But defeat forced the Republicans to come to terms with Prohibitionist sentiment and make concessions in almost every state and in the 1888 national platform, and without Willard and the WCTU it seems unlikely the Republicans would have capitulated. The WCTU, and especially Willard, did bring new life, enthusiasm, and glamor to the Prohibition party. Union support did not make it possible for the party to win any major elections, but certainly contributed to the general viability of the temperance cause. Prohibition and temperance legislation was voted on in several states where it would otherwise have been avoided—a clear gain for temperance that resulted from the WCTU's alliance with the Prohibition party. Once this was accomplished, however, its connection with the Prohibition party removed the Union from the mainstream of American party politics. Possibly by 1888, and certainly thereafter, the WCTU might better have followed a tactic later adopted by the Anti-Saloon League: the support of major party candidates committed to the cause, rather than of an independent party.[60]

Ironically Willard's faith in the efficacy of the Prohibition party wavered at the very time Foster led her contingent out of the Union to protest the WCTU's ties with the Prohibition party. Willard's political allegiances began to change in 1889, but not her faith in political parties as the most effective vehicle for political action. After the overwhelming defeat of the Prohibition party in the 1888 election, Willard began to consider a coalition of reform parties as the only hope for political success. Prohibitionists alone could not attract the necessary support. Willard looked toward a broad coalition of agrarians and labor, suffrage, and temperance adherents. Others in both the labor and farmers' movements shared her views. Three conferences from 1889 to 1891, aimed at achieving some kind of cooperation, proved abortive. Willard decided to take the lead and called her own conference in Chicago in January 1892 to plan strategy for the large Populist Party Convention, or Industrial Conference, scheduled for St. Louis in February 1892. Ignatius Donnelly, James Weaver, and Howard S. Taylor were at the Chicago meeting and under Donnelly's leadership were able to produce a consensus of opinion that they hoped could be used as the basis for the program to be adopted in St. Louis and that would lead to a merger of Populists and Prohibitionists.

The St. Louis convention was a bitter disappointment to Willard. The Prohibition party refused to join the reform coalition. Willard's old friend John St. John, whom she had enthusiastically supported in 1884, was among the Prohibition leaders who insisted on a stronger prohibition plank before joining the convention and who were determined to thwart Willard's efforts at union. As a result the reform element was divided and the St. Louis meetings failed to bring in the Prohibitionists. Willard's efforts for unity at the Prohibition convention in June were also unsuccessful, and fusion was defeated.[61]

Because Willard's attempts to establish a broad reform party failed, the Union membership was never confronted directly with the issue. Instead, over a period of years the WCTU gradually withdrew from direct party involvement. After the summer of 1892 Willard herself played a much less active role in the Prohibition party and politics generally. Her mother died in August of that year, and she began spending much of her time in England, away from the American political scene. As individuals, members of the WCTU continued to participate in Prohibition party councils, but the Union as a body was no longer firmly in the Prohibitionist camp. In 1894 the national WCTU convention "pledged prayers and influence to any party which puts Prohibition and Equal Suffrage into its platform" and once again failed to endorse the Prohibition party by name. Resolutions also commended the Kansas Populist party "for placing a Woman Suffrage plank in its platform" and the Republican party of Colorado for its commitment to woman suffrage.[62] The floor fight over extending endorsement to others than Prohibitionists was hot. Over a third of the delegates wished to support only the Prohibition party.[63]

Even so, Willard had not quite relinquished the coalition idea, and in

1894 she urged the Union to create a department of politics that would take the lead in once more trying to unite the Populists, Prohibitionists, and other reform elements before the 1896 presidential campaign.[64] The convention took no action, but in her New Year's message to the membership for 1895 Willard repeated her plea that every local Union invite to an informal conference in some member's home at least a dozen men and their wives in the community "who are either Prohibitionists or Populists to try to create understanding between the two movements." She saw this as "the most important request that I have ever made."[65] The 1895 convention did authorize the appointment of a committee to formulate plans for active political work in the 1896 campaign, and the Department of Christian Citizenship was created by the general officers.[66]

In 1896 the Prohibition party split. Its membership divided over whether to support a broad reform program or a single-issue approach, and the single-issue adherents were victorious. Although Willard privately favored the supporters of broad reform (who reorganized as the National party), she advised the Union to stay uninvolved and endorse neither side. In a sense she completely reversed her stance, for she wrote to the WCTU staff in the Chicago office, "Parties are of no account, they are of no more value than so many tin cans."[67] Neutrality was difficult to achieve, as state unions frequently took sides in the controversy. Willard warned, "All this looks as if we might go into [the] national [convention] divided, which would be a great pity. If they [state unions] could be made to split off and then become mere adjuncts of the party, that would suit some altogether too well."[68] The warmest debate of the 1896 national convention revolved around the resolution that expressed support for political parties. A noncommittal wording that promised to endorse any party that accepted temperance principles was amended from the floor to include woman suffrage as well as temperance. This meant the WCTU was endorsing the National party and its position on broad reform, since the Prohibition party was running on a single-issue platform.[69] There was no political endorsement from the convention in 1897. The Union was moving inexorably toward its eventual cooperation with the nonpartisan, single-issue Anti-Saloon League.

While the national Union's campaigns for woman suffrage and party alignments were the most dramatic and internally divisive aspects of the WCTU's political activities in the 1880s and 1890s, most Union political action took place on the local and state level, and being concerned chiefly with local option and prohibition, was noncontroversial within the Union. J. Ellen Foster reported in 1881 as Superintendent of Legislation that the WCTU circulated thousands of petitions for prohibition and local option that year. The Union had also proved a significant force in the adoption of prohibition by constitutional amendment in Kansas, and Iowa expected a prohibitory amendment to be ratified by the next legislature, which it was. Unions had supported unsuccessful prohibition efforts in eight other states, and local-option laws were passed or strengthened in three more.[70]

Local unions were active in local elections. In Owosso, Michigan, in April 1884 the local WCTU supported a temperance ticket for city officers and won the election with Republican party endorsement.[71] Before Atlanta's election for local option in 1885, Union women held daily prayer meetings, drilled both white and black children to sing temperance songs on the streets, made a "beautiful satin banner to go as prize to the colored club that could poll the most prohibitory votes," circulated petitions, and provided free lunch at polling places. Prohibition carried by 228 votes.[72] Even Bourbon County, Kentucky, was captured for local option in 1886 after hard work by Union women who saw victory here as an appropriate symbolic gesture.[73] Although only five states and the Indian Territory were under nominal prohibition at the end of the century, fourteen states had local option laws, fifteen states had conducted elections on the question of constitutional prohibition, and several others had considered prohibitory legislation.[74] The WCTU played a leading role in most of these campaigns, even though few of its members could vote.

Although most Union political attention on the state and local level in the 1880s was devoted to prohibitory legislation, the woman's ballot received increasing support. When a bill submitting the question of woman suffrage passed the New York Senate in 1880, Mary Hartt, president of the Brooklyn Union, reported that "the temperance women as a body, had not worked ten minutes . . . for it," but the next year J. Ellen Foster reported Union support for various suffrage measures in eight states.[75] Kansas adopted municipal suffrage for women in 1887, and the WCTU was very active in the campaign. A woman was nominated for mayor of Argonia that year, as part of an antisuffrage plot that the candidate herself described as an attempt to "slur the WCTU as well as myself, because I was the agitator, and they wanted to give equal suffrage the death blow"—but instead the people elected her by a two-thirds majority.[76] Michigan had had limited suffrage for women since 1874 in school elections; property-tax payers and mothers of children between five and twenty were eligible, but few actually voted. This changed as the WCTU grew in influence. In 1891 the Albion, Michigan, WCTU canvassed all eligible women voters and got them to the polls, where they elected a woman to the school board.[77] By 1892 women had full suffrage in Wyoming, municipal suffrage in Kansas, and at least limited school suffrage in twenty-three states and territories. By the end of the century four states had granted full suffrage. The WCTU had been active in all these campaigns.

The most successful (although nonpartisan) political campaign waged by the WCTU in the nineteenth century was for compulsory temperance education in the public schools. The national Union's first committee for what it always called "scientific temperance education" was appointed in 1879, after Willard invited Mary Hunt to address the convention. Hunt had devised a plan of graded temperance lessons for hygiene and physiology classes, and at the 1880 convention she suggested that local members visit schools and audit hygiene and physiology lessons and then urge school boards and superintendents to adopt Julia Colman's new elementary textbook, *Alcohol and Hygiene*.[78] By 1882 Hunt had convinced the American Medical Association to back temperance education.[79]

As with so many aspects of its programs, the WCTU first approached temperance education from the point of view of moral suasion, trying to convince teachers and school administrators to teach the dangers of using alcohol. But moral suasion was no more effective in temperance education than in anything else. Educating teachers proved slow and relatively unsuccessful, and by 1882 the WCTU was pushing for mandatory state laws requiring temperance instruction. As Hunt pointed out, "No study remains in the schools unless required by law and no teacher is prepared in a field unless the law requires it."[80] By the end of 1883, three states, Vermont, Michigan, and New Hampshire, had passed compulsory temperance education laws. New York followed the next year after a vigorous campaign led by the WCTU. Petitions were scattered over the state, and thirty-nine thousand signatures were presented to the legislature in a single day. One Union worker spoke sixteen consecutive nights promoting the bill, and hundreds of letters were written to clergymen and public officials asking for support.[81] The campaign snowballed. The Michigan law served as a model: it had two provisions, one requiring the schools to teach the harmful physical effects of alcohol, narcotics, and stimulants, and one requiring teachers to pass an examination on the effects of alcohol and narcotics. In a single year, 1885, nine more states joined the movement for compulsory temperance education.[82] Ten years later only three states were without legislation. By 1903 only Georgia held out.

In 1887 Congress passed stringent scientific temperance legislation for the District of Columbia and the territories. Mary Hunt masterminded the campaign in Congress herself. She arrived in Washington December 1, 1885, and did not leave until the bill passed both houses the following May. The bill was sponsored by Henry Blair of New Hampshire and Byron McCutcheon of Michigan. Letters and petitions elicited by Union members inundated the committees. The Senate finally agreed to take up the calendar out of original order, but the bill was buried in a subcommittee of the House Committee on Education that had "thus far only proved a sepulchre." The chairman, James N. Burnes, was most hostile and at first objected that such legislation would alienate the German vote important in Missouri, his home state; but Hunt produced hundreds of German signatures on WCTU petitions. Burnes then protested that there was only one good text on scientific temperance, and that the federal government should not abet a monopoly. The women loaded his desk with texts, good and bad, and assumed—probably rightly—that he did not know the difference. He next complained that the legislation was unconstitutional. Hunt searched the lawbooks and laid out the precedents. At last Burnes capitulated and permitted the bill to be reported out, and it passed without difficulty.[83]

In the legislative and congressional campaigns for temperance education, the WCTU perfected its lobbying skills. It was not unusual for superintendents of scientific temperance education to spend an entire legislative session in a state capital shepherding a bill to passage. In 1887 Ada Bittenbender, a Nebraska attorney, became national Superintendent of Legislation, and the following year she became the first salaried attorney for the WCTU, functioning as a paid lobbyist in Washington, testifying before congressional committees, and preparing model legislation, as well as presenting petitions.[84] The WCTU developed lobbying techniques in the 1880s and 1890s that were used successfully by the Anti-Saloon League in the twentieth century and that have formed the basis for most special-interest lobbying ever since.[85]

Obtaining compulsory temperance education legislation proved relatively easy. Enforcement and satisfactory textbooks posed larger problems. As more and more states passed laws, however, publishers began vying with each other to produce texts acceptable to the new market, and twenty-five texts met WCTU standards by 1891. Another problem that limited the program's effectiveness was that an estimated seven million elementary school age children in the United States were not in school because they had no schools to go to. Many of these were black children in the South. Senator Henry Blair sponsored a federal aid to education bill in the 1886–87 Congress, whose monies were to be dispensed to the states on the basis of illiteracy. The WCTU enthusiastically, if unsuccessfully, supported the bill. Ten thousand petitions that totaled 100,000 signatures, and 150,000 personal letters were sent to Washington. The bill passed the Senate but died in the House.[86]

By the mid-1890s opposition to curricular coercion was developing in the educational community; teachers resented being told what to teach and fought back. In 1895, when an attempt was made to amend the New York act of 1884 in order to specify the minimum amount of time devoted to alcohol education in hygiene and physiology courses, the New York teachers' state convention unanimously denounced the temperance education bill as "an insult to the teachers of the state and a menace to the principles of free school teaching." Seth Low, the president of Columbia College, was also opposed.[87] In 1893 a prestigious independent group, known as the Committee of Fifty, was organized to study the liquor problem and consider "the physiological, legislative and ethical aspects of the Drink-Question"; it was commissioned to determine the facts rather than advocate any theory or support any point of view.[88] Henry P. Bowditch of Harvard and C. F. Hodge of Clark University headed the subcommittee that compared current teachings and research in physiology and pathology with materials in school textbooks. They concluded that it was "not desirable to give systematic instruction to all children in the primary schools on the subject of the action of alcohol or of alcoholic drinks. To older children, and especially those in high schools, it does seem proper that instruction be given." The committee stressed, however, that instruction should be based on the facts, so that pupils could form their own educated opinions: they "should not be taught that the drinking of a glass or two of wine by a grown-up person is very dangerous."[89] While Willard late in her life would probably have agreed with this last proposition, most WCTU members could not, and certainly it was not one that Mary Hunt could accept. Moreover, if the recommendations in the report were followed, most schoolchildren would receive little or no temperance education. Less than 9 percent of young adults were high-school graduates as late as 1910.

In 1907 the WCTU ceased endorsing textbooks and concentrated thenceforth on prize contests, the donation of reference books to school libraries, and proselytizing among teachers. But its campaign for coercive temperance education had been almost universally successful in the nineteenth century and was to continue as a major force in the first two decades of the twentieth. It seems possible that temperance instruction in the schools of the 1880s and 1890s may well have played a significant role in creating the generation that accepted the Eighteenth Amendment and the Volstead Act.[90] Certainly, compulsory temperance education was one of the more lasting effects of WCTU political activity in the nineteenth century.

As noted in chapter 6, Willard in the last years of her life tried to move the Union from political action in support of specific legislation, such as prohibition, woman suffrage, and scientific temperance education, to support for a change in the system.[91] Although she joined the British Fabian Society (which developed into the Labour party) in 1893 and in that same year entitled her presidential address "Gospel Socialism," she was not successful in widening the WCTU's political aims to match her own. While that address invoked a strong socialist strain (referring to capitalists as "monstrosities") and called for "political machinery to dethrone those who reap the fruits but have not sown the seeds of industry," it propounded a political doctrine, unlike home protection, woman suffrage, and party allegiance, that she could not sell to the membership.[92] Gospel socialism was not to become the watchword of the WCTU. However, the Union enthusiastically supported Willard's other political goals and made them its own. Union membership by the 1890s wholeheartedly supported federal prohibition, almost universally demanded equal suffrage, and found Prohibition party membership more congenial than Willard herself did.

The most important long-range result of the WCTU's politicization was that a large group of women who previously had little experience in the political arena learned the practice of politics. Thousands of women participated at some level in political action, testifying before legislative committees, drafting and circulating petitions, writing legislation, and getting out the vote. Campaigns for scientific temperance education or local option were as crucial to this politicization as Willard's maneuvers on the national political scene, and perhaps more so. By the end of the century the WCTU was a substantial political force in the United States, and its membership was well trained in the art and craft of politics.

Cause for Serious
Reflection

CRISIS AND CHANGE, 1892–1900

The years 1892 and 1893 represent a watershed in the history of the WCTU. While the Union continued to grow until the passage of national prohibition and claimed half a million members in 1924, the rate of growth slowed perceptibly after 1892. The five-fold membership increase of the 1880s was never repeated, and the *Union Signal* wondered in an 1893 editorial, "Have we reached the limit?"[1] By 1910 the Union had fewer than a quarter-million members, while the General Federation of Women's Clubs, which held its first biennial national convention in 1892, had already passed the half-million mark. The period when the Woman's Christian Temperance Union was the largest organization of women in the United States was rapidly drawing to a close. Some of the reasons for the Union's decline in relative power and influence were internal, stemming from events and crosscurrents within the organization itself. Others reflected changes in the larger society and the way women perceived themselves within it, changes that shifted the relative position of the WCTU in the woman's movement as a whole.

A contributing factor in the Union's diminishing role in the woman's movement was the perceptible withdrawal of Frances Willard from leader-

The chapter title is a phrase used by Frances Willard, in her 1897 presidential address, to describe the conflicts and problems that confronted the Union; transcribed in the *Minutes* of the convention, 132.

ship and control. In the summer of 1892 Mary Willard, her octogenarian mother, died. This in itself should not have proved an emotional shock. It could hardly have been unexpected, and Willard had never been much at home, although she and her mother were ostensibly very close. But Willard mourned her mother with an exaggerated grief that no doubt reflected other frustrations and disappointments she was suffering at the time. Her political ambition to found a reform coalition had been unsuccessful, and broad political influence eluded her. There was a clique within the WCTU national leadership that was not personally loyal to her. Also, she had just developed a new affectional attachment that was to result in long absences from the United States.

Lady Henry Somerset, head of the English Union, came from Great Britain to Boston in 1891 to attend the first meeting of the World Woman's Christian Temperance Union, and there she met Willard. The two women were immediately attracted to each other, and Lady Somerset brought Willard back with her to England after Mary Willard's death, presumably for rest and healing. Willard not only adored her new friend, she also adapted easily to the life of the English nobility, enjoyed mingling with the British intelligentsia through the Fabian Society, and even took up the new fads of calisthenics and bicycle-riding. Somerset's wealth provided Willard with secretaries, travel money, and other luxuries. She was a new face on the English scene and attracted general press attention as well as acclaim from the feminist movement. Willard in her fifties was undoubtedly tired. She no longer possessed her earlier boundless energy, and life in the United States meant endless labor, travel, and speeches, and countless petty demands on her time. England on Somerset's estates meant stimulating company, ease, and freedom from everyday cares.

Willard's health had begun to fail, which gave considerable validity to the excuse that her precarious physical condition required the rest and relaxation she could only find abroad. She undoubtedly suffered from anemia and exhaustion. At one point in the spring of 1893 her illness was diagnosed as pernicious anemia, but there were conflicting reports about the seriousness of her condition. It seems likely that poor health was used on occasion without real cause to excuse her prolonged sojourns in England and explain her absence from the stormy 1893 national convention, the only one she missed in her lifetime.[2] Certainly she was ill in the spring, but much recovered by fall, when Anna Gordon cautioned her that poor health could not be used to explain her absence from the United States and the 1893 convention if she was able at the same time to publish a book on her mother, compile a handbook, and write a presidential address. Gordon suggested she stop writing.[3] As Harriet Kells, an editor of the *Union Signal*, wrote to Gordon, "Lots of people in our own ranks don't believe Miss Willard is sick . . . [and] one added the other day, 'or is it a bad case of Lady Henry?' "[4] But Willard was exhausted, depleted, and unwell at least part of the time; she was to die of the anemia, complicated by influenza, in 1898. Whether health was the real reason for her absences or not, Willard was out of the country for two years, from August 1892 to June 1894, except for a brief trip home to attend the 1892 convention. She returned to England in March 1895 and stayed abroad until late September. She also spent the months from May to November 1896 in Europe, but then remained in the United States until her death in 1898.

Willard's prolonged absences coincided with years of stress and crisis within the Union. First, the WCTU was experiencing severe financial problems for the first time since the mid-1870s. The panic of 1893 could not have come at a worse time, especially for the Union's affiliated interests— the Woman's Temperance Publishing Association, and the Woman's Temperance Building Association, which had just completed the Temple, the new headquarters for the national Union. The WCTU itself was less seriously overextended. Its income decreased, but not markedly. Some funds were lost in Chicago bank failures, and some by mismanagement. Five thousand dollars in bonds had been used by the treasurer over the previous five years to make up deficits that did not appear in financial reports and were unknown to officers and members. Salary cuts and a personal appeal from Willard for ten cents from each member got past that crisis, paid the Union's debts, and left the treasury with a surplus by 1894.[5] But the publishing company was harder hit. *Union Signal* circulation dropped to about 67,000, and many of its subscribers were in arrears. The publication for the YWCTU, the *Young Woman*, was discontinued and the *Young Crusader*, for children, was in danger but managed to survive. Income from job printing was off markedly. In fact, for several years in the 1890s receipts from the *Signal* were used to meet deficits incurred by the commercial printing department.[6] The new office building, home of the Union and its affiliated enterprises since 1892, was also in serious financial difficulties. Leases were canceled, office floors could not be fully rented, and the stock plummeted—the panic and ensuing depression had proved a disaster for Chicago Loop real estate.

If politics, the Union's relationship to the Prohibition party, was the major source of internal dissension in the 1880s, the Temple office building almost split the Union in the 1890s. The Union's publishing activities were concentrated in Chicago from 1883, and national headquarters was moved there in 1885 at Willard's request. The Chicago Union was the strongest in the country and was presided over by Matilda Carse, who was also president of the Woman's Temperance Publishing Association. Carse, a handsome, intelligent, energetic woman, who had emigrated from northern Ireland with her parents as a girl, found ample scope in the WCTU for her considerable talents. Widowed young and propelled into the temperance cause by the death of her small son under the wheels of a beer wagon driven by a drunken carter, she made the Union her life, and her gifts as a business organizer and financier were used in its service. Her quick success with the Woman's Temperance Publishing Association encouraged her to look for other business interests that would meet the WCTU's needs. The Chicago Central Union, of which she was president, had been conducting noon gospel meetings in the downtown YMCA since 1874, but in 1883 the YMCA's directors decided the building would no longer be open to women. Soon thereafter, Carse began to think in terms of a permanent home for noon meetings, the publishing company, the local union, and eventually the national offices. Her plans at first were modest. But she was by nature a speculator and entrepreneur, and in July 1887 she decided to proceed on her own and incorporate the Woman's Temperance Building Association. The national officers knew of her plans and approved with reservations, and Carse began to run a column in the *Union Signal* touting the project. The Nashville convention in November enthusiastically supported her, the women "vying with each other for the honor of donating the first hundred dollars." Willard was given the privilege.[7]

By then Carse's plan was both ingenious and ambitious. She would build a French gothic red granite and terra-cotta office building, twelve stories high, designed by the prestigious firm of Burnham and Root. She expected the building to be self-liquidating: office and meeting space for the Union and its related activities would be provided, but would occupy a small part of the building, and the substantial rental income from the other floors would eventually retire the bonds. Carse leased a prime site from Marshall Field, the Chicago department store tycoon, on the corner of LaSalle and Monroe streets and had little difficulty in selling stock and bonds to Chicago financiers. A few bonds were purchased by temperance women.

Construction began in the summer of 1890. In November two thousand children carrying banners and chanting "Saloons, saloons, saloons must go!" marched through the Loop to cornerstone ceremonies.[8] Originally Carse estimated the building would cost $800,000 but by the time it was ready to be occupied the figure had risen to $1,200,000.

Before ground was broken some WCTU leaders began to have second thoughts. Willard was apprehensive about building on leased ground.[9] The executive committee split 16 to 5 in its vote to endorse Carse's decision to go ahead with outside capital. Although the WCTU had no legal responsibility for the Temple project, several WCTU leaders, including Willard, were on its Board of Directors, Carse was president of the Building Association, and the columns of the *Union Signal* were freely used to advertise stock and appeal for contributions. In the spring of 1892 the WCTU moved into its new home, and second thoughts were smothered for awhile in optimism and pride, although actually the Union's share in ownership was small. The next winter strong criticism surfaced again. James B. Hobbs, a Chicago financier and one of the original incorporators of the Building Association, who later withdrew his support, was quoted in the *Chicago Tribune* as saying he opposed the project as finally conceived because it was much too ambitious for an organization like the WCTU: the Union at its present rate of purchase would be twenty years in obtaining a controlling share. Hobbs also impugned Carse's ability as a financier and businesswoman. Hobbs's wife, a devoted white-ribboner, had opposed the Temple project at every convention since 1887.[10]

While Hobbs certainly opposed the Temple, his newspaper attack had been inspired by dissidents within the Union itself. An internal feud in the WCTU now burst into the open. The *Tribune* story was generated not by Hobbs but by two of Carse's enemies in the WCTU offices, Esther Pugh and Caroline Buell, the treasurer and corresponding secretary of the national Union. Buell had opposed the Temple since 1889, and her concern about the wisdom of the undertaking was probably genuine. But the attack at this time was also part of a personal vendetta and a move for control of the Union by two women jealous of both Willard's and Carse's influence and power.[11] Carse was ill in California. Willard was, of course, in England. Although Carse hurried back from California and Anna Gordon was dispatched promptly from England to Chicago to investigate the fracas firsthand, Willard felt her loyalty to Lady Henry Somerset precluded leaving England at the time.[12] For awhile it looked as if Mary Woodbridge, the recording secretary, would also join the disaffected. She was not enthusiastic about the Temple and no admirer of Carse, but she stayed loyal to Willard and was not a party to the tale-bearing.[13] Mary Leavitt, the first round-the-world missionary and honorary world president, seems also to have been among the defectors, although she later concentrated her attacks not on the Temple but on Willard's long absences and neglect of her presidential duties. Leavitt also accused Lady Henry of being a hypocrite, of permitting wine on her table and owning pubs.[14]

Willard and Carse had made serious mistakes in their handling of the Temple project. They had underestimated the depth of rank-and-file concern about the Temple's financing, which had been expressed at the Denver convention in 1892.[15] Moreover, neither Willard nor Gordon had been in the Chicago office for months. Lillian Stevens lived in Maine and was also frequently absent. But Pugh and Buell were in Chicago, along with Woodbridge, and were increasingly involved with business activities of their own, including highly speculative real-estate developments, a woman's insurance company, and a baking company. For awhile they used the *Union Signal* and the prestige of the WCTU to promote these schemes. Fanny Rastall, business manager of the Woman's Temperance Publishing Association from 1890 through 1892, also participated in these private ventures.[16] As president of the Publishing Association, Carse was also publisher of the *Signal* and ultimately responsible for its business dealings. Carse fired Rastall in 1892 because of her suspect business interests, and Carse also ordered the *Signal* business office to refuse any future advertisements from the contingent led by Buell, Pugh, and Rastall.[17] Carse may have been playing at high finance in the Temple project, but not for personal gain. Her adversaries were trying to line their own pockets, and one of Willard's supporters believed Pugh was "prostituting the whole power of the W.C.T.U. to her own uses in her business enterprises. She *too* is but the agent of men—and not one of us knows if those enterprises are legitimate or otherwise."[18] As best she could from England, Willard supported Carse. Willard was editor of the *Signal* in 1893, a job she had assumed when Mary Allen West died. Although she did not as editor have direct responsibility for the paper's business policies, had she been on hand she might have exercised some restraint on the triumvirate. Hobbs's attack on Carse and the Temple project was only one facet of the larger picture. Willard's absence had created a leadership vacuum that others were jockeying to fill.

Carse was not without resources for fighting back. Phillip D. Armour, William Deering, and Marshall Field (despite his misgivings) were all heavy investors in the Temple and supported her. Many Union members showed their loyalty by continuing to send in small pledges and gifts. In one week Carse reported $125 in new pledges and $440 in payments on previous pledges—this after the panic that hit in June 1893 had compounded her troubles.[19] The failure of Carse's scheme to provide income for temperance work through rents from the Union-owned building was clearly a result of the panic. Instead of raising income for the Union, she now continually appealed to the membership for money to keep the enterprise afloat. Undoubtedly fund-raising for the Temple drained off money local unions might otherwise have used at home, and this upset the state unions. Vacant suites and canceled leases provided no profits. Without income to retire bonds, Carse attempted to obtain a controlling interest in Temple stock by floating another set of bonds to be used as collateral for stock Carse purchased.[20] This scheme might have worked had it not been for the panic, but now the stock could pay no dividends. The interest on $600,000 of building bonds had to be met as well as the interest on the Temple trust-fund bonds that had been used to purchase the stock. Eventually Carse was forced to use contributions not to buy stock or retire trust bonds, but to pay interest due on the building bonds. Of the $250,000 contributed from 1887 to 1898 (most of it in small amounts) by Union members, only about $30,000 was actually invested in stock, although $14,000 was also spent on furnishing Willard Hall, an assembly room in the Temple that was rented by the Chicago Union for the noon gospel temperance meetings and used for WCTU functions.[21] Contributions were also dissipated in the expenses of fund-raising.

The Temple issue consumed more and more time at national conventions. In 1893 all of one morning and most of the afternoon were spent in debate on the Temple.[22] In 1896 the discussion was again prolonged.[23] In 1897 only Willard's continuing support and her pledge that she would devote the next year to raising money for the Temple saved the project from outright repudiation. One-third of the Temple's offices sat vacant, $18,000 in past interest was due, and unencumbered stock owned by the WCTU was worth a mere $15,300.[24] But when Willard stood before the convention and said, "I dedicate my fifty-ninth year to the Temple . . . I have nothing on earth that shall not go into that enterprise. . . . Anybody that wants to follow, follow. Anybody that must falter, falter," her words brought tears to the women's eyes, "and the storm of applause was something never before heard" in a WCTU convention.[25] Most of the rank and file had a heavy emotional investment in the success of the Temple. A beautiful building embodied real accomplishment and tapped feminist pride. A Wisconsin woman wrote to Willard, "As I stood on the street opposite surveying the magnificent pile, I said to my husband, the W.C.T.U. must own it. My heart throbbed with delight that it was a woman's work that planned and completed such an undertaking."[26]

Chicago's businessmen also supported the Temple. Marshall Field stood by with offers of $50,000 in stock and cash, provided contributions could be raised to retire the trust bonds.[27] Field's exact relationship to the Temple is unclear. He owned the land on which it stood and was its principal private stockholder. Despite temporary unprofitability, the Temple was a prime piece of Loop office property and had considerable investment value. Field did eventually profit from the building, although he turned these profits over to another of his philanthropies. As a canny financier he could be expected to wish to keep his interest intact, but he appears to have sincerely and generously assisted Matilda Carse and the Union in their effort to become outright proprietors.[28]

Willard was making one last fund-raising effort for the Temple when she died in New York in February 1898. Fund-raising collapsed soon after, but at least it was possible for Willard to lie in state in the Temple's Willard Hall, where twenty thousand mourners came to pay their last respects. After Willard's death a special meeting of the WCTU Executive Committee was called in July 1898 to consider the status of the Temple. Twenty states were represented; the others were polled later by mail. The committee believed the WCTU should disaffiliate itself with the Temple and recommended the same to the national convention. Fifteen of twenty state conventions endorsed this action.[29] Passage would mean that the Union would no longer participate in fund-raising, that the *Union Signal*'s columns would be closed to the Temple management, and that the funds contributed by the membership would essentially disappear in a commercial venture owned by other investors. Opposition to disaffiliation was substantial. There were 364 delegates, and nearly one-third were unwilling to abandon the Temple. But without Willard to marshal support, and after Anna Gordon's speech that closed the debate, in which she told the delegates that worry over the Temple had been Willard's greatest burden in her last years and implied that it had hastened her death, there was no chance for Carse and the Temple. Marshall Field doubled his offer at the last moment,[30] but for naught: the national convention accepted the recommendation for disaffiliation by a vote of 197 to 118.[31]

The consequences of this protracted strife were wide and deep. During that period the Union's secondary leadership—the level just below the president—underwent almost complete change. At the 1893 convention, Mary Woodbridge replaced Caroline Buell as corresponding secretary, Helen Barker replaced Esther Pugh as treasurer, Lillian Stevens replaced Woodbridge as recording secretary, Clara Hoffman became assistant recording secretary, and several national superintendents were replaced. This was an upheaval even greater than Willard's triumph over Wittenmyer in 1879. By 1900 no offices were held by the women who held them in 1892, and among the entire 1892 roster only Lillian Stevens, by this time president, was still holding office. These changes in the top leadership of the Union were the direct result of the bickering and conflict that marked the Chicago group in 1892 and 1893.

Willard was the major force behind the changes, although she absented herself from the 1893 convention itself. She had the complete cooperation of Gordon, Stevens, Hoffman, and Somerset, who were there and did the actual maneuvering. Buell and Pugh were replaced as part of a purge of Temple opponents and also as punishment for being disloyal to Willard and using their offices to promote private gain. Most of the other replacements were made for similar reasons. Disloyalty to Willard was the more crucial factor in the ouster, for Willard and her associates found it easier to tolerate opposition to the Temple. Interestingly enough Buell, as corresponding secretary, presided at this stormy convention of which she was a prime target, and performed creditably. The pro-Willard forces thought they could "make the change in [corresponding secretary] much more easily without the President,"[32] and this was a major reason for Willard's remaining in England. The strategy worked but it might have backfired, and Willard took steps to make sure she would henceforth have a friend in the chair when she herself was absent. In 1894 Willard's supporters gave notice of a change in the bylaws that would provide for an executive vice-president, appointed by the president and ratified by the convention. At first this arrangement was opposed from the floor, since delegates feared Willard would appoint Carse, whom many were beginning to distrust. But Willard "asked for leave to speak and said she would appoint only a state president. At this a buzz swept over the hall. Carse was not a state president and Willard had undercut the opposition."[33] Willard appointed her good friend Lillian Stevens of Maine as vice-president. Stevens retained the office until Willard's death, when she automatically succeeded her.

Not all of the change in Union leadership in the 1890s was in response to conflict. Death and old age also took their toll. Julia Ames, associate editor of the *Union Signal*, and Mary Allen West, its editor, both died in 1892. Mary Lathrap and Mary Woodbridge died in 1895 and Sallie Chapin in 1896. Only seven members of the 1874 convention were present at the 1895 annual meeting, and only three of the sixteen officers chosen at the first convention—Willard, Eliza Thompson, and Zerelda Wallace—were still members of the Union.[34] The corresponding secretary reported in 1896 at the St. Louis convention that only six of the vice-presidents (who were also the state presidents), five of the departmental superintendents, and one of the organizers had been in office when the WCTU met in St. Louis twelve years before; sixteen of the departments were headed by women who had assumed their positions within the last two years. A single state had lost seven hundred members by death alone in 1895. But not all membership losses were due to death. The secretary also noted that many had left "for other forms of labor."[35] The WCTU made great efforts to attract new members in the middle and late 1890s, and there was some growth, but it was disappointing. From 1894 to 1896 the net increase was only slightly over two thousand.

At the same time the WCTU was beginning to feel the loss of the older generation, it was facing real competition as an organization for women and women's causes. Conservative upper middle-class women in the 1890s were drawn to the General Federation of Women's Clubs, which concentrated on education, self-improvement, and sociability rather than an activist program. Willard had addressed its first convention in 1892, but the range of its concerns was to be much narrower than that of the WCTU in the nineteenth century, and membership was thus more congenial and less demanding for conventional women than the reformist WCTU. Participation was largely passive, the level of commitment low. For example, the Federation did not endorse woman suffrage until just before the Nineteenth Amendment was ratified. Its third biennial convention was held in Louisville in 1896 to unify North and South and heal the wounds of the Civil War—the WCTU had embraced its southern sisters a generation earlier. Unlike the WCTU the Federation did not accept blacks at its conventions, for it dared not risk offending its southern members. The WCTU's racial policies were considerably more enlightened than those of the Federation, even at the turn of the century, when the Union was losing much of its reformist zeal.[36] However, the Federation gave women another choice, another organizational outlet, and one especially congenial to conservative women.

The Union also found it increasingly difficult in the 1890s to attract young women. Frances Willard had been youth's heroine in the 1880s, and young women had flocked to her cause. Jane Addams and Susan B. Anthony (who was growing old) were replacing her in the 1890s. The Chicago Columbian Exposition was a personal victory for Anthony. In contrast to her reception at Philadelphia in 1876, she was lionized and cheered by the Woman's Congress at the Exposition. Willard was in England, out of sight, in no position to share, much less rival, what one Union observer described as Anthony's "royal triumph."[37] The WCTU operated a booth at the fair; the literature proved popular and the sheer bulk of the polyglot petition, with its millions of signatures from around the world asking for temperance, attracted attention, but an exhibit could not make up for Willard's absence. Harriet Kells, managing editor of the *Union Signal*, wrote Willard that the WCTU "has been nothing literally before the great world at these wonderful Congresses, and every week teeming with chances."[38] Anthony *was* there and the *Signal* realized what was happening: "Nothing so clearly demonstrates the onward march of woman's—and of humanity's—cause as the love and veneration exhibited by our [the Union's] young women toward the one whose very name is a synonym for sex equality, Susan B. Anthony."[39] By the 1890s the National American Woman Suffrage Association competed with the WCTU for young women. At the same time, the WCTU competed for young college women with the Association of Collegiate Alumnae (later the American Association of University Women), founded in 1882 to provide a substitute for the sense of fellowship its members had experienced during their student days. The Collegiate Alumnae were an elitest group with rigorous admissions standards and snob appeal that the WCTU could never match.[40]

While radical young women sanctified Anthony and their college-trained sisters joined the Association of Collegiate Alumnae, the YWCTU seems to have concerned itself largely with busywork. Frances Barnes, national secretary in 1893, reported that one Y chapter in New York held meetings before the election, another educated a blind girl, and the Rhode Island Y's operated a "rest cottage" for working girls. Otherwise the Y's confined themselves to distributing temperance literature, assisting with Loyal Temperance Legion programs and conducting Demorest medal contests.[41] The exciting, innovative Union projects were not the work of the Y's but of older women, an indication perhaps that innovative young women, who had been attracted to the Union a generation earlier, now went instead to the settlement houses and the suffrage movement. The minutes of the conventions and the *Union Signal* frequently allude to the difficulty of enlisting the young.

The National American Woman Suffrage Association grew rapidly while the WCTU was struggling to hold its own. With only 13,000 paid members in 1895, the Association grew to between 70,000 and 100,000 by 1915, and support was much broader than its membership indicates—it was able to enroll half a million women for woman suffrage in New York state alone in 1915.[42] We do not know the age distribution of suffrage organization membership or that of the WCTU, but it seems probable that after the mid-1890s the suffrage cause attracted more young women than did temperance. The average age of the Ann Arbor, Michigan, Union in 1894 was fifty-two. Only one member was in her twenties and two were in their thirties. It was an aging group. Perhaps this was typical of the Union nationwide. However, one study of the age distribution of the leadership of the temperance and suffrage movements found no age difference between their leaders.[43] The young, however, are rarely leaders of long-established causes.

For whatever reason, the WCTU's program emphasis changed after Willard's death. The Union shifted to a single-issue approach, an emphasis on temperance. The 1897 convention passed resolutions favoring prohibition, woman suffrage (with an educational qualification), equal wages for women, the "social emancipation" of women, sabbatarianism, international arbitration, peace, and arbitration in railroad strikes. It went on record against prostitution, the double standard, lynching, prize-fighting, yellow journalism, tobacco, and narcotics.[44] The 1898 convention expressed itself on far fewer issues. It continued to support prohibition and temperance, limited suffrage, and sabbatarianism and to condemn the double standard and prostitution, but peace and international arbitration, labor questions, and equal wages for women no longer received attention.[45]

The change in tone between Willard's last presidential address in 1897 and Lillian Stevens's first in 1899 is even more dramatic. After the usual pleasantries, Willard spoke on peace and international arbitration as her first substantive topic. She next devoted time to national and state prohibition and the work of the Anti-saloon League, and followed with a wide-ranging discussion of social and political concerns that included the spoils system and political corruption, recreational centers (People's Palaces) for the masses, the double standard, the power of the press, the eight-hour day, the labor movement, poverty, social insurance, the initiative and referendum, the capitalist massacre of miners, starving Armenians, lynching, food reform, woman suffrage, and the fight for women's rights in the Episcopal church.[46] Stevens's first address was confined almost entirely to endorsing legislation to cure the alcohol problem. There was no mention of suffrage, women's rights, the kindergarten movement, labor, or poverty, although she did discuss peace and arbitration in general terms and commended reformatory prisons for women.[47]

The *Union Signal* reflected this change to a single-issue position. The paper that in 1896 had carried excerpts from Elizabeth Greenwood's sermon that began, "Our Age is predominantly the age of the people, or the Socialistic Age," heavily emphasized temperance, purity, and sabbatarianism by 1899.[48] The *Signal* carried a column labeled "Reform News" in the 1890s. During the four issues for October 1899, the column contained a total of sixty-eight items. An informal analysis of the contents showed that only eight of these sixty-eight did not concern temperance. On its other pages the paper carried one article on the initiative and referendum, one on the double standard, and one on vice. One editorial vilified polygamy and another lauded Admiral George Dewey, but all the rest addressed themselves to the temperance cause. Reports from state and local unions reflected the same trend: two reported sponsoring shelters for "betrayed girls," and one an adult education program for prisoners. All else was the battle against drink—except for the "About Women" column, a popular feature that had been published since the *Signal*'s early days, which contained brief items on women's accomplishments.[49] A similar analysis of the April 1899 issues showed only four items in the "Reform News" column not about temperance. There was one editorial on the disarmament conference, another on polygamy, and one on the concentration of wealth and its relation to poverty. Two state unions reported franchise work and one a school savings-bank program. There were two reports on Florence Crittenden homes and two accounts of purity meetings. The paper still carried

Lillian M. Stevens, President of the WCTU 1898–1914.

the column "About Women." All other news items, articles, editorials, and reports were concerned with temperance.[50] What was happening to Do Everything? Had Willard's admonition been forgotten?

The change in emphasis was immediate, abrupt, and dramatic. It could be described as resulting from the departure of Willard's influence. However, if Willard had died in the late 1880s, very probably this shift in program emphasis would not have taken place. There were conflicts, and certainly some of her ideas met with occasional reluctance among the membership in the 1880s, but overall the Union's program represented membership concerns. Willard was always the catalyst that galvanized and articulated support for the WCTU's program, but she did not create it from whole cloth.

Do Everything was probably losing favor even before Willard's death.[51] No clear evidence of this remains in the records. However, those who shared Willard's ideology responded strongly to the change in emphasis that followed her death and hinted this was a triumph for those already opposed to Do Everything. Wilbur F. Crafts, superintendent of the National Reform Bureau, urged the Union to keep the faith in a letter to the editor in the *Union Signal* in April 1898, saying the Do Everything policy was Willard's greatest contribution. Before her, "reformers had nearly all been 'one idea' people, who treated some one particular reform as a panacea, exaggerating its importance and failing to appreciate its need of cooperating moral forces. With her great heart she saw that all reforms were but fragments of one reform, the Christianizing of society."[52] The *Signal* carried editorials responding to criticism that the WCTU had been wrong in not confining itself to the single issue of temperance. The editors argued that under a single-issue program the Union's members "would have dwindled into a little band of 'fanatics who had lost all sense of proportion.' Our great leader's 'do-everything' policy saved us from that."[53]

What was cause and what was effect is difficult to sort out. Willard continued her interest in broad concerns and also moved toward the left throughout her life, but in the 1890s she was unable to carry the Union with her. Was this the result of her increasing radicalism, or was it that other organizations and movements, the settlement houses and suffrage associations, proved more attractive to radical women, leaving the Union with a majority who were social and political conservatives? Union members continued their work for temperance and a limited franchise and their fight against vivisection, the double standard, prostitution, and polygamy, but they no longer felt real sympathy with the labor movement. In 1900 the only long debate in the convention concerned the eight-hour day, an issue that had gained support easily in earlier years. There was a strong move to have this resolution stricken from the list altogether, although it was worded to emphasize the need for labor to support temperance.[54] The Union membership now saw the immigrant as a threat. They were satisfied with the capitalist system and once again ready to blame most social problems on the evils of drink.

Had Willard lived on, it seems possible the opposition to her leadership would have grown. She might well have been deposed by a more conservative woman, such as Lillian Stevens—who did succeed her. Stevens's husband was a wealthy grain and salt wholesaler. She was no socialist or radical reformer. She was a suffragist but at a time when suffrage was no longer the radical issue it had been in the 1870s and 1880s. By the 1890s the conservative native-born Anglo-Saxon community had been protemperance for years. Only Mormons condoned polygamy and no respectable person openly defended prostitution.[55] By the 1890s home protection was a phrase bandied about by successful politicians; it no longer belonged exclusively to activist women. At a time when the nation was engaged in the agonizing debate about the wisdom and propriety of a democracy's annexing the Philippines and Puerto Rico by force and becoming a colonial power, the WCTU preferred to concern itself only with "the imperative need of rescue work among the soldiers in Manila, tempted by innumerable saloons. . . ."[56] This would not have been the extent of their reaction earlier.

Most Union members were personally loyal to Willard as long as she lived but grew less enthusiastic about her ideas as the 1890s wore on. The membership had always been more conservative than its president. Willard had warned that "a one-sided movement makes one-sided advocates."[57] Her warning was coming true. The public image of the WCTU was changing—from the best, most respected, most forward-looking women in town to narrow-minded antilibertarians riding a hobbyhorse. The change was gradual and certainly not complete until the late 1920s, but it was under way.[58]

This Vast and

Systematic Work

AN ASSESSMENT OF THE WCTU

The Woman's Christian Temperance Union was unquestionably the first mass movement of American women. It had no competitors in size of membership or breadth and depth of local organization. It cut across sectional, racial, and ethnic boundaries, sheltering under its broad umbrella women from nearly every sector of American life. The Union penetrated into small towns and large cities. Among its members were seamstresses and the wives of artisans and clerks; women physicians, lawyers, clerics, and educators joined its ranks; the wives of business and professional men flocked to its banners. The Union also pioneered in being the first sizable organization controlled exclusively by women. Although women were major participants in church and charitable activities by the 1870s, that participation, except perhaps on the local level, was expected to stop short of leadership or control: women supplied the membership and men exercised the authority. From its beginning the Union excluded males from voting membership. As a result men never competed for leadership roles, and women ran the entire organization, including its affiliated business enterprises. Because the WCTU was entirely a women's institution, unlike the National American Woman Suffrage Association and the foreign missionary society movement, it became the major vehicle for active

The chapter title is from Frances Willard's "The Work of the WCTU," in Annie Nathan Meyer, *Woman's Work in America* (New York: Henry Holt, 1891), 406.

156

leadership by women on the local, state, and national levels. Frances Willard became a national heroine. The activities of the WCTU received national press coverage, and thousands of women in local Unions found their cause and their own contributions commented on from the hometown pulpit and reported in the local press. Through the WCTU, women became visible as leaders in communities and cities from coast to coast.

The reasons for the WCTU's success were many and varied, and several stemmed from the social and economic climate of the time in which the movement arose. The development of a sizable, relatively leisured middle class, which left women with time and resources to devote to voluntary organizations, was one factor that encouraged the Union's spectacular growth. The increasing urban population made it easy for women to meet and communicate with each other. The rising educational level gave women both experience with the world outside the home and the intellectual equipment to challenge male preemption of the public sphere. All contributed to the readiness of women to organize. Women's special vulnerabilities to the consequences of alcohol abuse by men helped to make temperance a cause women found most attractive. Congeniality to the Protestant churches, protective support of the nurturant home, and implicit acceptance of the moral superiority of women increased the Union's appeal. Its choice of a leader, Frances Willard, and Willard's choice of the Union as the organ through which she could work, greatly enhanced its success. Probably few other of her contemporaries could have so successfully combined daring innovation with womanly concern.

The WCTU also played a major role in heightening women's awareness. Starting with the Crusade itself, the Union became one of the most powerful instruments of women's consciousness-raising of all time. Through the Union women learned of their legal and social disabilities, gained confidence in their strengths and talents, and became certain of their political power as a group and as individuals. The Union elevated the personal and civic consciences of large numbers of women and provided the underpinning for the surge of interest in woman's suffrage after 1900 that made the Nineteenth Amendment possible. Before 1873 most Union women had worked only in their churches. By 1900 they had a full generation's experience behind them in political action, legislation, lobbying, and running private charitable institutions.

In 1870 the suffrage movement was more advanced in its demands than many women were prepared to venture. The movement asked for equal rights and the vote, a clear call for a place in public life. Most suffragists, especially the radical wing led by Elizabeth Cady Stanton and Susan B. Anthony, rebelled against the ideology of separate spheres of life for the sexes, and asked women to support changes in role and self-image that were radically different from existing norms. The immediate result for the suffrage movement was that it could not and did not succeed in attracting mass support for its goals until another kind of woman's movement had bridged the gap between the way most women perceived themselves and the equal rights stance of the militant suffragists. In discussing this aspect of the WCTU's role, Janet Zollinger Giele called the temperance woman a consolidator and the suffragist a pioneer.[1] This assessment is partly true. Temperance women were slower than suffragists to ask for the vote, but nineteenth-century Union activism in crucial ways made success possible for suffrage in the twentieth century. Most of all, the WCTU pioneered in local organization. As WCTU members, women learned how to organize, and eventually they put this knowledge to work in the campaign for the vote. And the Union was not always a follower. The suffrage movement advocated the woman's ballot earlier, but the Union was quicker to ally itself with organized labor, endorse the kindergarten, and advocate safer working conditions for women.

Ellen DuBois has argued that the WCTU's coming to terms with woman suffrage in the early 1880s demonstrates that the suffrage movement succeeded in making the woman's ballot the focus of nineteenth-century feminism.[2] Because suffragists explicitly demanded that women be admitted to the political sphere in the 1870s, they challenged the nineteenth-century concept that the public sphere was an exclusively male domain. DuBois among others has pointed out that the WCTU was able to join the suffragists in their goals while avoiding the issue of spheres through its emphasis on the home-protection ballot. It is true that WCTU women, as had Catharine Beecher's teachers before them, entered the public sphere in the 1870s (and some as late as the 1880s) only as guardians of the home. However, the union did not stay at this transitional phase for long. By the 1890s natural rights replaced home protection in the WCTU's arguments for the ballot. The Union's support of a dozen political and social causes put it clearly in the public sphere, and in fact it was a pioneer in its support of broad social reform movements that the suffrage movement for tactical reasons would not touch. Perhaps instead of being criticized for its oblique approach to the suffrage question, the Union should be credited with putting the focus of feminism on reform, on social feminism rather than the ballot, on emphasizing suffrage as only the means to a broader end. Indeed, to the extent that these broad aims were lost sight of in the first decades of the twentieth century, the ballot proved a sterile victory. The larger social and economic disabilities of women remained untouched, and the battle had to be fought all over again two generations later. But in the nineteenth century the WCTU did succeed in fastening its definition of social feminism on the woman's movement, and with its tens of thousands of members it did provide the mass base from which the twentieth-century suffrage movement could take off. Without the Union's legacy of activism and political experience, the suffrage cause could never have expanded as rapidly in its final two decades.

The WCTU also had an impact on the woman's movement abroad and provided a pattern for temperance activity in other parts of the world. Prior to the mid-1870s there were practically no women in the British temperance movement.[3] The involvement of women in temperance issues clearly spread from the United States, and the British Woman's Temperance Association was the direct result of the English tour of Eliza Stewart, the Ohio Crusader, in 1876.[4] By the end of the nineteenth century, temperance had become a recognized political issue in Great Britain, and the Liberal party placed it among the essential reforms for which it campaigned. In England the movement also attracted a broader base of middle and upper-class women than the suffrage organizations. The WCTU organizations in Australia and New Zealand, founded by Mary Leavitt in the 1880s, closely paralleled the American movement. The Union monopolized the woman's movement in Australia and New Zealand, just as it did in much of the American Midwest; it led the campaign and supplied almost all the organizational activity for woman suffrage in New Zealand. Originally in favor of universal suffrage like its counterpart in the United States, the New Zealand WCTU continued to mimic the American Union by eventually supporting a property qualification for the franchise.[5]

The WCTU was not only a mass movement that made substantial contributions to both the goals and the accomplishments of the nineteenth-century woman's movement; it also widely embraced diverse ethnic, sectional, and racial groups. Although thin in numbers, the mere presence of blacks, native Americans, and immigrants, and southerners too (who were numerically more important), contributed to the Union's claim to represent American womanhood. And like the conservative southerners, representatives from these minority groups attended conventions and were introduced from platforms, listened to in debate, and appointed to office. The evidence also confirms that while the Union was essentially middle and upper-class in its national leadership, lower-class women were able to find a meaningful niche in the Union. A black washerwoman occupied the position of Superintendent of Colored Work in Indiana in 1884. Skilled tradesmen's wives joined the Ohio Crusaders in 1873. A grocery clerk's wife shared responsibility with the wives of San Diego's leading business-men in managing a facility for indigent women and children in the 1880s. The *Union Signal*'s pages contain communications from many ordinary housewives in modest circumstances with no particular talents, as well as reports on the activities of their more gifted sisters. The more deeply one looks at the membership of the WCTU the more one perceives its diversity. Temperance touched a chord that united women of many backgrounds.

The demographic characteristics of the leadership of the WCTU have been examined several times. The Appendix of this volume summarizes earlier studies and presents the results of my own research on the topic. While membership in the WCTU covers a broad spectrum, all studies agree that the women who led the WCTU in the nineteenth century were primarily white, well-educated, economically prosperous native-born Pro-testants of Anglo-Saxon ancestry. With the possible exception of religious affiliation (the WCTU had a larger proportion of women who participated in enthusiastic religious sects, such as Methodism) Union leaders differ little from what we know of the leaders of other women's reform groups of the time.

In assessing why individual women joined the temperance movement, the most difficult question to answer is also one of the most crucial. How many members of the WCTU joined the temperance movement because they personally experienced the consequences of alcohol abuse? There is no way to determine the answer; the data do not exist. As far as one can tell, few women who were themselves abusers of alcohol were attracted to the WCTU. An occasional "fallen woman" rescued by Union members undoubtedly signed the pledge and perhaps became a dues-paying member of some local Union, but existing biographical data produce no evidence that sizable numbers of women entered the Union because of their own struggles with alcoholism. Clandestine drinking by middle-class house-wives was mentioned from time to time in both the *Union Signal* and annual reports, which shows that the WCTU was aware of the problem, but apparently Union members observed its presence only outside their own fold.

Several WCTU leaders, however, found temperance a congenial cause because of alcoholism in their families. The three Willard women all experienced considerable personal tragedy related to alcoholism. Mary Banister Willard's son, who was Frances Willard's nephew and Mary Hill Willard's grandson, was a chronic alcoholic for whom the family optimistically, tolerantly, and repeatedly found various forms of treatment.[6] Oliver Willard, Frances Willard's only brother, may also have had problems with alcohol, but the evidence is less clear. Georgia Hulse McLeod's son was an alcoholic. Eliza Thompson's son died in an institution for inebriates. Matilda Carse's son was run over and killed by a drunken drayman; every biological sketch of Carse attributes her commitment to temperance to this tragedy. An early Michigan WCTU leader, about whom there is little other information, was the wife of a reformed drunkard reclaimed by the Washingtonians.

Biographical sketches occasionally point out that a woman's interest in the movement was not related to problems with alcohol in her own family, that her motives were completely altruistic. Does this singling out of a few who were uninvolved indicate that there were personally compelling reasons for commitment to temperance on the part of many WCTU women? There is no way to answer this question. We do know that drunkenness was widespread in the United States in the nineteenth century. However, most of the available biographical information originated with the women themselves, and they were unlikely to acknowledge that personal relationships where alcohol was a problem brought them to the WCTU—rarely would they find it appropriate to expose the weakness of a close relative. Willard's friends and close colleagues knew the problems she faced with her nephew, but there was no hint of this in the public press. She did not suggest in print that a harsh life experience had propelled her to temperance, and this reticent stance may have been taken by many others.

Nonetheless, that temperance was chosen as the focal point of the only major woman's movement that grew spectacularly in the nineteenth century and attracted a substantial measure of mass support, is only partially explained by the social respectability of the temperance cause and its widespread acceptance among the Protestant churches. Temperance is primarily a problem of control. The inebriate has lost control, and it is difficult for either the alcoholic or those around him to reestablish that control. Women suffered from this lack of control in more than one way. A drunken relative might put their lives in disarray, but they also had no legal and political control over their own destinies. Ohio women who took to the streets in the Crusade of 1873–74 could not vote on the constitutional provisions that would regulate the liquor trade, and they were restive under that disability.

Perhaps the WCTU's success represented a symbolic crusade. Joseph Gusfield coined that phrase to describe the century-long temperance campaign that resulted in passage of the Eighteenth Amendment. He argues that temperance advocates used the temperance movement to legislate personal behavior for groups that were threatening the status and power of the dominant majority. He speculates about the loss of political control experienced by a native-born rural Protestant population that was being rapidly outnumbered by a massive wave of immigration from central and eastern Europe at the same time that its economic and social clout was threatened by the new industrial urban society.

However, the words "symbolic crusade" can be used in another way. Women's attraction to temperance in the last quarter of nineteenth century can be explained in terms of symbolism. Nothing was as destructive to a powerless woman's existence as a drunken husband. He could destroy both her and her family. Most of the fiction in the *Union Signal* repeats the same story over and over again: A woman and her children are abused and destroyed by a husband and father addicted to drink. The wife and mother has no legal remedies. She has no political remedies. She is forced to suffer from this lack of control. In the Crusade first, and later in the WCTU, women *were* taking control. The women who marched in Ohio shut down saloons. Mary Hunt and her cohorts successfully compelled legislatures to enact laws that required temperance education in the schools. Local option to close saloons became an alternative in hundreds of communities because of laws the Union shepherded through state legislatures. The WCTU was the major vehicle for the women's movement in the last quarter of the nineteenth century not only because of its impressively large membership, but also because it got things done. Women were taking real control over a part of their lives and the society to which they belonged. In this sense a symbolic crusade was under way. Temperance became the medium through which nineteenth-century women expressed their deeper, sometimes unconscious, feminist concerns.

Appendix

LEADERSHIP PATTERNS IN

THE WCTU

Three studies have been made of WCTU leaders. The first was undertaken in 1955, by Joseph Gusfield, who compared the class status of a relatively broad sample, drawn at twenty-five-year intervals, of WCTU women who were local officers between 1885 and 1950.[1] Using husbands' occupations to determine the socioeconomic status of WCTU women in the nineteenth and twentieth centuries, he demonstrated a dramatic change over time. Gusfield found that WCTU leadership at the local level was predominantly upper middle-class in the nineteenth century but shifted to predominantly lower-class and lower middle-class by 1950, the date of his last sample.[2] In the second study, based on a group of 153 leaders, Norton Mezvinsky confirmed Gusfield's findings of relative affluence and high social status, and he also showed that WCTU leaders were almost always native-born, of Anglo-Saxon ancestry, Protestant in religious affiliation, and above average in educational level.[3] He listed the names of the women in his sample, but he did not disclose how they were selected and made no breakdown of his data in terms of time. Nineteenth and twentieth-century leaders were lumped together. The third study presented a slightly different approach. Writing in 1961, Janet Zollinger Giele compared small samples, forty-nine in each, of the top leadership of the suffrage movement and the WCTU.[4] She found both groups above average in educational level, actively pursuing professional careers, and differing from each other only in religious

163

affiliation. Suffrage leaders were more likely to be affiliated with the Congregational, Unitarian, Quaker, and Episcopalian churches. Temperance women were largely Methodist, Baptist, and Presbyterian. Thus class, marital status, religious affiliation, level of education, and occupation of temperance women have all been investigated, and these studies indicate that the leadership of the WCTU in the nineteenth century was upper and middle class, Protestant, white, economically prosperous, and native-born with ancestors originating in the British Isles. With the possible exception of religious affiliation, Union leaders differ little from what we know of other women's reform groups of the time.

The data that I have collected break no new ground. However, they confirm and occasionally modify earlier studies. I accumulated data on two groups of WCTU women. The first group essentially collected itself. Biographical sketches of Union members appeared in two places in the WCTU files: in the *Union Signal* and in clippings carefully pasted into scrapbooks, first by Mary Hill Willard and later by Anna Gordon and other secretaries of Frances Willard. These materials are now easily available as part of the microfilm edition of the WCTU papers (see Introduction). The women whose biographical sketches appear in these sources represent women identified as prominent in the movement, rather than a systematic sample; they are simply the women who were important enough, newsworthy enough, powerful enough to merit attention from the press. The information is not uniform, and its usefulness is limited even for the simple categories into which it is arranged, for it is incomplete. The second sample group of WCTU women was derived more systematically, but the information is even less complete. I attempted to find biographical data on the national general officers and state presidents, who were ex-officio national vice-presidents, for the years 1884 and 1894, and the temporary and permanent national general officers and state representatives for 1874. In brief, I accumulated data on the national officers (which include the top state officers) at ten-year intervals.

The information on the self-selected "visible" group is more complete because these women were the objects of biographical attention in the press. Also, it was easier to find information on the 1894 officers than those from earlier decades, because booklets of biographical sketches were prepared for the national convention in 1895. It was hardest to find information on the officers for 1874.[5] Perhaps they had not yet become "visible."

Marital status—married at some time in life or never married—is the one characteristic for which data are complete. Of the 210 women who appear in these two samples, sometimes more than once, the single consistently verifiable fact is whether or not they have ever been married.[6] At a minimum this tells us something about nineteenth-century women. They apparently always revealed their marital status. Table 1 indicates that WCTU leaders who participated in the Union as officers were more likely to be married than those who were simply nationally visible leaders. Was prominence more easily achieved by single women without household responsibilities? Of group 1, the visible leaders, 20 percent were single. Mezvinsky found 24 percent of his WCTU leaders were single.[7] Giele's findings were almost the same, 23 percent.[8] However, only 5 percent of the national officers and state presidents were single in 1894. The percentage of single women was highest (10 percent) in the officer group in 1874. Nineteen of the "visible" women comprising group 1 were widows at the time they were most active as national leaders. There may have been others, since husband's date of death is not easily obtained. If the known widows are added to the category of single women, the percentage of single women becomes 38, far larger than previous studies have indicated. Several widows were young with small children; most, however, were older women with limited family responsibilities.

TABLE 1

Marital Status of WCTU Women

Marital Status	Group 1 (N = 110)	1874 Officers (N = 40)	1884 Officers (N = 56)	1894 Officers (N = 58)
Single	23 (20%)	4 (10%)	7 (12%)	3 (5%)
Married	87 (80)	36 (90)	49 (88)	55 (95)
Children*	50 (57)	9 (25)	18 (37)	14 (25)
No children*	14 (16)	5 (14)	2 (4)	5 (9)
No information on children*	23 (27)	22 (61)	29 (59)	36 (66)

*N = number of married women in each group, under the assumption that only married women had children.

Despite the large number of single women, many women with substantial family responsibilities did play active leadership roles. Martha McClellan Brown, one of the founders of the WCTU, had six children. She was married in 1858. Three years later she joined the Independent Order of Good Templars and began a lecturing career; a decade later she was Grand Templar of Ohio. Some of her children must have been small during her active career, since all had been born after 1858. J. Ellen Foster, an Iowa attorney and franchise chairman of the WCTU, was married early, divorced, and remarried in 1869. She had four children by her second marriage and was active in the WCTU from its inception. Her children must have been quite young during the years when she spent a great deal of time away from her home. Her second husband traveled with her on her southern tour in 1883, which indicates that his career was at least partially organized around hers.

The educational level attained by WCTU women was impressively high (table 2). Again, however, the visible leaders were far ahead of the officers. One-third of group 1 had been to college, but only in 1894 did the officer group match that record. Mezvinsky reports that 40 percent of the WCTU leaders in his sample had college or professional training beyond high school.[9] In a study of settlement-house workers Allen Davis found that 90 percent had been to college and 80 percent had bachelor's degrees. How-

TABLE 2

Educational Level of WCTU Women

Educational Level	Group 1 (N = 110)	1874 Officers (N = 40)	1884 Officers (N = 56)	1894 Officers (N = 58)
Common schools	8 (7%)	2 (5%)	4 (7%)	2 (3%)
Secondary education*	45 (40)	10 (25)	11 (20)	13 (23)
College†	35 (33)	5 (12)	14 (25)	21 (36)
Unknown	22 (20)	23 (58)	27 (48)	22 (38)

* Includes seminaries and high schools.
† Includes at least some postsecondary education, including Ph.D., professional training, etc.

ever, many of Davis and Mezvinsky's leaders were active in the twentieth century, when higher education was more common, and many of Davis's settlement workers were men.[10] Giele found that eleven (27 percent) of her forty WCTU leaders had received some higher education.[11]

Evaluating the professional and occupational activities of these women (table 3) presents more problems, especially for comparison with earlier studies. Remarkably few functioned solely as housewife-volunteers, a category I have defined as women who eschewed any kind of professional

TABLE 3

Profession or Occupation of WCTU Women

Profession or Occupation*	Group 1 (N = 110)	1874 Officers (N = 40)	1884 Officers (N = 56)	1894 Officers (N = 58)
Editor, author, lecturer†	30 (27%)	6 (15%)	9 (16%)	6 (10%)
Educator	33 (30)	7 (17)	10 (17)	16 (29)
Business or finance	4 (3.5)	1 (2.5)		1 (1.8)
Minister, evangelist	7 (6)	2 (5)	3 (5)	3 (5)
Attorney	2 (1.8)	1 (2.5)		
Physician	1 (.9)			1 (1.8)
Professional temperance worker	22 (20)	5 (12)	8 (14)	7 (12)
Housewife-volunteer (no other career)	28 (25)	5 (12)	9 (16)	6 (10)
Teacher briefly before marriage (no other career)	17 (15)	2 (5)	8 (14)	3 (5)
Unknown	12 (11)	21 (52)	26 (48)	23 (40)

* Several women functioned in more than one occupation and appear more than once in this table; therefore the percentages sometimes total more than 100%.

† This category includes only women who functioned as editors, authors, or lecturers in some other area than WCTU work, although many of them were also propagandists for the WCTU.

life for which they received monetary compensation (except a brief period as elementary schoolteachers before marriage). Only two (4 percent) of Giele's temperance leaders made motherhood and wifehood a career.[12] The figures in table 3 run considerably higher, but Giele's group was smaller and probably more consistently prominent. Mezvinsky labeled 10 percent of his women housewives.[13] Fully one-fourth of my group 1 appear to have functioned only as housewives and volunteers. The figure is lower for the officers, but since the number where vocation is unknown runs from 40 to 50 percent, the actual percentage of housewife-volunteers is undoubtedly much higher. An independent career is more likely than housewifery to be mentioned in biographical material.

Nearly one-third of group 1 and the 1894 officers pursued active careers as educators, principals, career teachers, college professors, or administrators. Mezvinsky found that over one-third of his leaders had been teachers at one time or another.[14] Giele reported that twenty-three of her forty-nine women had been teachers.[15] The number of editors, authors, and lecturers in my group was also relatively high, and in some cases the same women were also educators. Giele placed about half the women in her sample in a similar category (author, editor, lecturer, organizer), but she did not distinguish between those who were and were not professional temperance workers.[16] If professional temperance workers, all of whom were lecturers, authors, or editors, are added to the other publicists, 52 percent of group 1, or 56 percent of the women whose occupations are known, fall into that category. As in earlier studies, a few ordained ministers and professional evangelists appear, but the number is smaller than one might expect from a group heavily committed to religious proselytizing. But many more women preached or conducted services on occasion than appear in the figures—there was never any dearth of capable WCTU preachers to fill the Protestant pulpits of any convention city. To the extent that occupation indicates class, the data on occupation and profession confirm earlier findings that the WCTU leadership was a group of upper-class and upper middle-class women. None were engaged in menial occupations, unless one puts housewives in that category. However, given their husbands' social status (see table 7), most undoubtedly had servants who performed some of the household labor.

The temperance movement's reputation for being the domain of Methodists seems well deserved. As can be seen in table 4, no single sect or denomination came close to matching the popularity of the Methodist

TABLE 4

Religious Affiliation of WCTU Women

Religious Affiliation	Group 1 (N = 110)	1874 Officers (N = 40)	1884 Officers (N = 56)	1894 Officers (N = 58)
Enthusiastic Denominations				
Adventist	1			
Baptist	6	2	1	3
Christian	3	1	1	
Methodist	40	11	16	16
Total	50 (45%)	14 (35%)	18 (32%)	19 (33%)
Creedal Denominations				
Congregational	13	1	8	5
Episcopalian	5	1	1	2
Presbyterian	9	3	3	7
Quaker	7	1	3	3
Unitarian- Universalist	4		1	1
Theosophical Society				1
Total	38 (35%)	6 (15%)	16 (29%)	19 (33%)
Unknown	22 (20%)	20 (50%)	22 (39%)	20 (34%)

Episcopal church among WCTU women. But it is interesting that the Presbyterian and Congregational churches come next in popularity, and when the total number of women belonging to "enthusiastic" sects is compared with the total of those in creedal faiths (defined as those who emphasized doctrine and creed rather than revivalism and conversion experience), there is very little difference by the 1880s and 1890s. The religious proclivities of temperance women were less tied to Methodism and Baptism than has sometimes been thought. Three WCTU professional clergywomen belonged to the Congregational and Universalist churches, one was a Baptist, and one a Methodist. Mezvinsky found that fifty of his women belonged to creedal churches, compared to seventy-six (fifty-six of them Methodists) in the "enthusiastic" denominations.[17] Giele's data are not comparable because she used H. Richard Niebuhr's classification, which places Presbyterians in his "denominations of the frontier." Thirty of Giele's leaders belonged to these churches, and only ten to Niebuhr's "denominations of the established communities."[18] My findings seem to show that Methodists were certainly numerous in the WCTU (and since Methodists were the largest Protestant denomination in the United States, it is logical to find more of them), but beyond that fact, the Union was almost equally attractive to the major Protestant denominations. No Catholic or Jew appears in any of these samples. As pointed out earlier, Catholic women did not feel comfortable in the WCTU and segregated themselves into their own organizations. Davis found no Catholics among his settlement workers, but he did find twenty-two Jews.[19]

Table 5 confirms that WCTU women were usually native-born whites. If women whose ethnic origins are unknown are eliminated, the percentage is very high indeed, and the women in the unknown group almost all have Anglo-Saxon names. The few native-born whites who were not of English, Scotch, or Scotch-Irish stock derived from Dutch or French families. The

TABLE 5

Ethnic Background of WCTU Women

Ethnic Background	Group 1 (N = 110)	1874 Officers (N = 40)	1884 Officers (N = 56)	1894 Officers (N = 58)
Native-born white (English, Irish, Scotch ancestry)	91 (82.8%)	17 (42.5%)	30 (53.4%)	39 (67.2%)
Native-born white (other than above)	2 (1.8)		1 (1.8)	2 (3.4)
Foreign-born	4 (3.6)	1 (2.5)	1 (1.8)	
Black	1 (.9)			1 (1.7)
American Indian	1 (.9)			1 (1.7)
Unknown	11 (10)	22 (55)	24 (43)	15 (26)

foreign-born came almost entirely from Canada or the British Isles; one came from Denmark. The WCTU contained Scandinavian and German members who worked with their ethnic groups, but they were neither officers nor nationally visible (by my criteria) as leaders. The two black women worked with black unions. Lucy Thurman, a Michigan school-teacher and housewife, was national Superintendent of Colored Work in the 1890s. Georgia Swift King, a graduate of Atlanta University, was state president of Georgia Union No. 2, Georgia's black state union. The two American Indians were presidents of the WCTU in the Indian Territory. One, Jane Stapler, who was a personal friend of Willard, was the wife of a prominent Oklahoma merchant of Indian descent, and the daughter of a Cherokee chief. Little is known about Eva Ratcliff, president for the Indian Territory in 1894, except that she was a Presbyterian. However, the fact that there were any blacks or native Americans among the leadership sets the Union apart from other women's organizations in the nineteenth century. Giele reported no data on ethnicity; Mezvinsky found his group to be predominantly native-born whites of Anglo-Saxon descent.

The occupations of the fathers of WCTU women were difficult to obtain, and the unknown category is large. Where the information was available, table 6 shows the fathers of WCTU women belonged in large measure to the professional and business classes. Only two WCTU women were daughters of laborers and at least one of these laborers was skilled, being referred to as a mechanic. In group 1, 39 percent of the fathers, or nearly 80 percent of fathers with known occupations, were in business or the professions. Only 13 percent were farmers or laborers, and the farmers could well have been substantial landowners. Frances Willard's father was among them. He farmed for much of his life, but he was well educated and clearly belonged to the upper middle class in socioeconomic status. The four fathers tabulated under Other in group 1 were an architect, an inventor, an innkeeper, and an Indian chief, not exactly working-class occupations; the two listed for 1884 were an architect and a journalist. So few fathers' occupations are known for the officer group that meaningful conclusions cannot be drawn. Mezvinsky, Giele, and Gusfield collected no data on fathers' occupations. Davis found that his settlement-house workers were the sons and daughters of teachers and educators.[20]

Husbands' occupations were more easily ascertained, although the percentage of unknowns still ranges from 25 to 47 percent according to table 7. The number of WCTU women whose husbands were businessmen,

TABLE 6

Fathers' Occupations of WCTU Women

Father's Occupations	Group 1 (N = 110)	1874 Officers (N = 40)	1884 Officers (N = 56)	1894 Officers (N = 58)
Attorney	3 (2.7%)		2 (4%)	3 (5.3%)
Clergy	15 (13.7)	4 (10%)	5 (9)	4 (6.9)
Businessman, financier, industrialist	17 (15.4)	2 (5)	5 (9)	2 (3.4)
Educator	2 (1.8)		1 (2)	1 (1.7)
Physician	6 (5.5)	1 (2.5)		2 (3.4)
Farmer	13 (11.8)	4 (10)	6 (10)	7 (12)
Laborer	1 (.9)	1 (2.5)		
Other	4 (3.6)		2 (4)	
Unknown	49 (44.6)	28 (70)	35 (62)	39 (67.3)

bankers, or industrialists is impressive. This was not a movement of otherworldly do-gooders: the mainstream was behind it. Among the married WCTU women, 68 percent were married to men in business and the professions, 93 percent if the unknowns are eliminated. There is not a single laborer and only two farmers in the lot. The farmers disappear in the officer group, confirming the urban nature of the movement. In occupations labeled Other, group 1 includes a Civil War soldier, killed soon after his marriage and before his career began, a journalist, a professional politician, and a professional temperance worker. The 1884 group contains a druggist, a soldier, an editor, a professional temperance worker, a journalist, and an army officer. In 1894 there were an architect, an army officer, and an engineer. The two wives of army officers were presidents of the Kansas and Nebraska unions. Lurenda B. Smith was the daughter of a New York state Crusader, and was in her fifties when she headed the Kansas WCTU in the 1890s. Jennie Holmes was a teacher before her marriage at twenty-four. She moved with her husband, an army colonel, from Wisconsin to Tecumseh, Nebraska, in 1866. She described herself as

TABLE 7

Husbands' Occupations of WCTU Women

Husbands' Occupations	Group 1 (N = 87)	1874 Officers (N = 37)	1884 Officers (N = 48)	1894 Officers (N = 55)	San Diego Union* (N = 27)
Attorney	8 (9.2%)	5 (13%)	3 (6%)		3 (11%)
Clergy	14 (16.1)	4 (11)	8 (16.5)	7 (12.7%)	
Businessman, financier, industrialist	23 (26.4)	3 (8)	6 (12.5)	10 (18.1)	13 (48.1)
Educator	9 (10.4)	4 (11)	1 (2)	6 (11)	1 (3.7)
Physician	5 (5.7)	4 (11)	6 (12.5)	3 (5.5)	2 (7.4)
Farmer	2 (2.3)				
Laborer					
Other	4 (4.6)		6 (12.5)	3 (5.5)	4 (14.9)
Unknown	22 (25.3)	17 (46)	18 (37.5)	26 (47.3)	4 (14.9)

* Compiled from city directories, 1888 and 1890.

a suffragist and was elected to her local school board at a time when few women held elective office.

More WCTU women were wives of clergymen than wives of attorneys, physicians, or educators, a logical finding in view of the Union's strong religious emphasis. However, it is the large proportion of husbands who were entrepreneurs of one sort or another that underlines the mainstream character of the movement and also shows the strong support temperance received from the business community.

Gusfield also collected data on husbands' occupations, which he used as his determinant of class status. He found a high percentage of husbands in business and the professions in his 1885 sample, which included nearly two hundred women who were officers of local unions in thirty-eight cities in five states. But he also found nearly 30 percent whose husbands were engaged in skilled and unskilled labor. The wives of laborers were able to play a leadership role in local unions in the nineteenth century, although they do not appear on the state and national level.[21] The San Diego local Union founded and supported a home for dependent women combined with a child-care facility in the 1890s. Its Board of Management and Executive Committee were composed of twenty-seven local WCTU members. Many of their husbands (thirteen out of twenty-seven) were in business and industry: one was president of the San Diego Car Company, another was president of the Electric Railroad and Light Company, a third headed the Hotel Coronado, and one listed himself simply as a capitalist. However, among these twenty-seven local leaders were also the wives of two watchmakers, one county official, and a grocery clerk.[22] A grocery clerk's wife was sharing responsibility with the wives of the presidents of two major utilities for managing a charitable enterprise! Charles Isetts looked at Crusaders' husbands in Hillsboro, Ohio, and found that 75 percent of the marchers were married to men in white-collar occupations, and the rest to skilled craftsmen. Crusaders' families—which included almost all of Hillsboro County's richest citizens—controlled two-thirds of the county's wealth.[23] Nonetheless, a quarter of these women were the wives of men who earned their livings in the trades. Eliza Thompson marched the streets of Hillsboro with women far below her in social class. My own study of the Crusade in Adrian, Michigan, shows the same class range among participants. On the local level, unions included women from families with a broad range of occupations and wide variations in socioeconomic status. The middle and upper middle-class status of much of the WCTU's national leadership is unmistakable, but on the local level the spectrum is wider. The middle and upper classes may have been dominant, but the wife of the ordinary craftsman, mechanic, or clerk was not unrepresented. The movement was broad as well as large.

The relative importance of missionary-society and suffrage connections among WCTU leaders is indicated in table 8. Biographical material that recorded a specific connection with missions or a specific connection with suffrage was tabulated. Since most of the biographical sketches originated with the women themselves, mention of other active interests shows the importance a woman attached to them. Until the 1890s at least twice as many WCTU women mention their involvement with the missionary-society movement as mention suffrage connections. More important, there is practically no overlap; only two women appear in both groups. Did

TABLE 8

Identification of WCTU Women with Missions or Suffrage

Identification	Group 1 (N = 33)	1874 Officers (N = 12)	1884 Officers (N = 11)	1894 Officers (N = 15)
Missions	22	9	7	7
Suffrage	11	3	4	8

experience with missions preclude experience with the suffrage movement? Giele found much heavier participation by temperance women in the missionary-society movement than she found among her suffragists: seventeen of the temperance leaders in her group were involved with missions, but only one of the suffrage leaders.[24] However, my data show that this had evened out by the 1890s, perhaps foreshadowing the strong growth of suffrage as a vehicle for the mass women's movement in the twentieth century.

Notes

The microfilm edition of the Temperance and Prohibition Papers is described in full in the Introduction to this volume. Throughout the notes, references to material available in the microfilm edition have been abbreviated. These include citations of the *Minutes* of national conventions of the WCTU, the *Union Signal*, and numerous letters, clippings, and scrapbooks in the WCTU Series.

INTRODUCTION

1. Lathrap's speech and the proceedings of the convention are reproduced in full in the *Grand Rapids Daily Democrat*, May 30, 1878.
2. Forty-fourth Annual Report of the Superintendent of Public Instruction of Michigan, in *Joint Documents of the House and Senate of Michigan, 1880* (Lansing, 1881), v. 1, 415.
3. See Randall C. Jimerson, Francis X. Blouin, and Charles A. Isetts, eds., *Guide to the Microfilm Edition of the Temperance and Prohibition Papers*, The Michigan Historical Collections, The Ohio Historical Society, The Woman's Christian Temperance Union (Ann Arbor: University of Michigan, 1977), for a description of the Temperance and Prohibition Papers. The WCTU Series of the microfilm Temperance Papers, which includes the *Minutes* of the annual WCTU conventions, and the *Union Signal* Series, both of which are drawn from originals at the headquarters of the WCTU in Evanston, Illinois, and deposited in the Michigan Historical Collections of the Bentley Historical Library at the University of Michigan, Ann Arbor, have been used in preparation of this volume.
4. Jack S. Blocker, Jr., ed., *Alcohol, Reform and Society: The Liquor Question in Social Context* (Westport, Conn.: Greenwood Press, 1979); Larry Engelmans, *Intemperance: The Lost War against Liquor* (New York: Free

Press, 1979); William J. Rorabaugh, *The Alcoholic Republic: An American Tradition* (New York: Oxford University Press, 1979).

5. Andrew Sinclair, *Prohibition: The Era of Excess* (Boston: Little, Brown and Co., 1962), and Richard Hofstadter, *Age of Reform* (New York: Random House, 1955), are cases in point.

6. *Deliver Us from Evil: An Interpretation of American Prohibition* (New York: W. W. Norton, 1976).

7. *Symbolic Crusade: Status, Politics and the American Temperance Movement* (Urbana: University of Illinois Press, 1966).

8. Joseph Timberlake, *Prohibition and the Progressive Movement, 1900–1920* (Cambridge: Harvard University Press, 1963); John C. Burnam, "New Perspectives on the Prohibition 'Experiment' of the 1920's," *Journal of Social History* 2 (Fall 1968): 51–68.

9. Elizabeth Putnam Gordon, *Women Torch Bearers: The Story of the Women's Christian Temperance Union* (Evanston: National Woman's Christian Temperance Union Publishing House, 1924); Helen E. Tyler, *Where Prayer and Purpose Meet: The Woman's Christian Temperance Union Story, 1874–1949* (Evanston: Signal Press, 1949); Agnes D. Hays, *Heritage of Dedication: One Hundred Years of the National Women's Temperance Union* (Evanston: Signal Press, 1973).

10. Norton Mezvinsky, "The White Ribbon Reform, 1874–1920" (Ph.D. dissertation, University of Wisconsin, 1959); Samuel Unger, "History of the National Woman's Christian Temperance Union" (Ph.D. dissertation, Ohio State University, 1933). More specialized studies include Janet Zollinger Giele, "Social Change in the Feminine Role: A Comparison of Woman's Suffrage and Woman's Temperance, 1870–1920" (Ph.D. dissertation, Radcliffe College, 1961), and Joseph R. Gusfield, "Social Structure and Moral Reform: A Study of the Woman's Christian Temperance Union," *American Journal of Sociology* 61 (November 1955): 221–32.

11. Mary Earhart, *Frances Willard: From Prayers to Politics* (Chicago: University of Chicago Press, 1944).

12. Clark in *Deliver Us* devotes most of chapter 5 to the WCTU; Timberlake's *Prohibition and the Progressive Movement* discusses the WCTU's contribution to temperance education in the schools in chapter 2; Gusfield's "Social Structure and Moral Reform" analyzes the demographic characteristics of WCTU leadership. Jack Blocker discusses the WCTU primarily in terms of women's search for identity and its relationship to the Prohibition Party; see *Retreat from Reform: The Prohibition Movement in the United States, 1890–1913* (Westport, Conn.: Greenwood Press, 1976.)

13. Giele, "Social Change"; Ellen DuBois, "The Radicalism of the Woman Suffrage Movement: Notes toward the Reconstruction of Nineteenth Century Feminism," *Feminist Studies* 3 (Fall 1975): 63–71.

14. Earhart, *Willard*, 1–5.

CHAPTER 1

1. Henry William Blair, *The Temperance Movement: Or the Conflict between Man and Alcohol* (Boston: William E. Smythe Co., 1888), 504.
2. The words *feminism* and *feminist* pose special problems for the historian of nineteenth-century women's movements. These words were never used by the women themselves to describe either their ideology or their activities. As Linda Gordon, among others, has pointed out, the phrase used during this period in the United States to describe groups or campaigns aimed at "advancing" the position of women, was the "woman movement." *Feminism* and *feminist*, French in origin, were not used in the United States until early in the twentieth century, and they then refer to a specific ideology, the uniqueness of women, embraced by some advocates of women's rights; see Linda Gordon, *Woman's Body, Woman's Right: A Social History of Birth Control in America* (New York: Penguin, 1977), xiv. I use the term not in ways that it may have been used at specific points in past time, but in the dictionary sense of advocating legal and social changes that will establish political, economic, and social equality of the sexes.
3. Blair, *The Temperance Movement*, 592.
4. Alice Felt Tyler, *Freedom's Ferment: Phases of American Social History to 1860* (Minneapolis: University of Minnesota Press, 1944), ch. 13, contains a concise history of the early temperance movement. John Allen Krout's *The Origins of Prohibition* (New York: Knopf, 1925) is the classic work on the pre–Civil War period, recently supplemented and perhaps supplanted by William J. Rorabaugh's provocative study *The Alcoholic Republic: An American Tradition* (New York: Oxford University Press, 1979).
5. See Eleanor Flexner, *Century of Struggle: The Woman's Rights Movement in the United States* (Cambridge: Harvard University Press, 1959; reprinted New York: Atheneum, 1971), 181. Jed Dannenbaum, "Women and Temperance: The Years of Transition, 1850–1870," paper read at the Conference on the History of Women, October 21–27, 1977, St. Paul, examines the antebellum role of women in some depth.
6. Ida Husted Harper, *The Life and Work of Susan B. Anthony* (Indianapolis: Bobbs Merrill, 1899), v. 1, 64–66; Elizabeth Cady Stanton, Susan B. Anthony, and Matilda Joslyn Gage, eds., *History of Woman Suffrage* (Rochester: Charles Mann Printing Co., 1886), v. 1, 476.
7. Krout, *Origins of Prohibition*, chs. 2 and 3, discusses the Americans' use of alcohol. Brian Harrison, *Drink and the Victorians* (Pittsburgh: Pittsburgh University Press, 1972), 37–41, and Norman Longmate, *The Water Drinkers: A History of Temperance* (London: Hamish Hamilton, 1963), contain vivid accounts of nineteenth-century British attitudes toward strong drink, showing the problem was not peculiar to the United States. Rorabaugh's *Alcoholic Republic* discusses pre–Civil War American drinking habits in depth and detail.

8. Francis M. Whitaker, "A History of the Ohio Woman's Christian Temperance Union, 1874–1920" (Ph.D. dissertation, Ohio State University, 1971), 143.

9. John Marshall Barker, *The Saloon Problem and Social Reform* (Boston: The Everett Press, 1905; reprinted New York: Arno Press, 1970), 6, 8–9.

10. U.S. Bureau of Census, *Historical Statistics of the United States, Colonial Times to 1957* (Washington: Government Printing Office, 1960), 179.

11. Jon M. Kingsdale, "The 'Poor Man's Club': Social Functions of the Urban Working Class Saloon," *American Quarterly* 25 (October 1973): 472–73.

12. Blair, *Temperance Movement*, 363.

13. *Deliver Us from Evil: An Interpretation of American Prohibition* (New York: W. W. Norton, 1976), ch. 1.

14. Frances Willard, Annual Address, *Minutes, 1886 Convention*, 80.

15. Kingsdale, " 'Poor Man's Club,' " 482–83.

16. Ross Evans Paulson, *Women's Suffrage and Prohibition: A Comparative Study of Equality and Social Control* (Glenview, Ill.: Scott Foresman, 1973), 115.

17. Anthony as quoted in Aileen Kraditor, *Up from the Pedestal: Selected Writings in the History of American Feminism* (Chicago: Quadrangle Books, 1969), 159–61.

18. James H. Timberlake, *Prohibition and the Progressive Movement 1900–1920* (Cambridge: Harvard University Press, 1963), ch. 1, discusses prevalent attitudes toward drunkenness.

19. Flexner, *Century of Struggle*, ch. 4, has the best summary of women's legal position in the United States before the Civil War. Peter G. Filene in *Him/Herself: Sex Roles in Modern America* (New York: Harcourt Brace Jovanovich, 1975), 32–33, contains a good summary of women's legal position later in the century.

20. Gilbert Ostrander, *American Civilization in the First Machine Age* (New York: Harper and Row, 1970), 53.

21. Filene, *Him/Herself*, 33.

22. Flexner, *Century of Struggle*, 176.

23. The best recent analyses of "woman's sphere" are found in Barbara J. Berg, *The Remembered Gate: Origins of American Feminism; The Woman in the City, 1800–1860* (New York: Oxford University Press, 1978), 67–74, and Nancy Cott, *The Bonds of Womanhood: "Woman's Sphere" in New England, 1790–1835* (New Haven: Yale University Press, 1978). Although most theorists have tended to accept these evaluations, Joan Kelly has recently argued that there never were separate spheres. She believes the doctrine of spheres did not describe nineteenth-century society, but rather reflected its ideology. See her "The Doubled Vision of Feminist Theory," *Feminist Studies* 5 (Spring 1979): 216, 227.

24. Dannenbaum, "Women and Temperance."

25. Jill Conway, "Women Reformers and American Culture, 1870–1930," *Journal of Social History* 5 (Winter 1971–72): 164–77.

26. See June Sochen, *Movers and Shakers: American Women Thinkers and Activists* (New York: Quadrangle Books/The New York Times Book Co., 1973), 8–9, 65–66. William L. O'Neill, in *Everyone Was Brave: A History of Feminism in America* (New York: Quadrangle Books, 1971), 51, calls this same group the "social feminists."

27. Frances Willard, *Woman and Temperance* (Hartford, Conn.: Park Publishing Co., 1883; reprinted New York: Arno, 1972), 40.

28. Ruth Bordin, "Women March for Temperance: The Woman's Crusade in Adrian," *Michigan Chronicle* 15 (Winter 1980): 16–23.

29. Minutes, 1894, Ann Arbor, Michigan, Woman's Christian Temperance Union, Michigan Historical Collections of the Bentley Historical Library, University of Michigan, Ann Arbor.

30. Mary Ryan, "The Power of Women's Networks: A Case Study of Female Moral Reform in Antebellum America," *Feminist Studies* 5 (Spring 1979): 74.

31. See Susan J. Kleinberg, "The Systematic Study of Urban Women," in Milton Cantor and Bruce Laurie, eds., *Class, Sex and the Woman Worker* (Westport, Conn.: Greenwood Press, 1977), 25–26.

32. The best recent discussions of the changing status and growing importance of the middle-class woman in the nineteenth century are to be found in Keith Melder, *Beginnings of Sisterhood: The American Woman's Rights Movements, 1800–1850* (New York: Schocken Books, 1977), ch. 1; and William Chafe, *Women and Equality: Changing Patterns in American Culture* (New York: Oxford University Press, 1977), ch. 2. See also Martha Vicinus's introduction to her *Suffer and Be Still: Women in the Victorian Age* (Bloomington: Indiana University Press, 1972).

33. *Up from the Pedestal*, 14. In 1870 one out of every eight families had a servant. By 1900 the ratio had declined to one in fifteen. However, household conveniences were increasing rapidly in urban areas. By the 1880s the gas stove was replacing the coal range, and by 1890 many (even modest) city dwellings had cold and sometimes hot running water. See Sheila Rothman, *Woman's Proper Place: A History of Changing Ideals and Practices, 1870 to the Present* (New York: Basic Books, 1978), 14–16.

34. See Daniel Scott Smith, "Family Limitation, Sexual Control and Domestic Feminism in Victorian America," in Mary Hartman and Lois Banner, eds., *Clio's Consciousness Raised: New Perspectives on the History of Women* (New York: Harper Torchbooks, 1974), 122. Smith attributes this decline to what he calls "domestic feminism," women's insistence on control of their childbearing, probably through practice of coitus interruptus. See also Gordon, *Woman's Body*.

35. Urban places are defined as having a population of 2,500 or more, following census practice.

36. Robin Jacoby has argued that by the last decades of the nineteenth century, industrialization had created an unsatisfactory leisure for upper and middle-class women and an "oppressive" work life for their lower-class counter-

parts; see "The Women's Trade Union League," in Cantor and Laurie, eds., *Class, Sex and the Woman Worker*, 211.

37. See Chafe, *Women and Equality*, ch. 2.

CHAPTER 2

1. Parts of this chapter first appeared in "The Baptism of Power and Liberty: The Woman's Crusade of 1873," *Ohio History* 87 (Autumn 1978): 303–404, and were reprinted in Mary Kelley, ed., *Woman's Being, Woman's Place: Female Identity and Vocation in American History* (Boston: G. K. Hall, 1979), 283–95. The material is reprinted here with the kind permission of the publishers of *Ohio History* and Twayne Publishers, a division of G. K. Hall and Co., Boston.

For history and description of the Crusade see Mary F. Eastman, *The Biography of Dio Lewis, Prepared at the Desire and with the Cooperation of Mrs. Dio Lewis* (New York: Fowler and Wells, 1891), 65–66; see also Dio Lewis, "History of the Woman's Crusade," in *Prohibition a Failure* (Boston: James R. Osgood and Co., 1875), 227–28. Eastman's *Dio Lewis*, which incorporates many firsthand reminiscences, and Annie Wittenmyer's *History of the Women's Temperance Crusade* (Philadelphia: Office of the Christian Woman, 1878), contain the most complete contemporary accounts of the movement. Eliza Jane Thompson also wrote her memoirs, *Hillsboro Crusade Sketches and Family Records* (Cincinnati: Jennings and Graham, 1906), as did Matilda Gilruth Carpenter, *The Crusade: Its Origin and Development at Washington Court House and Its Results* (Columbus: W. G. Hubbard and Co., 1893). W. C. Steel's handbook for potential Crusaders and temperance advocates, *The Woman's Temperance Movement: A Concise History of the War on Alcohol* (New York: National Temperance Society Publication House, 1874), also contains eyewitness accounts. Most of the issue of December 20, 1883, of the *Union Signal*, the official organ of the WCTU, is devoted to reminiscences and evaluations of the Crusade. And T. A. H. Brown, a reporter for the *Cincinnati Gazette* who covered the Crusade for his paper, wrote a long, partially eyewitness account called "A Full Description of the Origin and Progress of the New Plan of Labor by the Women up to the Present Time," which appeared in Jane E. Stebbins, *Fifty Years History of the Temperance Cause* (Hartford, Conn.: J. P. Fitch, 1876). There have been three recent studies of the Crusade: Ruth Bordin, "A Baptism of Power and Liberty: The Woman's Crusade of 1873–1874," *Ohio History* 87 (Autumn 1978): 393–404, reprinted in Mary Kelley, ed., *Woman's Being, Woman's Place: Female Identity and Vocation in American History* (Boston: G. K. Hall, 1979), 283–95; Jack K. Blocker, Jr., "Why Women Marched: The Temperance Crusade of 1873–74," paper read at the annual meeting of the American Historical Association, December 28, 1977, New York; and Susan Dye Lee, "Evangelical Domesticity: The Woman's Temperance Crusade of 1873–74," paper read at the conference Women in New Worlds: Historical Perspectives on the United Methodist Tradition, February 2, 1980, Cincinnati.

2. Eastman, *Dio Lewis*, 126.

3. Elizabeth Putnam Gordon, *Women Torch Bearers: The Story of the Women's Christian Temperance Union* (Evanston: National Woman's Christian Temperance Union Publishing House, 1924), 13–14.

4. Thompson, *Crusade Sketches*, 59.

5. Ibid., p. 219. That Thompson attended Catharine Beecher's Cincinnati school is not without significance. As Katherine Kish Sklar has pointed out, Beecher was responsible in many ways for shifting "moral centrality away from the male clergy and placing it on women laity"; see *Catharine Beecher: A Study in American Domesticity* (New York: W. W. Norton, 1976), 86. Like the Crusaders, Beecher "not only wanted to 'save' the nation, she wanted women to save it" (ibid., 96). While Thompson did not at first see herself as an active moral leader, she adjusted quickly to the role and played it easily the rest of her life. Beecher's teachings may have had a lasting influence.

6. Frances Willard, "Field Notes," in *The Alliance*, June 6, 1876, scrapbook 4, WCTU Series, reel 30, frame 202.

7. Thompson, *Crusade Sketches*, 60–61.

8. Ibid., 61.

9. *Union Signal*, November 8, 1888, 5; also Thompson, *Crusade Sketches*, 62.

10. Thompson, *Crusade Sketches*, 63.

11. Eastman, *Dio Lewis*, 135–40.

12. Thompson, *Crusade Sketches*, 74.

13. Ibid., 75.

14. Techniques very similar to those used in the Crusade had been used by the New York Female Moral Reform Society in the 1830s in their campaign against houses of prostitution. In that movement the women hired male missionaries to descend on brothels and exhort patrons and inmates to give up their ways, and the "ladies" themselves also invaded the brothels, although not without male escorts. They prayed and sang hymns and were fully aware of the disruption their presence caused to the normal business activities of the houses. They also used the technique, later adopted by the Crusaders, of writing down the names of hapless patrons they encountered, especially if they were prominent in the business and professional life of the community. See Carroll Smith-Rosenberg, *Religion and the Rise of the American City: The New York City Mission Movement, 1812–1870* (Ithaca: Cornell University Press, 1971), ch. 4.

15. Thompson, *Crusade Sketches*, 79. Catholic priests also refused to join the Crusade in Adrian, Michigan; see Minutes, 1874, Adrian Ladies' Temperance Union, Michigan Historical Collections of the Bentley Historical Library, University of Michigan, Ann Arbor.

16. Thompson, *Crusade Sketches*, 80.

17. Gordon, *Women Torch Bearers*, 8.
18. Thompson, *Crusade Sketches*, 92.
19. Carpenter, *The Crusade*, 24–40.
20. Ibid., 43–44.
21. Ibid., 47–51.
22. Eastman, *Dio Lewis*, 200–202.
23. Gordon, *Women Torch Bearers*, 9. Many of these initial successes were shortlived. Hillsboro was still dry in the 1880s, but in many places the saloons were back within weeks or months.
24. *Union Signal*, September 30, 1923, 4.
25. Blocker, "Why Women Marched," 4.
26. Minutes, March 3–17, Adrian Ladies' Temperance Union, pp. 8–70.
27. Clipping, March 1874, Sarah Turner Papers, scrapbook 2, Michigan Historical Collections of the Bentley Historical Library, University of Michigan, Ann Arbor.
28. Clippings, *Adrian Daily Times*, March–June 1874, Turner scrapbook 2.
29. Turner scrapbook 2.
30. Minutes, March–August 1874, Adrian Ladies' Temperance Union, pp. 70–239. See Brown, "A Full Description," in Stebbins, *Fifty Years History*, 365, for an evaluation of the Adrian Crusade.
31. From the *Cincinnati Commercial* as quoted in W. C. Steel, *The Women's Temperance Movement*, 71.
32. Brown, "A Full Description," in Stebbins, *Fifty Years History*, 365.
33. Carpenter, *The Crusade*, 52–53.
34. Ibid., 84–85.
35. Thompson, *Crusade Sketches*, 102.
36. Ibid., 116; Minutes, 1874; Adrian Ladies' Temperance Union. Eliza Stewart secured the conviction of one saloonkeeper for illegal Sunday sales by marching into his saloon on Sunday, buying a glass, quietly making off with it before the seller was aware of what she was doing, taking it home, sealing it up, and using it as evidence in court (*Union Signal*, May 7, 1891, 8).
37. Brown, "A Full Description," in Stebbins, *Fifty Years History*, 437–42.
38. Sarah Bolton's reminiscences, *Union Signal*, December 20, 1883, 7–8.
39. Brown, "A Full Description," in Stebbins, *Fifty Years History*, 465.
40. Clipping from the *Alliance* (Ohio) *Monitor*, in scrapbook 4, WCTU Series, reel 30, frames 105–6.
41. Brown, "A Full Description," 469.
42. Norton Mezvinsky, "The White Ribbon Reform, 1874–1920" (Ph.D. dissertation, University of Wisconsin, 1959), 54–60.
43. Helen E. Tyler, *Where Prayer and Purpose Meet: The Woman's Christian Temperance Union Story* (Evanston: Signal Press, 1949), 17.
44. Blocker, "Why Women Marched," 4. Blocker counted actual numbers of women engaged in Crusade activity as recounted in 51 newspapers and journals published in 23 states, and estimates the numbers were at least three times as great.

45. See Frances Willard, *Woman and Temperance* (Hartford, Conn.: Park Publishing Co., 1883; reprinted New York: Arno, 1972). Of the ten temperance leaders who did not participate in the Crusade, three were not Americans and were living in England and Canada, three happened to be abroad when the Crusade occurred, and four were from areas of the country (New England and the South) where no Crusades took place. However, over one-half of the thirty came into public life by way of the temperance Crusade of 1873-74.

46. Ibid., 103-6. Woodbridge was a Congregationalist and the wife of a Ravenna, Ohio, merchant. Her father had been a judge and a member of the Massachusetts and Ohio legislatures.

47. Ibid., 88.

48. Ibid., 83-85.

49. *Deliver Us from Evil: An Interpretation of American Prohibition* (New York: W. W. Norton, 1976), 70.

50. Thompson, for example, was a person of considerable wealth. After she was widowed, the income at her disposal was reported at over $100,000 a year (*Union Signal*, August 20, 1891, 9).

51. Charles A. Isetts, "The Woman's Christian Temperance Crusade of Southern Ohio" (M.A. thesis, Miami University, Oxford, Ohio, 1971), 23-24.

52. Blocker, "Why Women Marched," 10. Blocker makes an impressive statistical argument for an abrupt increase in sale and consumption of alcoholic beverages in 1874. However, available figures are little more than estimates until quite late in the century. Even for 1873, the year Blocker cites for the big increase, the data base he uses changes from distilled spirits to distilled spirits plus beer and wine. Illegal production and sale of alcohol is also difficult to estimate. It is interesting to compare Blocker's conclusions with Mary Ryan's findings on the Utica moral reform societies, "The Power of Women's Networks: A Case Study of Female Reform in Antebellum America," *Feminist Studies* 5 (Spring 1979): 66-85. Sexual license appeared to be on the decline at the time Utica's moral reform societies were organized (Ryan, 71). Blocker finds alcohol abuse peaking at the time of the Crusade. However, Ryan contends that the Utica community's ability to set standards for acceptable sexual behavior had eroded. Geographical mobility for the young had removed parents from immediate control, and the direct influence of the churches on behavior was waning. Blocker finds a direct relationship between alcohol abuse and the Crusade; Ryan finds a more subtle juxtaposition in Utica.

53. Isetts, "The Woman's Christian Temperance Crusade," 49 and ch. 6.

54. Ryan, "Power of Women's Networks," 74.

55. The Crusade spread rapidly. In Michigan, for example, the first Crusade took place in Jackson in February. The Adrian Crusade began on March 4. Lansing, Grand Rapids, Coldwater, and Eaton Rapids followed within two weeks. Newspaper publicity seems to have facilitated the spread.

56. *Union Signal*, December 20, 1883, 6.

57. Mark Twain's article, originally published in the *London Standard*, was reprinted in the *Union Signal*, June 4, 1885, 5.
58. Mary Livermore in the *Union Signal*, December 20, 1883, 8.
59. Henry William Blair, *The Temperance Movement: Or the Conflict between Man and Alcohol* (Boston: William E. Smythe Co., 1888), 504.
60. Frances Willard, in her Introduction to Wittenmyer, *History of the Women's Temperance Crusade*, 15–21.
61. Mary Earhart, *Frances Willard: From Prayers to Politics* (Chicago: University of Chicago Press, 1944), 143. The attitude of suffragists toward the Crusade is interesting. Overall they felt that legislative halls rather than saloons were fit places for petitions. They found it "queer" that women who would not even ask for the vote had set the Crusade in motion, and they warned that only the vote changes laws, that rum-sellers whom the Crusade had intimidated would soon be back in business, and that suffrage was the cause that should receive women's attention. See Elizabeth Cady Stanton, Susan B. Anthony, and Matilda Joslyn Gage, eds., *History of Woman Suffrage* (Rochester: Charles Mann Printing Co., 1886), v. 3, 500–501.
62. Mark Twain in the *London Standard*, reprinted in the *Union Signal*, June 4, 1885, 5.
63. Charles A. Isetts, "A Social Profile of the Woman's Temperance Crusade: Hillsboro, Ohio," in Jack S. Blocker, Jr., ed., *Alcohol, Reform and Society: The Liquor Question in Social Context* (Westport, Conn.: Greenwood Press, 1979), 104–7.
64. Ibid.; Bordin, "Women March for Temperance: The Woman's Crusade in Adrian," *Michigan Chronicle* 15 (Winter 1980): 16–23; Blocker, "Why Women Marched," 17.
65. *Union Signal*, December 20, 1883, 8.
66. See above, p. 9 and note. These are the women Sochen defines as "pragmatic feminists" and whom O'Neill calls the "social feminists."
67. *Union Signal*, December 20, 1883, 8.
68. Elizabeth Greenwood in *Union Signal*, December 12, 1889, 9.
69. Ibid., 5.
70. Ibid., 8.
71. See Anne Firor Scott, "What Then Is the American, This New Woman?" *Journal of American History* 65 (December 1978): 679–703.
72. As quoted in Anna Adams Gordon, *Frances E. Willard* (Chicago: Lakeside Press, 1912), 85.

CHAPTER 3

1. The Ohio convention activity is described by a contemporary in Jane E. Stebbins, *Fifty Years History of the Temperance Cause* (Hartford, Conn.: J. P. Fitch, 1876), 474–86; it is thoroughly described and analyzed in Francis Myron Whitaker, "A History of the Ohio Woman's Christian Temperance Union, 1874–1920" (Ph.D. dissertation, Ohio State University, 1971).

2. This conference marked the beginning of the Chautauqua movement, a system of adult education that became very popular in the next decades. See Theodore Morrison, *Chautauqua: A Center for Education, Religion and the Arts in America* (Chicago: University of Chicago Press, 1974).

3. Mary B. Ingham, one of the organizing group, wrote a short memoir of the Chautauqua meetings that she read to the 1882 national convention on the origins of the Woman's Christian Temperance Union; it appears in the convention *Minutes* for that year and is also included in Frances Willard's *Woman and Temperance* (Hartford, Conn.: Park Publishing Co., 1883; reprinted New York: Arno, 1972), 121–26.

4. The members of the committee that issued the call were Mrs. D. Gause of Philadelphia; Mrs. E. J. Knowles of Newark; Mrs. S. J. Steele of Appleton, Wisconsin; Mrs. W. D. Barnett of Hiawatha, Kansas; Auretta Hoyt of Indianapolis; Mrs. Ingham Stanton of LeRoy, New York; Frances Crooks of Baltimore; and Emma Janes of Oakland, California. Steele was the wife of the president of Lawrence College. Hoyt had taught at Western College in Ohio. Janes was Vincent's sister-in-law. I have found no biographical information on Gause, Knowles, Barnett, Stanton, and Crooks, and they do not appear in Willard's *Woman and Temperance*. Presumably their roles as leaders in the woman's temperance movement were short-lived. Hoyt and Janes were the only two on the committee who were unmarried.

5. Sixteen women appeared on the list of temporary officers, twelve of them as vice-presidents for their states. Six of these twelve appear not to have remained prominent on the national level, and only one, Mrs. E. E. Marcy of Illinois, continued as permanent national vice-president for her state. The temporary general officers, Willing, Hoyt, Mary Burt, and Mary Ingham, remained active nationally but not as officers, as did four of the vice-presidents, Abbie Fisher Leavitt of Ohio, Zerelda Wallace of Indiana, Mary Lathrap of Michigan, and Mrs. S. J. Steele of Wisconsin. But none of these women played the key roles assumed by Wittenmyer and Willard once national organization had been accomplished.

6. *Minutes, 1874 Convention,* 5; Willard, *Woman and Temperance,* 128.

7. *Minutes, 1874 Convention,* 5–7; Willard, *Woman and Temperance,* 128.

8. John T. Cumbler, "The Politics of Charity: Sex and Class in Late Nineteenth Century Charity," paper presented at the meetings of the Organization of American Historians, April 1978, New York.

9. See Page Smith, *Daughters of the Promised Land* (Boston: Little, Brown, 1970), 181–89; and Barbara Welter, "She Hath Done What She Could: Protestant Women's Missionary Careers in Nineteenth Century America," *American Quarterly* 30 (Winter 1978): 624–38.

10. *Minutes, 1874 Convention,* 24–28.

11. *Minutes, 1874 Convention,* 29–30.

12. Clipping, *Cleveland Herald,* November 1874, scrapbook 4, WCTU Series, reel 30, frames 155–56.

13. Ibid.

14. The connection of both Leavitt and Wittenmyer with the women's mission-

ary society movement is significant. Page Smith has pointed out that the mission field was the place where women first obtained more or less equal professional status with men. Between 1840 and 1868 there were 148 women sent out as professional foreign missionaries. However, in the pre–Civil War period, with a few exceptions, these were wives of male missionaries. See Smith, *Daughters of the Promised Land*, 181, 189; and Welter, "She Hath Done What She Could," 625–27. In the South, where temperance was an exclusively male movement before the Civil War, women joined the missionary society movement first and then moved into the temperance movement. See Charles Pearson and J. Edwin Hendricks, *Liquor and Anti-Liquor in Virginia, 1619–1919* (Durham: Duke University Press, 1967), 197.

15. R. C. Wood to officers and superiors of the general hospital of the Western Medical Department, August 1, 1864, Annie Wittenmyer Papers, Library of Congress Manuscript Collections.
16. *Minutes, 1874 Convention*, 34.
17. *Minutes, 1874 Convention*, 36–37.
18. Mary Ingham in Willard, *Woman and Temperance*, 137.
19. Clipping, *Cleveland Advocate*, November 27, 1874, scrapbook 4, WCTU Series, reel 30.
20. Clipping, *Cleveland Herald*, November 1874, scrapbook 4, WCTU Series, reel 30.
21. Clipping, *Alliance* (Ohio) *Mirror*, undated, scrapbook 4, WCTU Series, reel 30.
22. Clipping, *Alliance Mirror*, undated, scrapbook 4, WCTU Series, reel 30.
23. Clipping, *Cleveland Advocate*, November 27, 1874, scrapbook 4, WCTU Series, reel 30.
24. Frances Willard, *Glimpses of Fifty Years: An Autobiography of an American Woman* (published by Woman's Temperance Publishing Association, 1889; reprinted New York: Source Book Press, 1970), ch. 18, 331.
25. Ibid., 334; Mary Earhart, *Frances Willard; From Prayers to Politics* (Chicago: University of Chicago Press, 1944), 149.
26. Willard, *Glimpses*, 334–35.
27. Ibid., 341.
28. Ibid., 337; Anna Gordon, *The Life of Frances Willard* (Evanston: National Woman's Christian Temperance Union Publishing House, 1914), 87.
29. Willard, *Glimpses*, 337.
30. Clippings, *The Traveler*, September 8–10, 1874, scrapbook 4, WCTU Series, reel 30, frames 104–6.
31. Letter, unsigned, to "Dear Children," September 13, 1874, WCTU Series, reel 11.
32. Willard, *Glimpses*, 339.
33. Clipping, *Temperance Herald*, undated, scrapbook 13, WCTU Series, reel 32, frame 80.
34. See Earhart, *Willard*, 93.

35. Ibid., 134.
36. Willard, *Glimpses*, 351.
37. Ibid., 69–70.
38. Ibid., 86–123.
39. Frances Willard to Annie Wittenmyer, March 29, 1875, WCTU Series, reel 11.
40. Willard to Wittenmyer, April 14, 1875, WCTU Series, reel 11.
41. Willard to Wittenmyer, March 29, April 9, April 24, 1875, WCTU Series, reel 11.
42. Treasurer's Report, *Minutes, 1875 Convention*, 50.
43. Clipping, September 1875, scrapbook 4, WCTU Series, reel 11.
44. *Minutes, 1875 Convention*, 49.
45. *Minutes, 1875 Convention*, 56.
46. Clipping, scrapbook 5, WCTU Series, reel 30, frame 267.
47. Mary Livermore to Willard, November 20, 1876, WCTU Series, reel 11.
48. Willard to Wittenmyer, December 11, 1874, WCTU Series, reel 11.
49. Ibid.
50. Ibid.
51. Report of the Committee on a Memorial to Congress, *Minutes, 1875 Convention*, 53; clipping, scrapbook 5, WCTU Series, reel 30, frame 267. This was not the first time women had testified before a congressional committee. Susan B. Anthony and Elizabeth Cady Stanton had testified before the District Committee in 1869 to urge that women be allowed to vote in the District of Columbia. See Ida Husted Harper, *The Life and Work of Susan B. Anthony* (Indianapolis: Bobbs Merrill, 1899), v. 1, 314. Victoria Woodhull had also testified on the suffrage question in 1871. See Eleanor Flexner, *Century of Struggle: The Woman's Rights Movement in the United States* (Cambridge: Harvard University Press, 1959; reprinted New York: Atheneum, 1971), 153.
52. Willard to Wittenmyer, December 11, 1874, WCTU Series, reel 11.
53. Willard to Wittenmyer, February 4, October 8, 1875, WCTU Series, reel 11.
54. See correspondence 1875 and scrapbooks 4, 42, and 57, WCTU Series, reel 3.
55. Willard to Wittenmyer, September 4, 9, 16, October 5, 8, 14, 1875, WCTU Series, reel 11.
56. Willard to Wittenmyer, September 16, October 25, 27, 1875, WCTU Series, reel 11.
57. *Minutes, 1875 Convention*, 47–63.
58. Willard, *Glimpses*, 352. Wallace originally opposed woman suffrage. May Wright Sewall reported she first met Wallace circulating temperance petitions that specifically stated that the signers were not advocating civil and political rights for women. When Wallace presented her petitions, however, she discovered that legislators paid attention only to the views of their constituents, and she became convinced that she too must become a con-

stituent. See Elizabeth Cady Stanton, Susan B. Anthony, and Matilda Joslyn Gage, eds., *History of Woman Suffrage* (Rochester: Charles Mann Printing Co., 1886), v. 3, 551–52.
59. *Minutes, 1875 Convention*, 65.

CHAPTER 4

1. Corresponding Secretary's Report, *Minutes, 1879 Convention*, 28–55.
2. *Minutes, 1876 Convention*, 93.
3. Treasurer's Report, *Minutes, 1879 Convention*, 21–24.
4. *Minutes, 1876 Convention*, 81; clipping, *Chicago Post*, September 22, 1876, scrapbook 4, p. 115, WCTU Series, reel 30.
5. Report of the Committee on Prison Reform, *Minutes, 1878 Convention*, 113–14.
6. Report of the Committee on Prison Reform, *Minutes, 1879 Convention*, 142.
7. *Minutes, 1878 Convention*, 105–9.
8. Ruth Bordin, "A Woman at Work," paper delivered at the Conference on the History of Women, St. Catherine's College, St. Paul, Minnesota, October 1975.
9. *Minutes, 1876 Convention*, 112–13. There was considerable general discussion in temperance circles about the Greek translation of the three Hebrew words for wine, and sanction only of *tirosh* (which meant unfermented wine), but this position received little support from the more reputable Biblical scholars. See Joseph Timberlake, *Prohibition and the Progressive Movement, 1900–1920* (Cambridge: Harvard University Press, 1963), 10–11.
10. Report of the Committee on Unfermented Wines, *Minutes, 1879 Convention*, 93–96.
11. Report of the Committee on Sunday School Work, *Minutes, 1879 Convention*, 81–86.
12. *Minutes, 1879 Convention*, 100–5, 120, 161.
13. *Minutes, 1878 Convention*, 41–42.
14. *Minutes, 1876 Convention*, 85; unidentified clipping, [October] 1876, scrapbook 4, p. 102, WCTU Series, reel 30.
15. Ibid.
16. The Prohibition party also supported prohibition, but it was still very small and received little support at the polls. In the 1876 presidential election it received only 9,737 votes. See Ernest H. Cherrington, *The Evolution of Prohibition in the United States of America* (Westerville, Ohio: The American Issue Press, 1920), 166.
17. Frances Willard, *Glimpses of Fifty Years: An Autobiography of an American Woman* (published by the Woman's Temperance Publishing Association, 1889; reprinted New York: Source Book Press, 1970), 351.
18. Willard to Wittenmyer, May 24, 1876, WCTU Series, reel 11. Mary Liver-

more, because her suffrage views were well known, was not permitted to speak at all (Willard, *Glimpses*, 351).

19. Anthony to Willard, September 18, 1876, WCTU Series, reel 11.
20. Clipping, *Zion's Herald*, August 1876, scrapbook 4, WCTU Series, reel 30.
21. As quoted in Mary Earhart, *Frances Willard: From Prayers to Politics* (Chicago: University of Chicago Press, 1944), 53.
22. Willard, *Glimpses*, 351.
23. Ibid., 401.
24. Earhart, Ellen DuBois, and Janet Zollinger Giele agree; see Earhart, *Willard*, 152, and DuBois. "The Radicalism of the Woman's Suffrage Movement: Notes toward the Reconstruction of Nineteenth Century Feminism," *Feminist Studies* 3 (Fall 1975): 68–69; and Giele, "Social Change in the Feminine Role: A Comparison of Woman's Suffrage and Woman's Temperance" (Ph.D. dissertation, Radcliffe College, 1961). William O'Neill disagrees and considers the home-protection strategy a mistake, saying that it changed the issue from an argument over principle to haggling over tactics; see *Everyone Was Brave: A History of Feminism in America* (New York: Quadrangle Books, 1971), 35.
25. *Woman's Journal*, October 11, 1879, 1.
26. Katherine Kish Sklar, *Catharine Beecher: A Study in American Domesticity* (New York: W. W. Norton, 1976), 96–97.
27. Willard, *Glimpses*, 351.
28. Ibid., 352.
29. *Minutes, 1876 Convention*, 115, 119. The resolution read that because woman is guardian of the home and the "greatest sufferer from the liquor traffic which is sanctioned and sustained by law," no place for the sale of intoxicants should be licensed without the consent of the voters (males) and of women over eighteen "by their signature to a petition for such license."
30. *Grand Rapids Daily Democrat*, May 29–30, 1879.
31. *Minutes, 1879 Convention*, 30, 43, 45, 49; Elizabeth Cady Stanton, Susan B. Anthony, and Matilda Joslyn Gage, eds., *History of Woman Suffrage* (Rochester: Charles Mann Printing Co., 1886), v. 3, 587–88.
32. Mary Livermore to Lucy Stone, November 11, 1877, Papers of the National American Woman Suffrage Association, Manuscript Collections of the Library of Congress.
33. Eleanor Flexner, *Century of Struggle: The Woman's Rights Movement in the United States* (Cambridge: Harvard University Press, 1959; reprinted New York: Atheneum, 1971), 151–52; Ida Husted Harper, *The Life and Work of Susan B. Anthony* (Indianapolis: Bobbs Merrill, 1899), v. 1, ch. 19; Stanton, Anthony, and Gage, eds., *History of Woman Suffrage*, v. 2, ch. 23. The best recent discussion of the split in the equal rights movement is in Ellen DuBois, *Feminism and Suffrage: The Emergence of an American Woman's Movement, 1848–1869* (Ithaca: Cornell University Press, 1978), chs. 2 and 3. (The National Woman Suffrage Association and the American Woman Suffrage Association merged in 1890.)

34. Harper, *Anthony*, v. 1, 200–204; Flexner, *Century of Struggle*, 153; and Lois
   W. Banner, *Elizabeth Cady Stanton: A Radical for Woman's Rights* (Bos-
   ton: Little, Brown, 1980), discuss the attitudes and actions of Anthony,
   Stanton, and Woodhull.

35. Flexner, *Century of Struggle*, 170–71; Harper, *Anthony*, v. 1, 477–79;
   Stanton, Anthony, and Gage, eds., *History of Woman Suffrage*, v. 3, 29–31.

36. *Minutes, 1877 Convention*, 163.

37. Willard to Wittenmyer, September 5, 1878, WCTU Series, reel 11.

38. Willard to Wittenmyer, January 20, 1879, WCTU Series, reel 11.

39. *Minutes, 1878 Convention*, 27–35.

40. *Minutes, 1878 Convention*, 108–10.

41. *Minutes, 1879 Convention*, 5, 17.

42. Ibid., 57–58, 64–65. In 1881 the provision was changed to a delegate for
   every five hundred dues-paying members.

43. Ibid., 59–61.

44. See especially Earhart, *Willard*, 173.

45. Gerda Lerner has argued that women wielded considerable political power
   in the nineteenth century through political pressure tactics, exercising the
   right of petition, lobbying, etc.; see "New Approaches to the Study of
   Women in American History," *Journal of Social History* 3 (Fall 1969):
   53–62.

46. Biographical information on the WCTU leadership came from a number of
   sources: Edward James, ed., *Notable American Women* (Cambridge: Harvard University Press, 1971); Willard's *Glimpses* and her *Woman and Temperance* (Hartford, Conn.: Park Publishing Co., 1883; reprinted New York:
   Arno, 1972); and WCTU publications and newspapers.

47. See Jill Conway, "Women Reformers and American Culture, 1870–1930,"
   Journal of Social History 5 (Winter 1971–72): 164–77.

48. See Allen Davis, *American Heroine: The Life and Legend of Jane Addams*
   (New York: Oxford University Press, 1973). Conway's "Women Reformers"
   and Davis have immeasurably enlarged my understanding of Willard's
   charismatic appeal.

49. Henry William Blair, *The Temperance Movement: Or the Conflict between
   Man and Alcohol* (Boston: William E. Smythe Co., 1888), 524–25.

50. *Union Signal*, November 24, 1887, 1.

51. This description is drawn from several clippings in scrapbooks 4 and 5,
   WCTU Series, reel 30, as well as from contemporary photographs.

52. Clipping, Newark, October 1876, scrapbook 4, p. 116, WCTU Series, reel
   30.

53. Clippings, ca. June 1875, scrapbook 4, pp. 85, 97, WCTU Series, reel 30. I
   found only one unflattering comment on Willard as a speaker. In 1875 when
   she was lecturing at the Milwaukee opera house, not on temperance, but
   delivering for a fee a set piece on success, "Who'll Win," a reporter described
   her as "eloquent" but having a "long-drawn way of delivery," and too closely
   confined to her manuscript (clipping, Milwaukee, March 22, 1875, scrapbook 4, WCTU Series, reel 30).

54. Clippings, *Portland Herald*, August 18, 1876, *Boston Herald*, August 11, 1876, scrapbook 4, p. 99, WCTU Series, reel 30.

55. Clipping, *Toronto Citizen*, ca. 1881, scrapbook 5, WCTU Series, reel 30, frame 303.

56. Belle Kearney, *A Slave Holder's Daughter* (New York: Abbey Press, 1900; reprinted New York: Negro Universities Press, 1969), 143.

57. Alfrieda Tilyard, *Agnes E. Slack: Two Hundred Thousand Miles' Travel for Temperance in Four Continents* (Cambridge, U.K.: W. Heffer and Sons, 1926), 224.

58. Eleanor Roosevelt was at a later time able to convey this same sense of concerned intimacy in her syndicated column "My Day."

59. Clipping, scrapbook 5, WCTU Series, reel 30, frame 277; *Minutes, 1873 Convention*, 135–36.

60. Clipping, *Washington Evening Star*, October 26, 1881, scrapbook 5, WCTU Series, reel 30, frame 305; *Louisville Lever*, November 4, 1882, scrapbook 7, reel 30, frame 472.

61. Clippings, *Boston Globe, Toledo Commercial, Cleveland World, Cleveland News and Herald*, November 12–13, 1884, scrapbook 11, WCTU Series, reel 31, frames 318ff.

62. Clipping, *Cleveland News and Herald*, November 13, 1894, scrapbook 11, p. 321, WCTU Series, reel 31, frame 238.

CHAPTER 5

1. Frances Willard, *Glimpses of Fifty Years: An Autobiography of An American Woman* (published by Woman's Temperance Publishing Association, 1889; reprinted New York: Source Book Press, 1970), 363.

2. President's address, *Minutes, 1880 Convention*, 15.

3. Cynthia M. Hanchett to Mary T. H. Willard, April 14, 1880, WCTU Series, reel 12.

4. Hanchett to M. T. H. Willard, April 23, 1880, WCTU Series, reel 12.

5. Hanchett to M. T. H. Willard, May 10, 1880, WCTU Series, reel 12.

6. Willard to M. T. H. Willard, April 10, 1880, WCTU Series, reel 12.

7. Willard to M. T. H. Willard, April 26, 1880, WCTU Series, reel 12.

8. Willard to M. T. H. Willard, October 17, 1880, WCTU Series, reel 12.

9. Anna Gordon to M. T. H. Willard, November 12, 1881, WCTU Series, reel 12.

10. Clipping, Frances Willard's column "Targets," no. 2, *Our Union*, 1876, scrapbook 4, p. 95, WCTU Series, reel 30.

11. *Minutes, 1880 Convention*, 19, 1.

12. Willard to Anna Gordon, May 14, 1881, WCTU Series, reel 12. Nanny was a nickname for Anna Gordon.

13. Willard to Gordon, March 26, 1881, WCTU Series, reel 12.

14. *Union Signal*, January 10, 1884, 11.

15. Letter to the editor by Sallie Chapin, *Union Signal*, May 17, 1883, 4.

16. Susan B. Anthony Papers, scrapbooks, Manuscript Collections, Library of Congress.

17. *Union Signal*, May 22, 1884, 9.

18. Ibid., 4.

19. *Glimpses*, 328. Anna Gordon, *The Life of Frances E. Willard* (Evanston: Woman's Christian Temperance Union Publishing House, 1914), 103, attributes this remark to Bishop Stevens of Charleston, South Carolina, who in the same introduction said that the initials WCTU stood for We Come To Unite the North and South.

20. Clipping, scrapbook 5, WCTU Series, reel 30, frame 289.

21. Clipping, scrapbook 14, p. 131, WCTU Series, reel 32. Scrapbooks 14 and 15 are almost entirely clippings describing Willard's southern tours of 1881 and 1882, and 16 covers the Louisville convention.

22. Willard to Gordon, April 13, 1881, WCTU Series, reel 12.

23. Clippings, *The Northwestern*, June 15, 1881, scrapbook 5, WCTU Series, reel 30, frame 287.

24. Clipping, *The Signal*, ca. August 1881, scrapbook 5, WCTU Series, reel 30, frame 300.

25. Clipping, *The Signal*, ca. August 13, 1881, scrapbook 5, WCTU Series, reel 30, frame 298.

26. Clipping, *Our Union*, May 1881, scrapbook 14, pp. 130–31, WCTU Series, reel 32.

27. Willard to Gordon, April 11, 1881, WCTU Series, reel 12.

28. Gordon to M. T. H. Willard, January 11, 1882, WCTU Series, reel 12.

29. Willard to M. T. H. Willard, January 25, February 25, 1882, WCTU Series, reel 12.

30. Gordon to M. T. H. Willard, January 11, 1882, WCTU Series, reel 12.

31. *Union Signal*, January 11, 1883, 9.

32. *Union Signal*, April 15, 1886, 5.

33. *Minutes, 1880 Convention*, 94, 108–13.

34. J. Ellen Foster in *Union Signal*, March 8, 1883, 11.

35. *Union Signal*, March 29, 1883, 1.

36. Clipping, *Louisville Commercial*, October 30, 1882, scrapbook 11, WCTU Series, reel 31, frames 238–39.

37. *Union Signal*, January 27, 1887, 10.

38. Edward James, ed., *Notable American Women* (Cambridge: Harvard University Press, 1971), v. 1, 321–22; *Union Signal*, March 10, 1887, 10; clipping, *Washington Post*, October 1881, scrapbook 5, p. 308, WCTU Series, reel 30.

39. Clipping, *Cincinnati Commercial*, October 25, 1882, scrapbook 11, WCTU Series, reel 31, frame 237.

40. Report of the Department of Southern Work, *Minutes, 1885 Convention*, cxv.

41. *Minutes, 1889 Convention*, 56–57.

42. Charles Chilton Pearson and J. Edwin Hendricks, *Liquor and Anti-Liquor*

in Virginia, 1619–1919 (Durham: Duke University Press, 1967), 199; Anne Firor Scott, *The Southern Lady: From Pedestal to Politics* (Chicago: University of Chicago Press, 1970), 136–40, 150.

43. Pearson and Hendricks, *Liquor and Anti-Liquor*, 222.
44. *Minutes, 1891 Convention*, 40.
45. Clipping, *Cincinnati Commercial*, October 25, 1882, scrapbook 11, WCTU Series, reel 31, frame 237; *Minutes, 1882 Convention*, lv.
46. *Minutes, 1886 Convention*, lc; *Minutes, 1887 Convention*, ccxiv–ccxvi.
47. Mrs. H. C. Fields of Leavenworth, Kansas, to Frances Willard, June 11, 1880, WCTU Series, reel 12.
48. Clipping, *Washington Evening Star*, October 27, 1881, scrapbook 5, WCTU Series, reel 30, frame 306.
49. *Union Signal*, May 24, 1884, 9.
50. *Union Signal*, December 10, 1891, 10.
51. *Minutes, 1895 Convention*, 208.
52. *Minutes, 1893 Convention*, 37–39.
53. *Union Signal*, October 11, 1900, 1.
54. Minutes, 1894, Ann Arbor WCTU, Michigan Historical Collections of the Bentley Historical Library, University of Michigan, Ann Arbor.
55. Clippings and correspondence concerning the exchange between *Fraternity* and Willard can be found in scrapbook 13, WCTU Series, reel 32, frame 213.
56. *Union Signal*, April 12, 1883, 13; April 19, 10; May 10, 9; August 2, 9.
57. *Minutes, 1886 Convention*, 47; *Minutes, 1887 Convention*, 14.
58. *Minutes, 1879 Convention*, 60.
59. *Minutes, 1885 Convention*, ix–x.
60. *Minutes, 1890 Convention*, 34–35. Surprising as it may seem I found no prejudice expressed against the native American in the *Union Signal*, in the *Minutes*, or in correspondence. Like the Asian Indian or Japanese woman, the native American seems to have been viewed by the WCTU as a piece of charming exotica. The native Americans who joined the WCTU appear to have universally adopted a white middle-class life-style. Stapler was a personal friend of Willard, who always stayed in her home when visiting the Indian Territory.
61. *Minutes, 1880 Convention*, 16.
62. *Minutes, 1882 Convention*, ix–xi; *Minutes, 1884 Convention*, xxxiv.
63. Welfare work among foreigners (in contrast to organization of the foreign-born into unions) is discussed in chapter 6.
64. *Minutes, 1881 Convention*, lxii.
65. *Minutes, 1881 Convention*, 26.
66. *Minutes, 1890 Convention*, 14, 19–20.
67. *Minutes, 1894 Convention*, 248.
68. *Union Signal*, January 1, 1891, 8.
69. *Minutes, 1892 Convention*, 55–57.
70. *Minutes, 1897 Convention*, 78.
71. Mary Livermore to [Mary R.] Smith, July 30, 1888, National American

Woman Suffrage Association Papers, Manuscript Collections, Library of Congress.

72. Joan Bland, *Hibernian Crusade: The Story of the Catholic Total Abstinence Union of America* (Washington: Catholic University Press, 1951), 91, 159.

73. For example, see her annual address, *Minutes, 1889 Convention*, 104.

74. Clipping, *Bridgeport* (Massachusetts) *Evening Farmer*, scrapbook 70, WCTU Series, reel 42, frame 143.

75. Clipping, *New York Herald*, October 24, 1895, scrapbook 70, WCTU Series, reel 42, frame 143; *Minutes, 1895 Convention*, 50.

76. Stevenson to Willard, January 7, 1895, WCTU Series, reel 23. The American Protective Association was a blatantly nativist organization.

77. Willard to Gordon, August 5, 6, 1891, WCTU Series, reel 17; Parkhurst to Willard, August 17, 1891, WCTU Series, reel 17.

78. *Union Signal*, March 12, 1885, 9, 12; *Minutes, 1886 Convention*, cxxxiii–iv.

79. *Minutes, 1887 Convention*, cxviii.

80. *Minutes, 1891 Convention*, 204–5.

81. *Union Signal*, March 14, 1884, 3; February 26, 1885, 6.

82. *Minutes, 1885 Convention*, 51–52. Their salaries were $100 a month plus expenses when in the field. They continued to take collections at meetings, and these were forwarded to the national treasurer through the treasurer of the state where they spoke.

83. Report of the Department of Organization, *Minutes, 1886 Convention*, cxci–ccliv.

84. *Minutes, 1898 Convention*, 165.

85. Minutes of the Executive Committee, November 14, *Minutes, 1889 Convention*, 72–74.

86. *Minutes, 1880 Convention*, 100–1, 122, 124, 136.

87. The *Union* was unequivocally opposed to merger. *Minutes, 1881 Convention*, cxix–cxxi.

88. *Minutes, 1883 Convention*, 31–36.

89. *Minutes, 1884 Convention*, 61.

90. *Union Signal*, January 23, 1890, 8.

91. *Minutes, 1886 Convention*, clxiii; *Minutes, 1888 Convention*, 229; *Minutes, 1889 Convention*, 33; *Minutes, 1890 Convention*, 8.

92. *Minutes, 1889 Convention*, 33.

93. *Union Signal*, January 23, 1890, 8.

94. *Minutes, 1883–98 Conventions; Union Signal*, 1883–84.

95. *Union Signal*, September 15, 1885, 1.

96. *Union Signal*, February 2, 1888, 1; February 19, 8.

97. Possibly these biographies represented preliminary work on *A Woman of the Century: Fourteen Hundred Seventy Biographical Sketches of Leading American Women* (Buffalo: Charles Wells Mouton), which appeared in 1893.

98. *Union Signal*, October 1, 1891, 1.

99. *Union Signal*, February–April, 1891.

100. *Union Signal*, March–April 1892.
101. See Janet Zollinger Giele, "Social Change in the Feminine Role: A Comparison of Woman's Suffrage and Woman's Temperance 1870–1920" (Ph.D. dissertation, Radcliffe College, 1961). As part of her study, Giele made a content analysis of the *Woman's Journal*, the organ of the suffrage movement, and the *Union Signal*, from 1885 to 1915, sampling issues at five-year intervals. She concluded that the suffrage journal pushed harder for general social reforms than the *Union Signal*. From her sample, she found 32 articles in the *Journal* that discussed the reform of societal agencies, as compared with 14 in the *Signal*. She also reports that 31 percent of the *Journal*'s articles asserted women's equality in matters of performance, competence, and citizenship, in contrast with only 3 percent in the *Signal*. In her analysis of articles giving arguments (e.g., in favor of home protection), she found the *Signal* more likely than the *Journal* to characterize men as inadequate in either general terms or family role. In fact, she believed the most striking difference between the two was that the *Journal* saw reform coming through the upgrading of women's status, especially in roles outside the home, while the *Signal* gave relatively more attention to the uplift of men and the quality of life within the home (ch. 8).

   Giele's study is invaluable, for it is the only quantitative comparison we have. However, the content analysis is less useful than it might be for an understanding of developments within the WCTU, because she does not break down her data by shorter time periods. Her tables lump together findings for the whole period, 1885–1915. In addition, her findings are used to point up the contrast between the WCTU and the suffrage group, rather than to show internal change within the WCTU as I have done. She was not able to take into account the substantial change in orientation in the *Union Signal* that occurred in the 1890s when the WCTU abandoned its commitment to general reform. It would be interesting to see what would happen if Giele's analysis were applied to the years 1885–1895 separately. I have read every issue of the *Signal* from 1883 to 1901, and impressionistic evidence indicates that the *Signal* actively supported a broad social reform program in the 1880s through the mid-1890s.
102. *Union Signal*, August 20, 1891.
103. *Union Signal*, April 24, 1884, 1.
104. In the *Union Signal* for January 2, 1890 there were 89 ads. Nineteen were for serials, books and pamphlets; 15 for medical remedies; 10 for food products; 8 for saleswomen or agents wanted; 7 for household appliances; 4 each for musical instruments, "reform" clothing, and other clothing; 3 each for schools and seed and garden products; 2 each for investments and jewelry; and 8 miscellaneous.
105. Julia Colman headed the Department of Temperance Literature for fifteen years. She wrote most of the materials it distributed. As Colman and her work became less important, overshadowed by the burgeoning Woman's Temperance Publishing Association, back-biting, resentment, and outright

conflict marked her relationship to the national leadership. She cared little for prohibition, suffrage, or general social reform, and wished only to point out the evils of drink. See *Union Signal*, November 10, 1887, 8; *Minutes, 1889 Convention*, 20–21; and Colman's letters in the Henry B. Colman Papers, Archives Division, State Historical Society of Wisconsin.

106.   Corresponding Secretary's Report, *Minutes, 1890 Convention*, 148–49, 157. Probably these figures are underestimates of the actual number of people involved. Local unions did not always fully report to national headquarters the money they raised and also did not always pay dues for all their local members.

CHAPTER 6

1.   *Minutes, 1891 Convention*, 93.

2.   See *Deliver Us from Evil: An Interpretation of American Prohibition* (New York: W. W. Norton, 1976), 51–53. Joseph Gusfield has also pointed out the relationship between the growth of temperance organizations and the dislocations caused by urbanization and industrialization; see *Symbolic Crusade: Status, Politics and the American Temperance Movement* (Urbana: University of Illinois Press, 1966), 79–80. Jack Blocker was first to emphasize that the temperance movement in the last quarter of the nineteenth century was not a rural movement but was based in small and large cities; see *Retreat from Reform: The Prohibition Movement in the United States, 1890–1913* (Westport, Conn.: Greenwood Press, 1976), 8–10.

3.   Ida Husted Harper, *The Life and Work of Susan B. Anthony* (Indianapolis: Bobbs-Merrill, 1899), v. 1, 117.

4.   See Ellen DuBois, "The Radicalism of the Woman Suffrage Movement, Stanton-Anthony Wing, 1867–1875," in Zillah R. Eisenstein, *Capitalist Patriarchy and the Case for Socialist Feminism* (New York: Monthly Review Press, 1979), 138–50; Barbara Harris, *Beyond Her Sphere: Women and the Professions in American History* (Westport, Conn.: Greenwood Press, 1978), 86, 129; and Lois Banner, *Elizabeth Cady Stanton: A Radical for Woman's Rights* (Boston: Little, Brown, 1980), 103, 116–17.

5.   *Minutes, 1882 Convention*, i–lxvi.

6.   *Minutes, 1883 Convention*, 5–7; *Minutes, 1896 Convention*, 1–8, 169–408.

7.   *Union Signal*, April 3, 1890, 3.

8.   *Minutes, 1890 Convention*, 55–60.

9.   *Union Signal*, June 11, 1891, 5.

10.   *Union Signal*, July 24, 1890, 9.

11.   *Union Signal*, September 14, 23, 28, October 3, 1893.

12.   *Union Signal*, March 10, 1887, 3.

13.   *Minutes, 1883 Convention*, xi–xiv.

14.   In contrasting the nineteenth and twentieth-century attitudes toward alcohol, Gusfield asserts that in the nineteenth century "the drunkard was neither

sick or foolish, he was sinful" (*Symbolic Crusade*, 30). This is only partly true even earlier in the century. The WCTU emphasized alcohol as an unhealthful, destructive poison from the beginning, and Benjamin Rush much earlier had viewed alcohol abuse as simply a health problem.

15. *Minutes, 1891 Convention*, 145.
16. *Minutes, 1891 Convention*, 146–48.
17. *Minutes, 1893 Convention*, 83. By this time Willard was spending much of her time in England with Lady Henry Somerset, who certainly believed alcoholic beverages could be used safely by many people, Somerset herself, deciding she must take the pledge if she intended to be a leader in the temperance movement, treated herself to a last glass of port before affixing her signature to a pledge. See Kathleen Fitzpatrick, *Lady Henry Somerset* (London: Jonathan Cape, 1923), 120.
18. *Minutes, 1882 Convention*, xiii.
19. *Union Signal*, December 2, 1886, 5; *Minutes, 1885 Convention*, iv; *Minutes, 1890 Convention*, 332.
20. *Minutes, 1889 Convention*, xxxiii–xl.
21. *Minutes, 1890 Convention*, 286–88.
22. *Union Signal*, July 9, 1885, 11.
23. *Union Signal*, January 20, 1887, 10.
24. Anne Firor Scott, *The Southern Lady: From Pedestal to Politics, 1830–1930* (Chicago: University of Chicago Press, 1970), 148.
25. *Minutes, 1894 Convention*, 171.
26. *Union Signal*, August 1, 1889, 1.
27. Miriam E. Rains, scrapbook, 1898–1942, San Diego Historical Society Library, Serra Museum, Presidio Park, San Diego.
28. *Minutes, 1880 Convention*, 136–37.
29. *San Diego Union*, June 17, 1890, 8.
30. Clipping, *Cleveland Leader*, November 22, 1894, scrapbook 70, p. 7, WCTU Series, reel 42.
31. *Union Signal*, January 25, 1883, 10.
32. *Minutes, 1883 Convention*, xxiii–xxvi.
33. *Minutes, 1887 Convention*, 12.
34. Frances Willard wrote her presidential address at one of the more successful of the schools in 1888. Its superintendent was the former WCTU state president of North Carolina (*Union Signal*, August 2, 1888, 9).
35. *Minutes, 1894 Convention*, 263–71.
36. *Union Signal*, March 27, 1890, 8.
37. *Union Signal*, March 20, 1890, 8. By 1895 over 18,000 children had been served.
38. *Union Signal*, April 30, 1885, 9.
39. See Jan Lundie, "To Provide a Home" (an unpublished paper) and clipping file on San Diego Children's Home, both in San Diego Historical Society Library, Serra Museum, Presidio Park, San Diego.
40. *Union Signal*, March 4, 1886, 12; *Minutes, 1885 Convention*, xxx–xxxvi.

41. See Superintendent Emma Wheeler's report, *Minutes, 1890 Convention*, 354–57.
42. See Mary Earhart, *Frances Willard: From Prayers to Politics* (Chicago: University of Chicago Press, 1944), 188, for an example of this misconception.
43. See Allen F. Davis, *American Heroine: The Life and Legend of Jane Addams* (New York: Oxford University Press, 1973), 55–60.
44. *Union Signal*, February 4, 1892, 8.
45. Davis, *American Heroine*, 60.
46. *Minutes, 1895 Convention*, 118.
47. *Union Signal*, November 21, 1895; March 5, 1896, 4–5; March 12, 1896, 2–3; *Minutes, 1895 Convention*, 118.
48. *Minutes, 1886 Convention*, 85.
49. The WCTU put this at $70 per capita in 1886 (*Minutes, 1886 Convention*, ciii). Jon M. Kingsdale, "The 'Poor Man's Club': Social Functions of the Urban Working Class Saloon," *American Quarterly* 25 (October 1973): 482, disputes this assumption. He estimates that liquor consumption never accounted for more than 5 percent of the working man's annual budget and that it generally contributed little to working-class poverty. Other historians of temperance, among them Norman Clark, do not necessarily agree; but it should be remembered that distilled spirits were cheap in the nineteenth century.
50. The Committee on Inducing Corporations to Require Total Abstinence reported for the first time in 1881 (*Minutes, 1881 Convention*, cxxii–xxiii). Resolutions had been passed in 1880 appealing to railroad and steamship companies to require employee abstinence as a safety measure (*Minutes, 1880 Convention*, 65–66).
51. *Minutes, 1886 Convention*, 86–87.
52. *Union Signal*, June 3, 1886, 20; Terence V. Powderly, *Thirty Years of Labor, 1859-1889* (Columbus: Excelsior Publication House, 1890), 601.
53. Powderly to Willard, December 12, 1886, WCTU Series, reel 14. A copy of Willard's letter, distributed as a printed document, is found in scrapbook 12, pp. 478–80, WCTU Series, reel 31, and in Frances Willard, *Glimpses of Fifty Years: An Autobiography of An American Woman* (published by Woman's Temperance Publishing Association, 1889; reprinted New York: Source Book Press, 1970), 363.
54. *Union Signal*, February 3, 1887, 1; February 10, 8.
55. Stone to Willard, March 28, 1887, as quoted in Earhart, *Willard*, 246.
56. Letters between them may have been removed from Willard's files, but the Terence Powderly Papers, Department of Archives and Manuscripts, Catholic University, Washington, D.C., contain few letters from Willard, all of them on business, and there are a few letterpress copies of letters to her.
57. See Earhart, *Willard*, 75.
58. See especially *Union Signal*, December 22, 1887, 5.
59. J. Blanchard to Willard, June 23, 1891, WCTU Series, reel 17.
60. *Minutes, 1890 National Convention*, 368–73.

61. *Union Signal*, July 14, 1892, 1; August 4, 9.
62. *Union Signal*, February 19, 1885, 3.
63. *Union Signal*, January 20, 1887, 12.
64. President's address, *Minutes, 1889 Convention*, 114.
65. *Union Signal*, December 1888–February 1889; April 4, 1889, 7.
66. *Union Signal*, September 7, 1893.
67. President's address, *Minutes, 1889 Convention*, 116.
68. *Union Signal*, March 21, 1889, 2.
69. President's address, *Minutes, 1889 National Convention*, 117.
70. *Union Signal*, February 23, 1893, 8.
71. *Minutes, 1886 Convention*, 40.
72. *Minutes, 1887 Convention*, 51, xxiv–xxx.
73. *Minutes, 1891 Convention*, 18.
74. President's address, *Minutes, 1881 Convention*, lxxiv.
75. *Minutes, 1885 Convention*, xlix. The superintendents were organizing institutes and lecture series on such topics as "What to Eat and Why," "The Problem of Nervousness," "The Skin and Its Care," and "Epidemics and Their Prevention" and lobbying with the fashion magazines for sensible dress. Kellogg's husband, John Harvey Kellogg, was superintendent of the Battle Creek Sanitorium, a fashionable nineteenth-century health resort.
76. *Minutes, 1886 Convention*, clxxvii.
77. *Minutes, 1884 Convention*, v; *Union Signal*, June 10, 1895, 8.
78. *Minutes, 1886 Convention*, lxxvii–lxxix.
79. *Union Signal*, October 30, 1884, 7.
80. *Union Signal*, April 8, 1896, 1, 6, 12; *Minutes, 1886 Convention*, 61, 80.
81. Anna Gordon to Mary Willard, October 4, 1881, WCTU Series, reel 12.
82. President's address, *Minutes, 1891 Convention*, 107.
83. *Minutes, 1887 Convention*, 61; *Minutes, 1888 Convention*, 118–23.
84. *Minutes, 1890 Convention*, 302–4. *Minutes, 1895 Convention*, 332.
85. *Union Signal*, March 18, 1886, 14; *Minutes, 1886 Convention*, xxxvii. Dr. Kate Bushnell, department evangelist and WCTU organizer, helped expose conditions in the Wisconsin pineries, where she found girls kept in stockaded dens guarded by bulldogs, girls enticed to the pineries by the promise of work and instead used as prostitutes, abused, and sometimes killed; law officers tracked down escapees, and in one instance a ball and chain was used to keep a girl from running away (*Minutes, 1888 Convention*, 141–42).
86. *Minutes, 1886 Convention*, 77.
87. *Minutes, 1894 Convention*, 329.
88. *Minutes, 1887 Convention*, clxxix–x.
89. *Union Signal*, March 8, 1888, 5.
90. Editorial, *Union Signal*, December 24, 1885, 3.
91. *Minutes, 1889 Convention*, 120.
92. *Union Signal*, June 3, 1893, 9. Suffragists were also protesting the double standard. Lucy Stone castigated the National Council of Women for "the shame of having *asked* such a male prostitute as Grover Cleveland if he

would receive them," especially since "they went from a 'social purity' meeting to be received by him" (Lucy Stone to Frances Willard, August 23, 1888, Lucy Stone Papers, Library of Congress Manuscript Collections).

93. In 1886 thirteen life-saving stations were in operation; Chicago had three, Nebraska had several, Indiana had two, and Iowa, Maine, Colorado, and Michigan each had one (*Minutes, 1886 Convention*, xxix–xliii). At least one WCTU home for girls entering the urban work force for the first time is still [in 1979] in operation: the Toronto WCTU administers and partially supports through endowment funds a temporary low-cost residence for young women coming to the city.

94. See David Pivar, *The Purity Crusade: Sexual Morality and Social Control, 1868–1900* (Westport, Conn.: Greenwood Press, 1973), 85.

95. *Minutes, 1886 Convention*, xxxv.

96. Carrie [no last name] to Mary Willard, November 15, 1887, WCTU Series, reel 14.

97. *Union Signal*, April 23, 1891, 8.

98. Bertha Palmer to Willard, December 15, 1891, WCTU Series, reel 17.

99. *Union Signal*, September 7, 1893, 6.

100. *Union Signal*, February 4, 1892, 8; July 13, 1893.

101. See Robin Jacoby, "The Women's Trade Union League," in Milton Cantor and Bruce Laurie, eds., *Class, Sex and the Woman Worker* (Westport, Conn.: Greenwood Press, 1977), 211. Aileen Kraditor, *Up from the Pedestal: Selected Writings in the History of American Feminism* (Chicago: Quadrangle Books, 1969), 13, states that the suffrage movement did not mention wages and labor conditions until 1900.

102. See correspondence March–May 1888, WCTU Series, reel 15; President's address, *Minutes, 1888 Convention*, 43–44.

103. Isabella B. Hooker to Willard, May 6, 1888, WCTU Series, reel 15.

104. *Union Signal*, February 9, 1893, 1.

105. *Union Signal*, June 29, 1893, 3.

106. President's address, *Minutes, 1891 Convention*, 87.

107. *Union Signal*, March 18, 1886, 15.

108. President's address, *Minutes, 1886 Convention*, 78.

109. *Union Signal*, January 8, 1891, 7.

110. President's address, *Minutes, 1889 Convention*, 122.

111. *Minutes, 1895 Convention*, 48. Although opposed by most liberals as well as society's conservative elements, divorce was rising during the Victorian era, from 1.2 per thousand marriages in 1860 to 4.0 per thousand in 1900. See William L. O'Neill, *Divorce in the Progressive Era* (New Haven: Yale University Press, 1967), for an analysis and description of nineteenth and early twentieth-century divorce patterns.

112. *Minutes, 1889 Convention*, 123.

113. See Daniel Scott Smith, "Family Limitation, Sexual Control and Domestic Feminism in Victorian America," in Mary Hartman and Lois Banner, eds., *Clio's Consciousness Raised: New Perspectives on the History of Women* (New York: Harper Torchbooks, 1974), 119–36. Smith sees the steady drop

in the birthrate in the nineteenth century as stemming from what he calls "domestic feminism," women's increasing insistence on control of their own bodies through family limitation, frequency of sex, or coitus interruptus. He argues that women moved from concern with their status in the marriage relationship to causes outside the home. See also Linda Gordon, *Woman's Body, Woman's Right: A Social History of Birth Control in America* (New York: Penguin, 1977). Gordon attributes the decline at least in part to early contraceptive devices.

114. *Union Signal*, July 3, 1890, 1. By "will" the *Union Signal* meant that a father could provide whatever guardian he chose in the case of his death, even if the mother was living and competent.

115. President's address as reproduced in *Union Signal*, November 27, 1890, 7. "Owner" is an awkward word, but it was the word used in connection with parental rights at the time.

116. *Union Signal*, August 14, 1890, 3. The WCTU's embracing of the natural-rights argument in the 1890s is interesting in light of the fact that the suffrage movement at this time was moving away from natural-rights arguments and emphasizing expediency; see Aileen Kraditor, *The Ideas of the Woman Suffrage Movement, 1890–1920* (New York: Columbia University Press, 1965), ch. 6, and her *Up from the Pedestal*, 18.

117. For an example see *Union Signal*, May 21, 1891, 8.

118. *Minutes, 1890 Convention*, 370.

119. *Union Signal*, May 4, 1893, 8.

120. *Minutes, 1893 Convention*, 78–79. See above, 60–61.

121. William L. O'Neill, *Everyone Was Brave: A History of Feminism in America* (New York: Quadrangle Books, 1971), ix.

CHAPTER 7

1. *Minutes, 1880 Convention*, 24.

2. *Minutes* as quoted in Frances Willard, *Glimpses of Fifty Years: An Autobiography of An American Woman* (published by Woman's Temperance Publishing Association, 1889; reprinted New York: Source Book Press, 1970), 380.

3. Mary B. Willard, *The Story of a Great Conviction* (Chicago: Woman's Temperance Publishing Association, n.d.), 9–10.

4. *Minutes, 1893 Convention*, 349.

5. *Minutes, 1883 Convention*, xvi.

6. See Norton Mezvinsky, "The White Ribbon Reform, 1874–1920" (Ph.D. dissertation, University of Wisconsin, 1959), 221–22.

7. See Earhart's *Frances Willard: From Prayers to Politics* (Chicago: University of Chicago Press, 1944), 226. Earhart argues that the WCTU was instrumental in encouraging the Republican party's interest in woman suffrage.

8. *Union Signal*, May 15, 1884, 10.

9. *Union Signal*, March 6, 1884, 1.
10. *Union Signal*, September 12, 1889, 8.
11. *Union Signal*, March 21, 1889, 8.
12. *Minutes, 1892 Convention*, 113.
13. *Minutes, 1894 Convention*, 47.
14. *Union Signal*, January 10, 1884. The pattern followed by the WCTU was the reverse of that taken by the suffrage movement. Suffrage organizations originally stressed the natural-rights argument and then shifted to an emphasis on expedience (that is, the argument that women's votes were necessary to achieve societal reform) by the end of the century; see Aileen Kraditor, *The Ideas of the Woman Suffrage Movement, 1890-1920* (New York: Columbia University Press, 1965), and her Introduction to *Up from the Pedestal: Selected Writings in the History of American Feminism* (Chicago: Quadrangle Books, 1969). Settlement-house workers like Jane Addams were also advocating the vote for women by the 1890s as the only way to clean up city government and make the city safe for children—another form of home protection; see William Chafe, *The American Woman: Her Changing Social, Economic and Political Roles, 1920-1970* (New York: Oxford University Press, 1972), 3-22.
15. See Eleanor Flexner, *Century of Struggle: The Woman's Rights Movement in the United States* (Cambridge: Harvard University Press, 1959; reprinted New York: Atheneum, 1971), 185; Mezvinsky, "White Ribbon Reform." ch. 8.
16. *Minutes, 1887 Convention*, xix; *Union Signal*, September 12, 1889, 8; see Norman Clark, *The Dry Years: Prohibition and Social Change in Washington* (Seattle: University of Washington Press, 1965), 35-39, 46-52, for an analysis of the effect of temperance on suffrage reform.
17. Anthony to Willard, March 21, 1890; Philena Johnson to Willard, October 10, 1890; Blackwell to Willard, October 2, 1890, WCTU Series, reel 16.
18. *Minutes, 1894 Convention*, 59.
19. Anthony to Willard, January 23, 1896; B. Sturdevant Peet to Willard, January 25, 1896; L. M. N. Stevens to Willard, January 31, 1896, WCTU Series, reel 23. K. Stevenson to Willard, April 2, 1896; Anna Gordon to L. M. N. Stevens, June 25, 1896, WCTU Series, reel 24. Willard's official reason for changing the venue of the convention was inability to obtain low railroad rates to the West Coast. She did not believe the Union membership would take well to her deferring to Anthony's wishes. In any case the California amendment lost.
20. *Minutes, 1896 National Convention*, 52.
21. *Minutes, 1899 National Convention*, 24-25, 33-38.
22. *Woman's Journal*, November 21, 1891, 1.
23. See Kraditor, *Ideas*, ch. 6.
24. See, for example, the editorial in *Woman's Journal*, December 8, 1894, 1: "Do those in favor of woman suffrage who demand 'universal' suffrage without any educational qualifications, realize that while our question is

pending . . . these steadily increasing thousands are a sure and mighty force to join the enemy, already organized, to hold the women of this nation subject to a foreign vote?"

25. Clipping, *Zion's Herald*, August 1896, scrapbook 4, p. 101, WCTU Series, reel 30; *Union Signal*, July 12, 1888, 4.
26. *Minutes, 1895 Convention*, 46.
27. *Union Signal*, February 20, 1890, 2.
28. *Union Signal*, January 17, 1895, 4.
29. *Minutes, 1891 Convention*, 159–60.
30. See Norman Clark, *Deliver Us from Evil: An Interpretation of American Prohibition* (New York: W. W. Norton, 1976), 69–71, and Ernest H. Cherrington, *The Evolution of Prohibition in the United States of America* (Westerville, Ohio: The American Issue Press, 1920), ch. 6.
31. *Glimpses*, 375–76.
32. *Minutes, 1880 Convention*, 24.
33. *Glimpses*, 382–83. See also Earhart, *Willard*, 210–15, and *Glimpses*, 376–82.
34. *Minutes, 1882 Convention*, 28.
35. J. Ellen Foster to Willard, April 2, 1884, WCTU Series, reel 13.
36. See *Union Signal*, September–October, 1884.
37. *Minutes, 1883 Convention*, 41; *Union Signal*, August 21, 1884, 8.
38. *Minutes, 1884 Convention*, 28.
39. *Minutes, 1884 Convention*, 66–70.
40. *Minutes, 1884 Convention*, 22–24; *Union Signal*, October 30, 1884.
41. *Union Signal*, November 20, 1884, 1.
42. *Union Signal*, November 27, 1884, 8.
43. *Union Signal*, December 18, 1884, 8.
44. *Minutes, 1887 Convention*, 54.
45. *Minutes, 1886 Convention*, 55.
46. Gordon to Mary T. Willard, October 23, 1888, WCTU Series, reel 15.
47. Foster to Willard, November 10, 1888, WCTU Series, reel 15; Anna Gordon to Mary Willard, April 2, 1888, WCTU Series, reel 15.
48. *Union Signal*, June 28, 1888, 8, 9; July 5, 1; July 12, 4, 5.
49. See scrapbook 21, pp. 14–80, WCTU Series, reel 34.
50. Anna Gordon to Mary Willard, September 18, 1888, WCTU Series, reel 15.
51. *Union Signal*, July 19, 1888.
52. Clipping, *Pittsburgh Dispatch*, July 24, 1884, scrapbook 21, p. 14, WCTU Series, reel 34.
53. Thompson to Willard, July 12, 1886, WCTU Series, reel 14; September 6, 1888, WCTU Series, reel 15. Twelve old Crusaders publicly endorsed the Prohibition party in early 1889, in separate statements, all of which view WCTU support of the party as following logically from the aims of the Crusaders to abolish the saloon; see *Union Signal*, February 14, 1889, 2–3, 8–9.
54. *Union Signal*, June 25, 1885, 1.
55. *Minutes, 1889 Convention*, 45.

56. Clipping, *Chicago Times*, January 28, 1890, scrapbook 13, WCTU Series, reel 32, frame 95; *Union Signal*, January 30, 1890, 4.
57. Wallace to Willard, December 17, 1889, WCTU Series, reel 16.
58. J. Ellen Foster et al., *The Truth in the Case: Concerning Partisanship and Non-Partisanship in the WCTU* (n.p., 1889), 24. This pamphlet was the Non-Partisan WCTU's reply to a forty-four page pamphlet, *The Facts in the Case*, circulated by the national WCTU.
59. Ibid., 26–34.
60. See Clark, *Deliver Us*, 74–79, for an assessment of the WCTU–Prohibition party alliance.
61. Earhart, *Willard*, 227–42, and Jack S. Blocker, *Retreat from Reform: The Prohibition Movement in the United States, 1890–1913* (Westport, Conn.: Greenwood Press, 1976), chs. 2 and 3, examine in detail Willard's efforts to form a reform coalition.
62. *Minutes, 1894 Convention*, 49–51.
63. The vote was 108 to 62. Clipping, *Cleveland Leader*, November 22, 1894, scrapbook 70, pp. 6–7, WCTU Series, reel 42.
64. President's address, *Minutes, 1894 Convention*, 104.
65. *Union Signal*, December 27, 1894, 4.
66. *Minutes, 1895 Convention*, 53, 60.
67. Willard to "Dear Sisters," June 12, 1896, WCTU Series, reel 24.
68. Willard to L. M. N. Stevens, July 1, 1896, WCTU Series, reel 24.
69. *Minutes, 1896 Convention*; clipping, *Chicago Tribune*, November 19, 1896, scrapbook 70, p. 238, WCTU Series, reel 42.
70. *Minutes, 1881 Convention*, xv–xviii.
71. *Union Signal*, May 8, 1884, 5.
72. *Union Signal*, December 24, 1885, 5.
73. *Union Signal*, November 25, 1886, 1.
74. See Cherrington, *Evolution of Prohibition*, chs. 6 and 7. Local option did not disappear with repeal. "Drys" won a local option election in Zeeland, Michigan, in August 1979.
75. Hartt to Willard, May 12, 1880, WCTU Series, reel 12; *Minutes, 1881 Convention*, xv–xviii.
76. S. M. Salter to Willard, August 25, 1887, WCTU Series, reel 14.
77. *Union Signal*, September 17, 1891, 1.
78. *Minutes, 1880 Convention*, 106–8.
79. See Joseph Timberlake, *Prohibition and the Progressive Movement, 1900–1920* (Cambridge: Harvard University Press, 1963), 40–50, for a useful summary of early alcohol research. Little research was done before 1860 on the effect of alcohol on the human body, but in 1866 a British physician, Benjamin Richardson, exploded the myth that alcohol was a source of human warmth and proved that it actually chilled the body instead. It was not until 1892 that a German scientist discovered that alcohol was a depressant rather than a stimulant, and studies of the relationship of insanity to alcohol abuse were only begun in 1896. Whiskey and brandy were not

removed from the pharmacopeia until 1915. The WCTU was much quicker to repudiate the beneficial physical effects of alcohol and see its dangers.

80. *Minutes, 1883 Convention*, lxxvii.
81. *Union Signal*, March 13, 1884, 1, 4; March 27, 4.
82. *Minutes, 1885 Convention*, ccxi.
83. Report of Mary H. Hunt, *Minutes, 1886 Convention*, cciii–vii.
84. *Minutes, 1888 Convention*, 48.
85. Gerda Lerner, "New Approaches to the Study of Women," in Berenice Carroll, ed., *Liberating Women's History* (Urbana: University of Illinois Press, 1976), 354, points out that women's groups were the first to use the pressure-group tactics common today.
86. *Minutes, 1887 Convention*, cxliv–lv; Blair to Willard, March 7, 1886, WCTU Series, reel 14; *Union Signal*, March 11, 1886, 1, December 1, 1887, 20–21.
87. *Union Signal*, August 8, 1895, 8.
88. John S. Billings, ed., *The Liquor Problem: A Summary of Investigations Conducted by the Committee of Fifty, 1893–1903* (Boston: Houghton Mifflin, 1905), 4. The committee's membership was indeed impressive; Seth Low (chairman), President Charles Eliot of Harvard, President William Preston Johnson of Tulane, Francis Peabody, Zebulon Brockway and Frederick Wines (both prominent penologists), and Bishop Edward G. Andrews of the Methodist church were among its members.
89. Ibid., 35–36.
90. A detailed account of the WCTU's scientific temperance campaign and the reaction to it may be found in Mezvinsky, "White Ribbon Reform."
91. Also see above, 107–8, 116, and below, 154–55.
92. President's address, *Minutes, 1893 Convention*, 110, 106.

CHAPTER 8

1. *Union Signal*, August 3, 1893, 8.
2. See WCTU Series, reel 19; much correspondence from March to May 1893 deals with Willard's health.
3. Gordon to Willard, October 30, 1893, WCTU Series, reel 20.
4. Kells to Gordon, May 20, 1893, WCTU Series, reel 19.
5. *Minutes, 1894 Convention*, 21–22; correspondence, October 1893, WCTU Series, reel 20.
6. *Minutes, 1895 Convention*, 347–48; *Minutes, 1896 Convention*, 424–25; *Minutes, 1900 Convention*, 102–3; *Union Signal*, November 25, 1897. In 1903 the WCTU purchased the *Union Signal* from the Woman's Temperance Publishing Association, and the printing department was leased to a commercial printer. Matilda Carse's publishing empire was essentially dismantled by 1900; Carse herself had been replaced as president of the Association in 1898 (*Union Signal*, November 24, 1898; *Minutes, 1900 Convention*, 47, 102–3).

7. The pledging was more enthusiastic than the paying. Only one-sixth of the 1887 pledges had been paid by the next convention (*Minutes, 1888 Convention*, 246).

8. *Union Signal*, November 6, 1890; *Chicago Globe* as quoted in *Minutes, 1890 Convention*, 393.

9. Willard to M. T. H. Willard, April 19, 1888, WCTU Series, reel 15.

10. Clipping, *Chicago Tribune*, February 25, 1893, in scrapbook 13, WCTU Series, reel 13, frame 123; *Union Signal*, April 6, 1893.

11. *Minutes, 1889 Convention*, 78; Helen Barker to L. M. N. Stevens, February 25, 1893, and Clara Hoffman to Stevens, February 28, 1893, WCTU Series, reel 19.

12. Lady Henry Somerset was facing a challenge to her continued leadership of the British Union at its national convention, and a death in her family forced her to cancel many speaking engagements, some of which Willard filled on her behalf. Willard was popular in England and could always draw a crowd, and she certainly contributed to Somerset's retaining the presidency of the British Woman's Temperance Association.

13. L. M. N. Stevens to Anna Gordon, March 8, 1893, WCTU Series, reel 19.

14. Leavitt's letters to Willard and others have disappeared from the WCTU correspondence, but are alluded to in other correspondence from 1893 to 1897, WCTU Series, reels 19–24. See also *Union Signal*, June 1, 1898. Mary Earhart, who had access to some papers that are no longer available, saw Leavitt as Willard's primary enemy, despite their long friendship, and attributed this to her concern with Willard's political radicalism and to jealousy of Somerset (*Willard*, 352–66). Earhart also believed that Woodbridge wanted to oust Willard as president, but evidence for this no longer exists; what little remains runs to the contrary.

15. The *Minutes* and the *Signal* do not carry detailed accounts of the Temple debate at that convention. However, dissension is frequently alluded to in letters from the state presidents to Lillian Stevens after the Hobbs's attack in 1893; see correspondence, March 1893, WCTU Series, reel 19.

16. *Union Signal*, February 2, 1893; Katherine Stevenson to Gordon, May 13, 1893, and Harriet Kells to Willard, May 14, 1893, WCTU Series, reel 20.

17. Harriet Kells to Gordon, May 20, 1893, WCTU Series, reel 20.

18. Harriet Kells to Willard, May 14, 1893, WCTU Series, reel 20.

19. *Union Signal*, August 17, 1893, 5.

20. See the account of the 1893 convention debate, *Union Signal*, November 2, 1893, 15–16.

21. *Union Signal*, November 25, 1897, 4–5.

22. *Minutes, 1893 Convention*, 99–102; clipping, scrapbook 11, p. 64, WCTU Series, reel 31; *Union Signal*, October 26, 1893, 8, 9, 14, 15–16.

23. *Minutes, 1896 Convention*, 44.

24. Debate on this issue is reproduced verbatim in the *Union Signal*, November 25, 1897.

25. *Union Signal*, November 25, 1897, 16.

26. Carrie M. Stair to Willard, January 10, 1896, WCTU Series, reel 23.

27. *Union Signal*, March 4, 1897, 5.
28. See John W. Tebbell, *The Marshall Fields: A Study in Wealth* (New York: E. P. Dutton, 1947), chs. 3–5.
29. *Union Signal*, August 4, October 27, 1898.
30. *Minutes, 1898 Convention*, 48–49; *Union Signal*, November 24; December 1, 1898, 12.
31. *Minutes, 1898 Convention*, 48. The Temple no longer exists. It was torn down and replaced by an office building before 1936.
32. Gordon to Willard, September 12, 1893, and other correspondence September–October 1893, WCTU Series, reel 20.
33. Clipping, *Cleveland World*, November 17, 1894, scrapbook 11, p. 117, WCTU Series, reel 31.
34. *Union Signal*, August 8, 1895, 8; December 6, 8.
35. *Minutes, 1896 Convention*, 77, 85, 88, 111.
36. For a discussion of the General Federation of Women's Clubs see William L. O'Neill, *Everyone Was Brave: A History of Feminism in America* (New York: Quadrangle Books, 1971), 84–90.
37. Harriet Kells to Willard, May 20, 1893, WCTU Series, reel 19.
38. Kells to Willard, September 24, 1893, WCTU Series, reel 20.
39. *Union Signal*, November 2, 1893, 2.
40. O'Neill analyzes the Association of Collegiate Alumnae in *Everyone Was Brave*, 77–84.
41. *Union Signal*, December 28, 1893, 10. Demorest medals, named after William Demorest, fashion arbiter and prohibitionist, were awarded young people for prizewinning temperance orations.
42. Janet Zollinger Giele, "Social Change in the Feminine Role: A Comparison of Woman's Suffrage and Woman's Temperance 1870–1920" (Ph.D. dissertation, Radcliffe College, 1961), 83.
43. Ibid., 281–82.
44. *Minutes, 1897 Convention*, 48–51.
45. *Minutes, 1898 Convention*, 65.
46. *Minutes, 1897 Convention*, 73ff.
47. *Minutes, 1899 Convention*, 85ff.
48. *Union Signal*, December 31, 1896, 2.
49. *Union Signal*, October 1899.
50. *Union Signal*, April 1899.
51. Earhart believes this very strongly and attributes the growing strength of opposition to Willard in the 1890s to this trend (*Willard*, 356–7).
52. *Union Signal*, April 28, 1898, 6.
53. *Union Signal*, October 6, 1898, 8; November 17, 8.
54. *Union Signal*, December 27, 1900, 4.
55. One of Mary Leavitt's quarrels with Willard's attachment to Lady Henry Somerset revolved around Somerset's support of licensed and inspected prostitution at British army bases in India as the lesser of two evils. Even here the Willard-Somerset axis was moving to the left.
56. *Union Signal*, January 18, 1900, 1.

57. Frances Willard, *Do-Everything: A Handbook* (Chicago, n.d.), 5.
58. See Joseph R. Gusfield, "Social Structure and Moral Reform: A Study of the Woman's Christian Temperance Union," *American Journal of Sociology* 61 (November 1955): 221–32, for an analysis of the class status of the WCTU membership. Gusfield's study is discussed further in the next chapter and the appendix.

CHAPTER 9

1. See Janet Giele, "Social Change in the Feminine Role: A Comparison of Woman's Suffrage and Woman's Temperance 1870–1920" (Ph.D. dissertation, Radcliffe College, 1961), 101–8.
2. Ellen DuBois, "The Radicalism of the Woman's Suffrage Movement: Notes toward the Reconstruction of Nineteenth Century Feminism," *Feminist Studies* 3 (Fall 1975): 66–69.
3. See Brian Harrison, *Drink and the Victorians* (Pittsburgh: Pittsburgh University Press, 1972), for a detailed study of the early British temperance movement. Harrison barely mentions women except to remark that a few Quaker women were active in the temperance cause.
4. See Norman Longmate, *The Water Drinkers: A History of Temperance* (London: Hamish Hamilton, 1963), 216.
5. Ibid., 151; Richard J. Evans, *The Feminists: Woman's Emancipation Movements in Europe, America and Australasia, 1840–1920* (New York: Barnes and Noble, 1977), 68, 151.
6. Willard's correspondence in the WCTU papers contains much information on her newphew's problem.

APPENDIX

1. See "Social Structure and Moral Reform: A Study of the Woman's Christian Temperance Union," *American Journal of Sociology* 61 (November 1955): 221–32.
2. Ibid., 231.
3. "The White Ribbon Reform, 1874–1920" (Ph.D. dissertation, University of Wisconsin, 1959).
4. "Social Change in the Feminine Role: A Comparison of Woman's Suffrage and Woman's Temperance, 1870–1920" (Ph.D. dissertation, Radcliffe College, 1961).
5. In addition to the material in the *Union Signal* and the WCTU scrapbooks, I have collected data for this survey from the biographies in Edward James, ed., *Notable American Women* (Cambridge: Harvard University Press, 1971); Frances Willard, *Woman and Temperance* (Hartford, Conn.: Park Publishing Co., 1883; reprinted New York: Arno, 1972); Mary Livermore

and Frances Willard, *A Woman of the Century: Fourteen Hundred Seventy Biographical Sketches of Leading American Women* (Buffalo: Charles Wells Mouton, 1893); Ernest Cherrington, ed., *The Standard Encyclopedia of the Alcohol Problem*, 6 vols. (Westerville, Ohio: American Issue Publishing Co., 1925–30); Louise E. Van Norman, *An Album of Representative Prohibitionists* (New York: Funk and Wagnalls, 1895); George Bungay, *Pen Portraits of Illustrious Abstainers* (New York: The National Temperance Society, 1881); Clara C. Chapin, *Thumbnail Sketches of White Ribbon Women* (Chicago: Woman's Temperance Publishing Association, 1895); B. F. Austin, *The Prohibition Leaders of America* (Ottawa, 1895); and several house histories of state unions which contain biographical sketches.

6. In assembling data on 1874 I could find no information on sixteen out of forty women except marital status and the state where they were living. For 1884 this was true for fifteen of fifty-six, and for 1894, five of fifty-eight.

7. "White Ribbon Reform," 73.

8. "Social Change," 153.

9. "White Ribbon Reform," 73, 329.

10. See Allen Davis, *Spearheads for Reform: The Social Settlements and the Progressive Movement* (New York: Oxford University Press, 1967), 33.

11. "Social Change," 148.

12. Ibid., 149.

13. "White Ribbon Reform," 73.

14. Ibid., 73.

15. "Social Change," 152.

16. Ibid., 149.

17. "White Ribbon Reform," 330.

18. "Social Change," 157; see Niebuhr's *The Social Sources of Denominationalism* (New York: Henry Holt and Co., 1929).

19. *Spearheads*, 27, 265.

20. Ibid., 265.

21. "Social Structure," 230–31.

22. The names of these women were obtained from the *Report of the Woman's Home Association and Day Nursery*, 1891, in the papers of the San Diego Children's Home, San Diego Historical Society Library, Serra Museum, Presidio Park, San Diego. Husbands' occupations were taken from *Directory of San Diego City and County* (San Diego, 1888) and *Directory of San Diego and Vicinity for 1889–90* (San Diego, 1890).

23. Charles Isetts, "A Social Profile of the Woman's Temperance Crusade: Hillsboro, Ohio," in Jack S. Blocker, Jr., ed., *Alcohol, Reform and Society: The Liquor Question in Social Context* (Westport, Conn.: Greenwood Press, 179), 10.

24. "Social Change," 159.

Index